Women in the Developing World:
Evidence from Turkey

Nermin Abadan-Unat

MONOGRAPH SERIES
IN WORLD AFFAIRS

Graduate School of International Studies

UNIVERSITY OF DENVER

VOLUME TWENTY-TWO

Book One
WOMEN IN THE DEVELOPING WORLD:
EVIDENCE FROM TURKEY
Nermin Abadan-Unat

MONOGRAPH SERIES IN WORLD AFFAIRS

A Quarterly
Graduate School of International Studies
University of Denver
Denver, Colorado 80208

Editor .... Karen A. Feste
Managing Editor .... Millie Van Wyke

Send manuscripts in triplicate to Karen A. Feste, Editor, Monograph Series in World Affairs, Graduate School of International Studies, University of Denver, Denver, Colorado 80208. Manuscripts already published, scheduled for publication elsewhere, or simultaneously submitted to another journal are not acceptable.

MONOGRAPH REVIEWERS
Volumes 20 and 21

The editor appreciates manuscript evaluations provided by the following people during the past two years.

Bernhard Abrahamsson, U.S. Merchant
  Marine Academy
Chadwick Alger, Ohio State University
Michael Altfeld, Michigan State University
Jennifer Bailey, University of Denver
Asma Barlas, University of Denver
Frank Beer, University of Colorado
Roger Benjamin, University of Pittsburgh
Bruce Berkowitz, University of Minnesota
Thomas Biersteker, Yale University
Eric Browne, University of
  Wisconsin-Milwaukee
Robert Butterworth, Alexandria, Virginia
Louis Cantori, University of
  Maryland-Baltimore
Asa Clark IV, U.S. Military Academy
Stephen Douglas, University of
  Illinois-Urbana
Raymond Duvall, University of Minnesota
David Freeman, Colorado State University
John R. Freeman, University of Minnesota
David Garnham, University of
  Wisconsin-Milwaukee
Judy Gillespie, Boston University
Charles Gochman, University of Pittsburgh
Ted Gurr, University of Colorado
Michael Haas, University of Hawaii-Manoa
Michael Handel, U.S. Army War College
Charles Hermann, Ohio State University
Ladd Hollist, Brigham Young University
Francis Hoole, Indiana University-
  Bloomington
James Jankowski, University of Colorado
Robert Jervis, Columbia University
Eric A. Jones, Brigham Young University
Peter Katzenstein, Cornell University
Charles Kegley, University of
  South Carolina
Robert Kvavik, University of Minnesota
Marion Knodler, University of Denver
Jacek Kugler, Vanderbilt University

Victor Le Vine, Washington University
Jack Levy, University of Texas-Austin
Fred Lister, Ralph Bunche Institute
Patrick McGowan, Arizona State University
Manus Midlarsky, University of Colorado
James Morrow, Michigan State University
James Murdock, Northeast Louisiana
  University
Max Nieman, University of
  California-Riverside
Michael O'Leary, Syracuse University
Michael Patton, University of Minnesota
Fred Pearson, University of
  Missouri-St. Louis
Bennett Ramberg, University of
  California-Los Angeles
Barbara Salert, Washington University
Ahmed Samatar, St. Lawrence University
Martin W. Sampson III, University of
  Minnesota
Todd Sandler, University of South Carolina
Philip Schrodt, Northwestern University
John Schwartz, University of Arizona
Robert Shelton, Oak Ridge National
  Laboratory
George Shepherd, University of Denver
Randolph Siverson, University of
  California-Davis
Theda Skocpol, University of Chicago
W.A.E. Skurnik, University of Colorado
Theresa C. Smith, Macalester College
Alan Sobrosky, U.S. Army War College
Michael Stohl, Purdue University
Michael Sullivan, University of Arizona
Mark Tessler, University of
  Wisconsin-Milwaukee
John E. Turner, University of Minnesota
Paul Viotti, U.S. Air Force Academy
John Walton, University of California-Davis
Michael Don Ward, University of Colorado
Spencer Wellhofer, University of Denver

WOMEN IN THE DEVELOPING WORLD: EVIDENCE FROM TURKEY

Nermin Abadan-Unat

Foreword by
Elise Boulding

Volume 22
Book 1

MONOGRAPH SERIES IN WORLD AFFAIRS

Graduate School of International Studies
University of Denver
Denver, Colorado 80208

Library of Congress Cataloging-in-Publication Data

Abadan-Unat, Nermin, 1921-
    Women in the developing world.

    (Monograph series in world affairs; v. 22, bk. 1)
    Bibliography: p.
    1. Women in development — Turkey. 2. Women's rights — Tur
3. Women, Muslim — Turkey. I. Title. II. Series.
HQ1726.7.A63 1986   305.4'2'09561   85-28915
ISBN 0-87940-080-3

© University of Denver (Colorado Seminary) 1986.
Printed in Taiwan, ROC

ABOUT THE AUTHOR

NERMIN ABADAN-UNAT is Professor of Political Sociology at the Faculty of Political Science, Ankara University, Ankara, Turkey. She earned her Ph.D. as a Fullbright scholar at the University of Minnesota in 1953. Dr. Abadan-Unat has served as president of the Turkish Social Science Association, and two years as contingent senator in the Turkish Senate. She is the author of several books and articles, including *Turkish Workers in Europe, 1960-1975* (1976); *Migration and Development* (1976); and *Women in Turkish Society* (1981).

ACKNOWLEDGMENTS

I wish to acknowledge those whose advice and assistance have been most helpful. My first thanks go to Karen Feste, Denver University, Graduate School of International Studies, who encouraged me to submit the various papers presented and whose encouragement and valuable criticism were of immense importance. The managing editor of the Monograph Series in World Affairs, Millie Van Wyke, provided valuable suggestions and comments. Finally I would like to express my sincere gratitude to Professor Joseph S. Szyliowicz and Professor E. Thomas Rowe from Denver University, GSIS, who invited me as a guest professor in summer 1984 and furnished me the opportunity to forge precious bonds with Denver University. Any errors of content or omission are, of course, my own. Sincere appreciation goes to Samantha Hawkins for her great help in editing and typing.

We also wish to acknowledge the following publishers for granting reprint permissions: *Journal of the American Institute for the Study of Middle Eastern Civilization, The Middle East Journal,* Croom Helm, Indiana University Press, *International Migration Review,* and E. J. Brill.

CONTENTS

Women in the Developing World:
Evidence from Turkey

FOREWORD

By Elise Boulding
Professor Emerita, Dartmouth College

A monograph on women and development in the Turkish context has special interest because of Turkey's unique developmental path in the twentieth century. Will the story for women also be unique, or will it bear the earmarks of the familiar cultural dualism which characterizes countries of both North and South? Professor Abadan-Unat is well qualified to tell us, as a distinguished social scientist who has also had a political career and has been at the center of the interesting developments in her country in recent decades.

There was already a century of progressive thinking behind the radical secularization which Turkey, the center of the old Islamic Empire, initiated in the early 1920s. The adoption of the Swiss Civil Code and associated changes under the leadership of the charismatic Kemal Ataturk can be thought of as one of the great utopian ventures of the modern era. With one stroke of the pen women had political, economic and legal rights that most of their sisters in other Moslem countries still do not have- even if those rights came in the strictly patriarchal mold of Swiss law. The Code gave them educational opportunities which equal those of Western women, and it produced a generation of professional women with more status and authority, and in greater numbers, than their counterparts in any Western country. Professor Abadan-Unat poses two questions: Can equality for women be enacted by law, from the top? And is equal participation of women necessary for development?

Her answer to the first question is sobering for those who are putting major efforts into legislative action, though perhaps not surprising to sociologists: law alone cannot do this. Each successive government after the initial pioneering secularizers has been more conservative than its predecessor, and the number of women in parliament has gradually

3

decreased. Rights have been curtailed. Traditional Islamic family values have been reasserted. The second question gets a more positive answer. Participation In the labor force continues to increase, and Turkish women are visible nationally and internationally in public life. This participation certainly has something to do with Turkey's leadership role in development in its part of the world.

Clearly, law does not operate in a vacuum. The author points out that industrialization itself is a powerful force propelling women into the labor force, whether domestically or as migrant workers abroad. Husbands are often the first to push their wives into jobs when demand for female labor is high. From the women's side, their motive for working is household-related; wages mean purchasing power. Professor Abadan-Unat's research findings make no distinction between working class and professional women. Professional women, whether in government or the private sector, resemble their working class sisters in holding traditional, family-oriented values; they see their work as contributing primarily to their standard of living, not as a career in itself. Education has not meant liberation in terms of women's sense of autonomy, of claiming new status. The conclusion is that the participation of women in the labor force and in public life is a misleading indicator of equality. It helps development, but it may not help women in the larger social sense.

Since it is well established that attitudes change more slowly than overt behavior, one might speculate that attitude change is taking place beneath the surface, but may not show for some time yet. After all, law is precisely aimed at behavior, in the hope that attitudes will follow. What are the long-run forces at work that may contribute to a future mindset for women of autonomy, without which equality has no meaning? Economic forces have already been mentioned. Continued exposure to crises, and a rapid rate of social change in the environment so that traditional behaviors are maladaptive for survival, is another suggested by the author. My own work, which she cites, provides some evidence for this crisis theory of role change. Unfortunately, as we have both noted, participation in wars of liberation give women the requisite experience of change but subsequent political quiet gives men the opportunity to send women back to their homes. Again, the time factor is important. Traditional attitudes take a lot of wearing down.

There are circumstances under which the crisis theory works, and some of Professor Abadan-Unat's most important research centers on one of those circumstances: migration. A woman migrant does not automatically become an autonomous person. She may be overwhelmed by the alien surroundings and not be able to manage anything but a survival adaptation. However, when resourceful women who have handled past change experiences well are in the migrant situation, they are able to take in the new information they need, find a support system, and handle resource allocation and decision making well. This is most apt to happen when the woman has been sent ahead where there is demand for female labor, the husband using this advance migration as a legal device for his own migration. When the husband arrives, he faces an autonomous wife; either he adapts or there is separation. Similarly, when wives are left behind to manage the family homestead while the husband emigrates, they gain autonomy through successful decision making. The returned husband has to adapt to to an autonomous wife, or divorce ensues. What is important in both cases is that women have learned to see themselves differently while learning to cope with a changed environment. What Professor Abadan-Unat deplores is that so few women have as yet learned to see themselves differently.

The task of learning to see themselves differently is perhaps the major task that confronts the women's movement on every continent, in countries of every degree of industrialization. In the end, both men and women must see themselves and each other differently, for true "development" to take place. That will not happen soon. Yet Professor Abadan-Unat's monograph conveys a strong positive message about development as process. Since law is interactive with economic forces, changing the law is important. Turkey would not be the exciting blend of Islamic East and Euro-North American West that it is without the new constitution of the 1920s, nor would Turkish women be leaders in public life without that constitution. Women would not be international leaders in the professions of the sciences, law and medicine without the education which followed the constitution. When it is time for the next step down the long road of human and social development, Turkish women will be among the first to be ready to take it.

INTRODUCTION

Change in the status of women in the Muslim world, following upon increased contact with and openness to the West, most often proceeded relatively rapidly. In reforms relating to women, Turkey was far and away ahead of other Middle Eastern societies. This process began back in the nineteenth century, but, contrary to some expectations, was not initiated by the women themselves. Although some women such as daughters of scholars, generals, and judges were privately educated at home and eventually became famous as writers, composers and calligraphers, the restrictive rules in force during the imperial reign of the Ottoman did not furnish any opportunity for an opening of restrictions. Aside from the imperial harem, city women rarely left the house, and even when they did were hemmed in by administrative decrees.

The initiative actually came from men. The first move in this direction is tied up with a process defined by political scientists as "defensive modernization." Due to the rapid advances of science and technology in the eighteenth century, the Ottoman Empire suffered a succession of military defeats. This situation worried mostly the men of the sword, who were the first to feel the need for essential reforms and were desirous of adopting Western ways. These endeavors culminated in the reorganization of the army and of the educational system. Interestingly, these political choices closely affected women's opportunities for acquisition of professional skills in health as midwives and in education as teachers.

During the second half of the century, the strong desire to modernize Ottoman society as quickly as possible increasingly preoccupied the minds of Ottoman elites as well. For Young Turks and their reformist and nationalist sympathizers the status of women constituted, among others, a criterion for progress toward a new, Western-oriented social order. Indeed women's place in society became one major issue in the political ideologies to spread. Thus one of Turkey's most influential philosophers and mentors of Ataturk, Ziya Gokalp, wrote "in the future Turkish ethics must be founded upon democracy and feminism, as well as nationalism, patriotism, work and the strength of the family."

Similarly another influential politician, Ahmen Agaoglu, stressed that progress in the Islamic world depended upon two factors: literacy and the emancipation of women. Thus the emancipatory process of women became a part of the nationalist revolutionary movement, which paved the ground for Ataturk's deep rooted reforms, realized after the establishment of the Turkish Republic.

Obviously no society can be totally changed solely through legal and educational reforms. However the discarding of the totality of Islamic laws, namely the Sharia, as it was realized in 1926 with the adoption of the Swiss Code, remains in its magnitude a unique experience in the whole Islamic world. To assume that this far-reaching political decision has totally changed the inherent value system of the cultural outlook of Turkish society would be erroneous. No doubt a great number of conflicts, especially individual ones, have arisen around the old and new values which were transformed into binding norms. It is undeniable that the traditions of Islam concerning women are still too strong to be termed a mere residue. They permeate Turkish society in breadth and in depth and are at the bottom of male/female relationships even in public institutions. They induce Turkish women to keep a subservient role relative to men and encourage them to remain passive about and insensitive to their social situation. In the past as today motherhood and support for husband and children remain the highest values to cherish. While this mentality still exercises a considerable influence in rural areas and small towns, Turkish women in large cities and metropolitan areas have achieved success in combining a strictly biologically defined role with jobs and careers outside the home. Considering the extraordinarily rapid degree of urbanization they more and more are becoming full members of society.

The attitudes of Turkish women in public administration in the judiciary and in parliament, when more closely scrutinized, reflect to some degree this contradicting position of being desirous to achieve full equality in public life, while clinging to traditional values in private life. This situation is more than ever encouraged by the images conveyed in the mass media. Furthermore a strong tradition of centralized government and restrictive laws concerning associational activities discouraged a higher degree of participation and initiative in solving problems pertaining to working women.

In spite of the continuing impact of traditional values stemming from a strong patriarchy inspired mentality, the process of social change continues to produce a new generation of self-assertive women. Turkey, which has changed in the last twenty years from a predominantly agrarian society into an urban and industrialized one, witnesses the decline of the extended family, and the growth of female labor force both in industry and the services, the direction new generations are embracing seems to be clear: to embrace and enlarge the legacy of Ataturk to its women.

The selection of articles presented in this modest volume are divided into three parts. Part I represents an introduction to the historical background of the emancipatory process of Turkish women, and the impact of the War of Independence (1919-1922) on the status of women. Part 2 focuses on the process of modernization, the various factors which induced major changes in the socio-economic context, particularly the impact of external migration on sex role and family structure. Part 3 deals with the role and functions of Turkish women in government and the judiciary.

In summary, empirical data of recent years reveal that four groups among Turkish women seem to have adopted significantly new attitudes and standards. Each group—the newly urbanized women, product of depeasantization, the Turkish migrant women worker abroad, the female relatives of migrant workers left behind and the middle-class professional women—is acquiring a different set of modernizing values.

PART 1
POLITICAL DIMENSIONS

1

MOVEMENTS OF WOMEN AND NATIONAL LIBERATION: THE TURKISH CASE

Generally speaking a social movement emerges from given socio-historical conditions of dissatisfaction and strain. However as H. Blumer[1] states, the areas of social movements "are not chartered effectively". They start out as a vague, general, episodic expression of a fundamental search for new directions (general amorphous movement). It then becomes fairly rationalized and conscious; it probably creates an articulated ideal image of the future, an ideology and finally it formalizes and structures its existence and plans its specific course of action (specific crystallized movement). This model is justifiable insofar as it is the outcome of a logical questioning of the concrete socio-historical situation from which the movement has arisen.[2] The problem to be discussed in this paper deals with the question of whether or not a social movement, such as women's rights and political participation, has the chance to survive and to continue, or does it require additional political and ideological support. Since this problem is closely related to social change and sex roles, a short overview of the theoretical approaches is necessary.

The sociological, anthropological or social psychological theories (Goode 1963, Bott 1957) seem to point ultimately to changes in all requirements of the economic system as the prime moving forces of shifts in sex roles or in changes in the status of women. A different approach centered upon social crisis furnishes an additional dimension. According to this approach, rapid modernization as well as war and crisis often seem to bring women into the "male" position, at least for some

---

Reprinted from the *Journal of the American Institute for the Study of Middle Eastern Civilization* Vol. 1, Nos. 3-4:4-15. Autumn-Winter 1980-81.

time (Boulding, 1966), a fact which may be interpreted as a national mobilization of all resources. In times of crisis, economic or military demands may, at least temporarily, lead to a breakdown of cultural norms and ideals pertaining to men's and women's tasks. Thus the crisis theory serves to illustrate the role of time necessary for changing ascribed roles. Again the possibilities and limitations for sex role change inherent in a society are likewise demonstrated during crises. Finally this approach is most useful to make the sharp distinction between the effects of unifying nationalistic movements versus ideologically oriented action towards permanent structural change.

The sudden appearance of Turkish women in public life toward the end of World War I and their political and military participation during the War of Independence (1919-1922) and the slowing down of mass movements of women after the proclamation of the Republic may serve as a case study, which helps to illustrate how a national crisis may induce deep changes in social values without explicitly redefining sex roles and individual goals and aims. Before analyzing the particular historical facts of the Turkish case, a general evaluation of the dominant legal and cultural system of the Moslem countries in the Middle East seems to be indispensable.

WOMEN IN THE MIDDLE EAST

The traditional status of women in Moslem society can be explained by the symbiotic interaction between the prescribed acknowledgement of economic and moral responsibility toward all kinswomen and the principles of familial "honour" which depend upon attributes of female sexual purity. Control over Moslem women is solely the province of male relatives, — "The Harem and their cousins" as Germaine Tillion has named it so eloquently—who are expected to provide economic support for their women at all times, irrespective of the women's marital status. This has led to the combined effect of the traditional patterns of female seclusion and exclusion.[3] Only Turkey since the establishment of the Republic, which has totally repudiated the validity of the Sharia (religious legal norms) and to some extent Tunisia, may be exempted partly from this pattern.

EMANCIPATION EFFORTS DURING THE OTTOMAN EMPIRE

Within the Ottoman empire a series of initiatives to oppose or decrease this traditional life style began as far back as the first half of the 19th century. Intellectuals in favour of a radical Westernization of Turkish society demanded the abolition of polygamy, free choice of feminine garments, freedom of choice in matters of marriage, free circulation in the streets, and the establishment of girl's schools on all levels. However the beneficiaries of some of these innovations undertaken during the reign of Abdülaziz (1861-76) and Abdülhamit (1876-1909) were strictly classbound. Only girls of wealthy families, educated either by European governesses or attending foreign schools, were exposed to "Western" ideas and consequently began to exercise some kind of social criticism.[4]

After the return to constitutional monarchy in 1908, bolder steps such as the promotion of women's higher education institutions, discarding of veils, special lecture series for women, publishing of women's photos in the daily press, etc. were undertaken. But in this case again it was predominantly the women of the capital, Istanbul, who benefited from these changes. The editorial attitude of some women's journals of this period are indicative; they have an ambiguous character, they defend more liberal views, yet want to be loyal to the values of the establishment. For instance, the journal *Mahasin*, published in 1908, stated on the one hand that the slavery endured by women is the product of 600 years of tyranny and repression, but on the other hand maintained that it was "shameful for a woman to solve an equation or undertake a surgical operation!"[5]

The real impetus for a more comprehensive change came during World War I. Actually the existence of a small female labor class, mostly employed in the textile and food sectors, had become already noticeable in 1908, when striking women textile workers got involved in clashes with the police.[6] Yet only a huge challenge, such as the entrance of the Ottoman empire in World War I, could so suddenly catapult a new contingent of veiled and secluded women into public life. The jobs offered to women in ammunition and food factories enlarged the size of the working class. Parallel to this growth were banks, postal services, central and municipal administration and hospitals that opened their doors to women as well. In 1915, Princess Emine Naciye, wife of Enver Pasha, one of the leading figures of the ruling triumvirate, created an association to promote employment of women. During the same year an imperial decree (*irade*) permitted civil servants to discard the veil during office hours. However, these changes accelerated by the demands of the war machine, did not meet general approval. Though women were beginning to contribute to the functioning of public offices, they were often forced by the police to return home if their skirts were shorter than the officially prescribed length.[7] It should not be overlooked that during all the years of World War I, women passengers boarding Istanbul ferry boats operating on the Bosphorus and to the Islands, were not permitted to sit on the deck, they were confined to the lowest cabins.[8] Evidently the size of the female labor vanguard entering economic life was much too small to produce any effective structural changes. As Nadia H. Youssef insists, the real and lasting breakthrough is when the average female participates in a non-agricultural occupation. As long as this percentage remains excessively low and confined to one or two big cities, the social role of women remains exclusively domestic and maternal.[9] This explains also why women in the Ottoman empire only concentrated on more personal freedom, education and rights within marriage, at a period when their sisters in the West had already started to ask for political rights.

It was the tremendous shock which shook the country due to the defeat of the Ottoman army on more than one front, the humiliating clauses of the armistice of Mondros, the landing of Greek troops in Izmir and finally the occupation of Istanbul by British troops, which mobilized Moslem women of all walks of life. A national crisis contributed among other things to the rising consciousness of all Turkish women. Traditions and morals were pushed aside; Turkish women and Turkish men began to raise their voices and appeal to world public opinion.

THE POLITICAL ACTIONS OF TURKISH WOMEN PRIOR TO AND DURING THE WAR OF INDEPENDENCE

The sudden emergence of Greek troops in Anatolia on May 15, 1919 as the result of a special clause in the armistice, served as the catalyst for a nationwide wave of protest. In almost all cities of Turkey, open air meetings were organized with large numbers of women present. The threat directed toward disbanding national unity and independence forged strong bonds of solidarity between men and women of all strata. At these open air meetings — in Denizli, Kastamonu, and Tavas on May 16, 1919, in Giresun, Trabzon, Zonguldak, and Edremit on May 17, 1919—Turkish women and men expressed common feelings of distress and sorrow. These waves of protest not only served as a unifying factor in political action, but pushed women into the limelight of politics. Four days after the landing of Greek troops in Izmir, the students of the Istanbul Women's University, founded in 1914, together with members of the Progressive Women's Association, organized a sizeable meeting at the mausoleum of Mehmet the Conqueror.[10]

Istanbul, being the capital, became the scene of a chain of large-scale meetings. During the second half of May 1919, the squares of almost all major districts of Turkey's largest city witnessed the collective protest of its Turkish population. On May 19, 1919 in Fatih; May 20 in Üsküdar, May 22 in Kadiköy, May 23 and 30 in Sultanahmet Square, huge crowds, surpassing even an estimate of 100,000 at the last meeting, pledged themselves to the restitution of freedom and independence. At all of these meetings famous women writers, teachers, and students made important and relevant political speeches. Many of them had never spoken in public before.

At one of the largest meetings on Sultanahmet Square, May 19, 1919, Halide Edip a well-known writer and educational leader said:

> Turks, Moslems! We are living through our darkest hour! It is like night — the blackest of nights. But we will tear down this darkness and greet the morning sun... Swear your allegiance to the Ottoman flag and take your oath to die if need be. Even though we do not have weapons in our hands, there is a more effective weapon than them all: God and His Justice... Cannons and rifles may be destroyed, but God and Justice are imperishable. We, Turkish mothers, have sufficient nationalistic feelings to spit at these cannons. We demand, together with our men, a courageous, strong, representative government![11]

At the second meeting on this same square on May 23, she invited the huge crowd to resist and die for the freedom of the country. The Ottoman government, sympathizing with the British government, unwilling to take any contradictory measure, finally incited the court martial of "Kürt" Halide Edip. Meanwhile the War of Independence had started under the inspiring leadership of Mustafa Kemal. Halide Edip, together with her husband, fled from Istanbul, joined the national armed forces of Mustafa Kemal and soon became the first woman sergeant. Many of her experiences later served as a source of inspiration for her novel, "The flame Shirt" (Atesten Gömlek).[12]

But not only distinguished and already famous Turkish women participated in these political actions. Professional women as well as students, pushing aside the values of the past, such as modesty and submission to men, emerged as strong and influential public leaders.

Nakiye Elgün, Chairman of the Teachers Association, said at the Üsküdar meeting of May 20, 1919, "We shall not give up an inch of Turkish soil. Moslem brothers, you are not alone in this fight. Behind you are your grief-stricken, ill-fated mothers, sisters!"[13]

Representatives of the women's association such as Sabahat Hanim, addressed the crowds at the Üsküdar meeting on May 20, 1919, on behalf of the "Association of Progressive Women" as follows: "Today Izmir has been usurped by the Greeks. Tomorrow they might demand Konya, Bursa or even our beloved Istanbul. Shall we remain silent and accept all of these in a fatalistic mood? No, believing in a progressive social order for women in the future, I repeat: we, women, must take the lead in this fight for our most fundamental rights!"[14]

The younger the speaker, the more concrete her proposals. At the Kadiköy meeting of May 22, 1919, a student representative, Münevver Saime, said: "As a daughter of a nation whose freedom has been confiscated, I want to point out how to march toward independence. The time has come for few words and big deeds, not for sitting down and weeping. Nothing is to be gained from tears and lamentations. What we must do is to organize ourselves and act!"[15]

She too had to flee from Istanbul to Anatolia, where she joined the nationalist army. She actively participated in the War of Independence, and was known to many as "Soldier Saime". Wounded, she was later awarded the highest distinction, the Medal of Independence.

Equally indicative is the conclusion of a speech by another famous woman writer, Şükûfe Nihal, on the second meeting of Sultanahmet, May 30, 1919: "Do you know why all this disaster came upon us? Because we remained silent, we did not rebel against injustice. *If we were given the right to vote*, if there would have been a representative parliament and we would have a trustworthy cabinet, these days would not have come upon us!"[16]

This last paragraph, which implies less the political rights of women, than franchise in general, reflects one of the major arguments which led to the early establishment of a Turkish parliament in Ankara on April 23, 1920. The affinity between democratic demands for an enlarged political participation and the right of self-determination were formulated from the onset and defended by the leaders of the nationalist revolution as well as representatives of the nation.

WOMEN AND MILITARY ACTION

Next to the writers, teachers, and students who served to mobilize Turkish public opinion around the nationalist cause, history has also recorded a small but significant number of Turkish heroines, who actively fought on the battlefields. The likelihood that a much larger number of these partisan Anatolian women have been overlooked by official records is very great. Cahit Çaka, a Turkish historian who concentrated his efforts to unearth the contributions of Turkish women during the War of Independence, reports a number of important accomplishments solely realized by voluntary women soldiers such as Makbule from Gördes, who fought for months with her husband as a guerilla and was finally killed in combat in 1921. Similarly, the voluntary commander of a battalion on the south flank, Tayyar Rahmiye, organized an assault against the French at Osmaniye and was killed in action on July 1, 1920.

Again in the south, a woman named Hatice from Külek, joined the troops of Emin and Derviş. Upon the information that the French troops wanted to break through the siege at Posanti in the direction of Tarsus, she managed to obtain the confidence of the French, acted as a guide, led them to an ambush position at Karaboğaz, later returned with one hundred armed men and engaged herself in a decisive battle. Evidence of female participation in military action is indeed surprisingly high. The newspaper *Türkoğlu,* published in Bolu, near Ankara, reported on October 30, 1921, the names of twelve peasant women who fought all the way through the battle of İnönü with their own means of transportation. One among them was promoted to sergeant for her excellent organization for sending supplies to the front.[17]

The heroic deeds of Turkish women were not only recorded by historians, but passed also into the records of the new Turkish parliament. On January 30, 1921, at its 140th session, the representative of Bursa, Emin Bey, requested the awarding of the Medal of Independence to Nezahat, the daughter of Halit Bey, for her heroic deeds during the battle of Gördes and İnönü. Called by a number of speakers "the Turkish Jeanne d'Arc", this little girl, who started her career as an eight year old on the battlefield and was twelve at the time of this debate, was even proposed to be honoured with a promotion to general. But members of parliament such as Hamdi Namık from Izmir, desirous of maintaining a certain age standard in connection with the award of this supreme medal, proposed to grant Nezahat "a gift which could be used later for her trousseau..."[18]

POLITICAL ORGANIZATIONS OF WOMEN DURING THE WAR OF INDEPENDENCE

Parallel to the spontaneous mass action and individual participation on the battlefield, new types of women-sponsored organizations emerged. Until the War of Independence women's associations were almost uniquely preoccupied with educational and social welfare issues. The forging of a new nation also changed this conventional trend.

The first organized women's movement in Anatolia started in Erzurum. After a gathering in the mosque, telegrams were sent to the representatives in Istanbul of the United States and the Allied powers. The telegram read in part: "Oppression and cruelty have become common events in the occupied territories of Izmir, Antalya and Maraş. How can it be acceptable that after the signature of an armistice, occupation can take place? The British, the French and the Italians have stated that they desire peace without either annexation of territory or war indemnity. *We, the women of Erzurum*, are drawing the attention of the Allies to these facts!"[19]

The next step was the establishment of a special political organization constituted solely by women. The major source of inspiration for this unexpected move, was no doubt Mustafa Kemal's appeal to the whole nation on May 28, 1919, in which he urged men and women of Turkey to combat the enemy with all available means.

The first positive echo came from the women of Sivas (Central Anatolia) who under the leadership of Melek Hanım, wife of Reşit Pasha, the governor, and other women teachers, founded the "Anatolian Women's Association for Patriotic Defense" on November 5, 1919. Its by-laws, comprising eleven articles, published on November 8, 1919 in the newspaper "National Will" (*Irade-i Milliye*) states as its main aim and purposes the following ideas:

— To underline the indivisibility of all territories conceded to the Ottoman state by the armistice of Mondros,
— To strengthen the bonds of solidarity between Moslem men and women,
— To prevent disruptive, secessionist actions initiated by Greek and Armenian ethnic groups in these regions, while pledging to respect their religious beliefs and traditions.[20]

This association, administered by a board of sixteen women, succeeded in establishing many branches all over Anatolia with a large membership. These branches were as follows: Amasya, Kayseri, Niğde, Erzincan, Burdur, Pınarhisar, Kangal and Kastamonu.

The major activity of this organization, which actually was less a spontaneous grouping of women activists than a gathering of wives, daughters and sisters of Ottoman bureaucrats,[21] was to influence European public opinion by sending elaborate telegrams of protest to responsible authorities, further organizing open air meetings, and by collecting all kinds of donations.

The style and topics selected by the leaders of this organization indicate the prevailing political nature of their preoccupation. In a telegram sent to the ambassadors of France, the United States, and Italy in Istanbul, the president Melek Reṣit and general secretary Ṣefika Kâmil state on January 12, 1920:

> 1— We vigorously protest against the arbitrary action of the occupying powers executing a person, carrying a gun without administering any judicial inquiry,
>
> 2— We totally reject the decision of the occupying forces which stipulates that in case of an injury or death of one French soldier two local persons will be selected at random and executed.[22]

It might be advanced that some of the initiatives undertaken by this women's organization were actually part of the proposals of Mustafa Kemal's headquarters. But even if this were the case, this group of devoted, politically inexperienced pioneering women accomplished an important function in mobilizing national and international public opinion around the cause of national independence.

AFTERMATH: COMPREHENSIVE LEGAL REFORMS WITHOUT THE SUPPORT OF A MASS MOVEMENT

Following the massive support of Turkish women during the War of Independence briefly sketched above, how was the status of Turkish women changed? Did the support of this effective social movement spur further progressive policies or were the coming reforms the deed of one single farsighted man, Mustafa Kemal Atatürk?

The founder of the new Turkish state, a fierce opponent of autocratic rule, attached great importance to representative government. This explains why he succeeded in reconvening the dissolved Ottoman parliament as early as April 23, 1920 under the name of the Turkish Grand National Assembly. This assembly was the arena for sharp political fights. Although officially there were no political parties, two competing factions, representing traditional and progressive views, constantly clashed. This fact was to play a decisive role in matters relating to women. At the very moment when the vague, episodic expression of the women's movement was about to become an articulated ideal image of the future, the traditional forces in parliament blocked the way. Although Mustafa Kemal publicly acknowledged the heroic deeds of the Anatolian women in his speech of February 3, 1923 and promised that "Turkish women should be free, enjoy education and occupy a position equal to that of men; they are entitled to it," the divisive composition of the first Turkish Grand National Assembly ·obliged him to postpone most of his reformist plans. And the zest displayed by the Anatolian women had somehow also disappeared. With peace a return to conventional sex roles had taken place. Society at that point did not look upon its women as equal to men. Two parliamentary debates in particular may serve as examples for this negative attitude. Both the first relating to a bill concerning syphilis control (session 122, 1921)[23] and the second dealing with the electoral law,[24] turned into violent discussions. Defenders of women's rights (Emin Bey and Tunalı Hilmi Bey) were not granted the floor, they were grossly insulted and the sessions were suspended. Proposals such as those compelling women to undergo medical control and including the female population in calculations for the size of voting districts were bluntly refused. The decision of the Ministry of Education of the period to invite the female teacher corps to the National Convention of Education led to a general investigation and finally ended with the resignation of the incumbent minister.

However Mustafa Kemal, during his various visits to the countryside, continued to declare himself in favour of egalitarian measures. He argued in Konya (March 21, 1923), about six months before the proclamation of the Republic, that "the fact that women who are subject to much less encouraging conditions have been able to march along with men, sometimes even ahead of them, is clear-cut proof of their equality and their outstanding ability!"[25]

At this very period, the position of educated, active Turkish women indicates a rather ambivalent standing. The situation shortly before the adoption of the Swiss Civil Code helps to explain this ambiguity better. In the parliament an attempt was made to codify the Family Law bill, drafted in 1917. The commission in charge approved of marriages at the age of 9 for girls and 10 for boys and of polygamy. Furthermore, it gave women the right to divorce their husbands only under certain conditions, but the men's right to repudiate their wives was upheld. At this point the very mild, almost unnoticeable reaction of educated women was criticized by the Turkish press.[26]Even feminists such as Halide Edip Adıvar, expressed their criticism, not from the point of view of women's rights, but rather from the angle of conditions favouring a harmonious marital life. How can such passivity be explained? The answer lies first in the cultural dualism, which persists in spite of economic participation of women in many contemporary societies. In Turkey, once peace was restored, the vigorous impetus for women's initiatives had disappeared. Furthermore, the rather élitist approach of Mustafa Kemal Atatürk to social change preferred the persuasion of public opinion rather than open controversies with opposing climates of opinion.

Thus the most comprehensive change in the legal status of women within the whole of the Middle East was realized through the farsighted plans of one statesman and his dedicated inner circle.

Atatürk, anxious to present to the world a "modern face" was determined to fight against the conservative forces gathered around the Ministry of Sharia. He first severed the ties between state and religion by abolishing the Caliphate on March 23, 1924. On that very same day he enacted a law on education bringing all religious schools under unified control. Atatürk then proceeded from here on to use legal codification as an accelerator for social change. On February 17, 1926, a slightly modified version of the Swiss Civil Code was adopted in one session, where only speeches in favour of the Code were made.[27]

For Atatürk and his followers, the granting of equality before the law among men and women was the realization of a promise given long before, but even more than that, it was a symbol to the world that the new Turkey was adamant "about reaching the level of contemporary civilization."

Thus the major rights conferred upon Turkish women were predominantly the result of the relentless efforts of a small "revolutionary élite," for whom law-making was the primary tool of social change rather than the product of large-scale demands expressed in mass meetings.

A similar trend can be traced on the issue of granting political rights to Turkish women. These rights were given to them about 15 years earlier than to their French counterparts, yet it is hard to pretend that this additional dimension of emancipation was the result of a heavy campaign, backed by urban and rural potential women voters.

Requests in this direction were articulated mainly by speakers and members of the Women's League, a women's association located in Istanbul with a predominant membership of professional women. This association amended its by-laws in 1927 and started to pronounce itself in favour of political rights. Its president, Nezihe Muhittin, declared: "Revolutions are born out of just demands. We shall continue to put forward our claims at each election and in the end we shall obtain the right to vote as citizens."[28] Yet, it would be erroneous to state that the League exercized a determining influence on this issue. The agenda-setting function of political rights for women was not exercized by a selected women's organization, but directly by Atatürk himself. Ignoring this issue for about four years following the transition to a secular civil code, the question suddenly appeared in parliament in 1930. On the very same day Professor Afet Inan in Atatürk's People's House gave a formal lecture defending the necessity of granting men and women the right to participate in public affairs. The Turkish Grand National Assembly unanimously amended the municipal law (April 3, 1930) and thus enabled Turkish women to participate in municipal elections.[29]

It is equally indicative that the proposal for the amendment of the Constitution of 1924, which represents the final step for the participation of Turkish women at general elections, took its inspiration from the discussions of the "inner circle" of Atatürk. As Afet Inan related in her writings, "...on June 4, 1933 a lively discussion among the closest friends of Atatürk around his dinner table in Çankaya took place. The topic of discussion was the balance sheet of the first ten years of the Republic. The essence and meaning of democracy being discussed in detail, it was again Atatürk who maintained that any system which does not provide women equal political rights with men, cannot qualify as truly democratic."[30]

How decisive the course of such closed discussions happened to be is illustrated with the following example again related by Afet Inan. "One evening in winter 1934, Atatürk and his prime minister, Ismet Inönü, came to my library. Atatürk said to me 'Kiss Inönü's hand and thank him!' Surprised, I asked why. Atatürk replied, 'It is Inönü who will propose a constitutional amendment to grant Turkish women complete political rights!'"[31]

Indeed on December 5, 1934 Articles 5, 11, 16, 23, and 58 of the Constitution were amended, the age limit for voting raised from 18 to 22 and the genders "men and women" explicitly cited. Among the various speakers of this historical session, Sadri Maksudi (Şebin Karahisar) strongly emphasized that "this government has to be congratulated because only countries without democratic systems are depriving their women of political rights!" These amendments were unanimously accepted by 258 members, 58 were not present.[32]

How should one evaluate this additional move toward more liberties? Is it the fruit of an independent action or rather complementary to a more comprehensive set of policies? The latter seems to be the case. Considering that Turkish women because of historical reasons were excluded from active economic participation due to the Ottoman Empire's traditions in the nineteenth century, and because of their segregation in public life as a result of Islam's definition of women as inferior to men, it is not surprising that they never developed a genuine and effective Turkish suffragette movement. Arguments put forward by various writers such as increasing pressure from women's associations

(Tezer; Inan, 1957) appear to have no direct relation to the problem. Thus the hypothesis, eloquently defended by Şirin Tekeli, a young political scientist, seems to offer the most persuasive and plausible explanation.[33] Accordingly, Atatürk was extremely anxious not to be associated with any kind of fascist movement. With the increasing weight of fascist régimes in the West, he attempted to avoid classification under the same label. This explains why he stressed in an interview given to the *Vossische Zeitung* that "revolution and dictatorship, even if necessary, can only be used for a short time." In order to prove his genuine belief in a true democratic system, even when implementing a tutelary democracy, Atatürk, by granting political rights to the women of Turkey and later by nominating fifteen distinguished representatives to parliament, attempted to prove to the West that he placed his country ahead of some others "with the highest levels of civilization."[34]

CONCLUSION

This model of modernization of Turkey, while reflecting the vanguard of liberation in the Middle East, is not unique. Tunisia, under the leadership of Bourguiba, appears to have followed a similar path. This obliges developmentalists to use certain social indicators such as legal equality, the right to vote, etc. in a very specific historical context. As Nadia H. Youssef correctly emphasizes,[35] women's rights and status in most developing nations are *nationalistically* rather than *individualistically* grounded. In other words, the concept of improving women's status is closely associated in the Moslem world with their potential contribution to national development rather than with their own self-realization and self-actualization. The results of that orientation are ambivalence and tension between the drive to develop, to become "modern" (economically, emotionally and socially) and the wish to reaffirm certain traditional bases of life.

Although migration, urbanization and industrialization have abolished innumerable constraints on present-day Turkish women and in spite of Turkey's large, knowledgeable and powerful women's élite in all professions and spheres of public life,[36] the impact of a cultural dualism based on Islam versus secularism, has not been eliminated. Neither does the existence of a multi-party system, compelled to function through compromises usually given toward traditionalism, contribute to reducing the huge gap between the economically independent urban woman and her dependent, unpaid, virtually illiterate rural sister.

Thus, if war, participation on the battlefront, and the fight for national liberation serve only as a crisis catharsis, a transitional vehicle for major modifications in women's social status are basically the product of the will power of charismatic leaders, is there another solution? The answer probably lies in having parties in power continue systematic efforts to make known the suffering of women under the "double oppression" of traditional roles and marginal working conditions. Only when the liberation of women from various societal constraints, mostly anchored in the prevailing cultural system, becomes an independent political goal, sustained by appropriate organizations and mass movements, can the evolutionary pattern toward more social justice and equity between sexes be accelerated. Otherwise the most comprehensive legal reforms will continue to maintain the major division between women, between those who are educated, urban, and economically independent and those who are illiterate, rural, and economically dependent.

Fortunately the heirs of the Atatürk legacy to womanhood, especially in recent years, have grasped the vital importance of the reinforcement of legal reforms to enhance their impact on society's fabric and public opinion.

NOTES

1. Blumer, H., "Collective Behaviour" in J. Gittler, Ed. *Review of Sociology Analysis of a Decade,* New York, J. Wiley, 1957, p. 127.
2. Koutopoulos, K.M. "Women's Liberation on as a Social Movement" in Constantina Safilios-Rotschild, *Toward a Sociology of Women,* Xerox Corp., 1972, p. 355.
3. Youssef, Nadia H., "Women in the Moslem World," in B. Ilglitzin and R. Ross, Eds. *Women in the World,* Clio Books, Oxford, 1976, p. 204.
4. Abadan-Unat, N., "Social Change and Turkish Women, 1926-1976," in N. Abadan-Unat, Ed. *Women in Turkish Society,* E.J. Brill, Leiden 1981, p. 6.
5. *Mahasin,* 1908, No. 7.
6. Coşar, Ö.S., "Çakırcah Mehmet Efe," *Milliyet,* June 9, 1973.
7. Inan, A., *The Rights and Duties of Turkish Women in History,* (in Turkish., *Tarih Boyuncu Türk Kadnumin hak ve görevleri, Ankara 1975, Millî Egitim Bakanlıgi,* 3rd Ed., *p. 97.*
8. *Inan, A., op.cit., p. 204.*
9. Youssef, N.H., *op.cit.,* p. 204.
10. Inan, A., *op.cit.,* p. 104.
11. Arıburun, Kemal, *The Istanbul Open Air Meetings During the War of Independence* (in Turkish) *Millî Mücadelede Istanbul Mitingleri* Ankara 1951, p. 12-13.

12. Taskıran, T., *Women in Turkey,* Istanbul, 1976, Redhouse Publ. p. 51.
13. Arıburun, K., *op.cit.,* p. 23-24.
14. Ibid. p. 21-22.
15. Ibid. p. 34-35.
16. Ibid. p. 50.
17. Çaka, C., *War and Women in History* (in Turkish, *Tarih Boyunca Harp ve Kadın*), Ankara, 1948, Askerî Fabr. Basımevi, p. 57.
18. Taskıran, T., *Turkish Women Rights* (in Turkish, Türk Kadın Hakları), Ankara 1973, Basbakanlık Basımevi, p. 81.
19. Çaka, C., *op.cit.,* p. 41-43.
20. Inan, A., *op.cit.,* p. 124.
21. The breakdown of the 16 members of the executive committee elected on February 19, 1920 at Sivas is quite revealing. Four teachers, five wives of top ınilitary and civilian administrators, and seven wives of notables. Similarly the executive committee of the Kangal branch comprises nine wives, daughters, mothers of military and civilian bureaucrats, one teacher, and three wives of notables. Inan, A., *op.cit.,* p. 128-129.
22. The newspaper "Will of the People" (Iradei Milliye), January 12, 1920.
23. Taskıran, T., *op.cit.,* p. 63.
24. Taskıran, T., *op.cit.,* p. 64.
25. *Atatürk Speeches and Declarations* (in Turkish, Atatürk'ün Söylev ve Demeçleri, II), "A Talk with the Women in Konya", March 21, 1923, p. 147-148.
26. In the winter of 1923-1924, the Istanbul *Aksam* newspaper carried several such articles. "Loyalty to Tradition" by A. Agaoglu, December 26 1923, "Decision of the Family Law" by N. Sadak, January 7, 1924, Halide Edip. "What are the Intentions of Our Women?" February 9, 1924.
27. Sükrü Kaya, speaker for the judicial commission in parliament, presented the new code with the following justification: "The commission believes that the Swiss Civil Code is most relevant to the Turkish character and its needs. It comprises in itself all the principles that human perception can assemble in the name of justice and human rights. The new law incorporates such principles as monogamy and the right to divorce-principles which are required for a civilized nation". *T.B.M.M. Tutanakları,* (Record of the Turkish Grand National Assembly), February 17, 1926.
28. *Cumhuriyet,* June 6, 1927.
29. Inan, A., *op.cit.,* p. 165.
30. Ibid. p. 175.
31. Ibid. p. 175.
32. Ibid. p. 188.
33. Tekeli, S., *A Comparative Study on the Status of Women in Politics* (in Turkish unpublished manuscript, Kadının Siyasal Hayattaki Yeri üzerinde Karsılastırmaı bir Arastırma), Istanbul 1977, p. 272-273.
34. Tekeli, S., *op.cit.,* p. 282-284.
35. Youssef, N.H., *op.cit.,* p. 203.
36. Abadan-Unat, N., "The Modernizatioh of Turkish Women," *Middle East Journal,* Summer 1978.

2

THE MODERNIZATION OF TURKISH WOMEN

Turkey has long been cited as the most important pioneer in the Middle East in modernizing the life of its female population. Now, 50 years past, we have to ask: How was it possible to transplant completely alien laws to a country of totally different culture and be able to administer this legislation with success for about half a century? The answer lies as much in the attachment to the values produced by Western civilization which Atatürk so fervently attempted to implant in Turkish society as in the changes produced by the slow but constant evolution which already began during Ottoman rule. Although these early attempts did not result in any successful and meaningful reform, it was these kinds of social challenges that prepared the ground for the later decisive and deep changes.

Indeed, emancipation of women began in Turkey in the first half of the nineteenth century. Those in favor of radical Westernization of Turkish society asked for the introduction of monogamy into the Imperial Household, including the elimination of the Sultan's *odalık* (concubine); free choice of feminine garments; non-interference by the police in the private lives of women; greater consideration toward women in general; freedom of choice in matters of marriage; the suppression of intermediaries in marriage arrangements; the creation of a medical school for girls, the adoption of a European civil code; the abolition of polygamy in general and the outlawing of repudiation, that is, arbitrary and summary divorce.[1]

Reprinted from *The Middle East Journal* Summer 1978, pp. 291-305.

Another group of intellectuals of that period, deeply imbued with ideas of Turkish nationalism, who deemed the call for European education nothing but Montmartrian immorality deplored polygamy, repudiation and the veil.

Even the Islamic traditionalists who advocated segregation were ready to concede women the right to dispose of their own property, to walk alone in the streets, to frequent women's organizations and to attend primary and secondary schools.

Although women's life in the Ottoman Empire was hemmed in by innumerable restrictions, it would be erroneous to assume that they were completely passive sufferers. Their struggle for more and better education was carried on vigorously in the last quarter of the nineteenth century. As a matter of fact, as early as 1863, under Sultan Abdul-Aziz, a college for the training of women teachers was founded in Istanbul, followed by the opening of primary schools for girls. The first women's magazine, entitled *Progress* (*Terakki*), appeared in 1869.[2] Under Sultan Abdulhamit another weekly, called *The World of Women*, began publication. Its contributors and editorial staff were all women. Women writers of that time were no longer mere poets singing of love, of nightingales and nature; they studied deeply the social and educational questions which affected their lives.[3]

Turkish women got their real chance in 1908. The return to constitutional monarchy brought into positions of power men whose political and social creed laid strong emphasis on women's education. During this period women started to organize themselves. The first women's club, *Taali Nisvan*, not only invited lecturers and opened courses, but founded, under the vigorous and energetic leadership of Halide Edib, the famous writer, day care centers for children. During the Balkan war, the women's section of the Red Crescent, founded in 1877, trained the first nurses. After the creation of a kind of "women's university" (*Nisvan Darüflünun*), regular courses for women students were started on February 7, 1914, at the University of Istanbul. In January 1914 the first seven Muslim female employees were recruited by the telephone company in Istanbul.[4]

Nevertheless, all these innovations and achievements were the accomplishment of members of a privileged, urban élite. The majority of the Muslim-Ottoman population still clung to the idea that there is definite male supremacy. Well known writers such as Namık Kemal and Tevfık Fikret repeatedly deplored the traditional anti-feminine attitude in the realm of education.[5]

It was the abrupt entrance of the Ottoman Empire into World War

I which helped the Turkish middle class urban women enter new fields of activity such as employment in post offices, banks, hospitals, and municipal and central administration. Although unaffected by the suffragette movement which was raging in Europe during the first quarter of the twentieth century, Turkish women, when confronted with concrete situations of national distress, quickly gained political consciousness. Its most obvious evidence was the astonishingly high participation of women protesting in the Square of Sultan Ahmed in May 1919 against the occupation of Izmir by the Greeks. The support of educated women as well as countless anonymous peasant women at the front or in auxiliary services represents an important aspect of Turkey's struggle for independence.

This also explains why Atatürk started his speech on February 3, 1923, with acknowledgement of the deeds of Anatolian women. Rightly he promised: "The Turkish women have fought bravely for national independence. Today they should be free, enjoy education and occupy a position equal to that of men; they are entitled to it."[6]

LEGAL EMANCIPATION

The bold reform undertaken by Atatürk, especially in regard to the status of women, was a gigantic swing towards the West, which no other Islamic society had ventured.[7] By liberating Turkish women, he wanted to lay the foundation for more egalitarian and harmonious family life. He wanted Turkish women to have the same goals as men, that is to develop a life style that uses their energies and capabilities in such a way that they function in their various roles efficiently and productively. Atatürk was determined to liberate women from their secondary and subdued role that consisted solely of being a commodity of exchange, a producer of offspring, in short, an object. He said in March 1923: "Our enemies claim that Turkey cannot be considered a civilized nation, because she consists of two separate parts: men and women. Can we shut our eyes to one portion of a group, while advancing the other and still bring progress to the whole group? The road of progress must be trodden by both sexes together, marching arm in arm...."[8]

Of all Atatürk's Westernizing reforms, the emancipation of women carries a double distinction: it definitely represents priority over a number of planned innovations — as an example one can cite the administrative decision of İstanbul's head of the police four days before the proclamation of the Turkish Republic to abolish the segregated compartments on the streetcars of İstanbul, October 24, 1923[9]—and the fact that none of the vital innovations concerning women were embodied in any law. Whereas the turban and fez were outlawed by the Hat Law (No. 671-25.11.1925), only local ordinances were directed against the veil. But Atatürk was not satisfied simply by introducing bold innovations in relatively narrow, élitist circles. He wanted, above all, to change the fate of Turkish women at large. And because of his remarkable attachment and respect for law and organization,[10] he set out to introduce a completely new legal framework for the regulations of family relationships in order solidly to implant his most cherished ideal, equality between men and women.

The most important date for the advancement of Turkish women was the adoption of the Swiss Civil Code on October 4, 1926. With the adoption of a complete system of Western private law, Turkey's legislators wanted to emphasize the importance they placed on the initiative of equality before the law irrespective of sex and the strengthening of the status of Turkish women within the family. This decision, qualified in legal terms as "reception", made polygamy illegal, gave the right of divorce to women as to men, made civil marriage obligatory, by its significant silence allowed marriage between Muslims and non-Muslims, and removed any difference between men and women in terms of inheritance.[11] In one respect, however, the weight of custom had forced a change in the new code. The minimum ages for marriage, which was 20 for men and 18 for women in the Swiss Civil Code, were reduced first to 18 and 17 and, later, in June 1938, to 17 and 15 respectively.

The Turkish Civil Code, in line with its Swiss prototype, does not allow absolute equality between husband and wife. The husband is the head of the family, the wife must follow the husband, who alone is entitled to choose a domicile, unless the wife, by applying to the court, can justify on acceptable grounds such as health, *etc.*, her own choice. The wife is required to participate in the maintenance of the household by assuming tasks in the household. If the wife wants to practice a profession, she has to obtain the open or tacit consent of the husband; in case of refusal she may apply to the court for arbitration. Since the law is based on a system of separate ownership of property, she may dispose freely of her material goods and has unlimited rights of ownership over all her acquisitions.[12]

The Turkish Civil Code grants both sides the right to ask for divorce. The grounds for divorce can be classified in two groups: specifically stated ones of desertion, ill treatment or adultery, and those of a general nature such as incompatibility of character. Since the adoption of the Turkish Civil Code divorces have rapidly increased; divorce is mostly sought in large cities, by couples married from six to ten years. The majority of the divorces are those of childless couples and the most frequently quoted grounds are incompatibility of character, followed by desertion.[13]

Another innovation brought about by the Turkish Civil Code is temporary separation of the marriage partners (Art. 38) with a duration of one to three years. At present much discussion goes on in the media about the rigidity of the Turkish jurisdiction in regard to divorce, favoring a more flexible approach to dissolved unions with little hope for reconciliation.

Legally, religious marriages are not recognized. They may be carried out after the civil ceremony. However, religious practice as the sole basis for marriage is still widespread in the countryside under the name of "Imam marriage". The absence of formal registration of a large number of newly formed households has given way to urgent demands in the field of legitimization of children. The recognition by law of these children born out of wedlock has been realized by a sequence of special laws: No. 2330-1933, No. 4727-1945, No. 5524-1950, No. 6650-1956. The total figure for registrations under these laws is 7,724,419 children.[14] Since then another set of laws has been discussed and promulgated which concerns the registration without a fine of children born of illegal unions, the enlargement of the competence of local authorities in terms of recognition of these illegitimate children and the establishment of a legal link between the child and the mother. These laws are No. 461-11.3.1964, No. 554-8.4.1965, No. 578-17.4.1965.[15]

The legal emancipation certainly strengthened the position of Turkish women within the family. With the threat of repudiation, of polygamy, being banned at least partially — and especially among the younger generation — a new concept of family life has emerged which is based on mutual rights and duties. Equality within the family not only changed the status of women once they were widowed or orphaned by equalizing inheritance, but also by supplying the women with some kind of coercive legal power. In case of adultery, if the husband's involvement was proved *in flagrante*, the Penal Code provides — upon grievance on behalf of the other spouse — a penalty for both partners of from three to 30 months. (T.C.K. Art. 141). These penalties can be dispensed in case the plaintiff, in this case the wife, takes back her complaint.

Even so, traditional institutions such as the paying of the bride price and elopement of minors — punishable by law — are still exercizing their influence because their disappearance largely depends on the economic evolution of society.

STATUS OF WOMEN IN URBAN AND RURAL SETTINGS

The extraordinary change of the status of Turkish women, be it within the family or in a larger context, is closely related to de-peasantization and rapid urbanization. Since Turkish society bears a strong, homogeneous Muslim character, traditions, mores and even superstitions still prevail wherever rigid social stratification patterns remain intact. As Fatima Mernissi pointed out,[16] Muslim sexuality is a territorial one, a sexuality whose regulatory mechanisms consist primarily of a strict allocation of space to each sex. The universe of men is related to the universe of religion and power and the universe of women to the domestic universe of sexuality and the family. Wherever rural women are living in a secluded *Gemeinschaft* type of community, little attempt is made to make use of personal abilities for the development of a free personality.

This general trend has been upheld by empirical findings of social scientists such as M. Kiray and D. Kandiyoti. It appears evident that only where changing economic conditions of village life have produced a new type of community life do attitudes toward family permissiveness and liberalism to women substantially change. Turkey, especially since 1950, has undergone rapid change in rural areas, largely provoked by the mechanization of farming[17] as well as internal and external migration.[18] As a result, various forms of modernization, including a growing awareness of political issues, can be witnessed in rural areas as well as urban areas. However, the strong-hold of traditionalism, especially in regard to women's status, still remains in rural regions.

The great discrepancy between rural and urban centers no doubt explains the sharp difference of skill acquisition, educational level and vocational orientation between rural and urban women. In spite of the rapid degree of urbanization — the annual average rate of population growth in large cities was 5.2 per cent in 1940-50, nine per cent in 1950-60 and 11.1 per cent in 1960-70—Turkey is still an agrarian society.[19] Sixty-two per cent of its population of 40 million lived in rural settlements in 1973. Again, 75 per cent of its active population of 10.9 million belongs to the peasant class. When we consider that 49 per cent of this active population is female and that in Turkish villages,[20] females between the ages of seven and 70 are engaged in all kinds of agricultural activities, one comes to the conclusion that half

32

of the agricultural output of Turkey lies on the shoulders of its female peasant population, who still are far from being able to benefit from the legal reforms implemented half a century ago.

This fact becomes even more relevant when considering its relationship to literacy and fertility. According to the census of 1970, out of a total population of 29.4 million who are six years old and above, there were 8.7 million (62 per cent) women versus 4.6 million (38 per cent) men who were registered as analphabets. If one considers those primary school graduates who completed only a three year education and had no opportunity to do any reading after that time, the actual rate of illiterates no doubt will be even higher. This situation has an important impact on various factors, especially the rate of fertility.

While the fertility rate in the urban sector amounts to three per cent, it climbs to seven per cent in rural surroundings. Until the early 1960s, the Turkish government's official stand was for the encouragement of population increase. It was only after 1960 that the idea that existing policies might be in opposition to national goals gained some recognition. Thus a change in the existing laws was formulated in the first Five Year Plan, which went into effect in 1963. A General Directorate of Family Planning was subsequently established within the Ministry of Health and, in 1965, the sale of contraceptives and the dissemination of information concerning them were legalized. However, the impact of family planning still remains limited owing to the fact that, among the rural population, it is predominantly women who already have an average of four to five live or eight to ten live/still births who are volunteering for the usage of intrauterine devices and other contraceptives.

While the average number of children in rural areas of Turkey is 6.12 it is around 3.88 in urban areas. Further broken down, we see that it totals to 3.30 in Ankara, 2.91 in İzmir and 2.65 in Istanbul.

It is often claimed that the most important determinants of fertility are the level of education and level of income. Both of these determinants are closely related to urbanization and industrialization, since increased urbanization also means increased literacy and a higher degree of education. While the average amount of fertility among illiterate women is 4.2 children, this average falls to 3.2 among literate, to 2.8 among primary school graduates, to two among secondary graduates and to 1.4 among university graduates.[21] The same trend can be witnessed in terms of income.

According to S. Timur's findings the number of children among married women between 14-44 averaged according to yearly income, indicates that persons with the lowest income (11-500 TL) had 4.6, and those with the highest yearly income (4,000 and above) only 2.7 births.[22] The relationship between fertility and income level has been verified through other empirical findings as well. Ç. Kağıtçıbaşı has shown within a comparative survey on the value of children that case studies in Turkish urban or rural settings produce quite different attitudes towards children. Comparing urban middle SES respondents with urban low SES and rural respondents, it came out that while the modal value of children for urban middle class is providing happiness, for rural respondents it is providing financial help. These value variations also reflect the life styles and basic needs of various social classes. While psychological benefits are important for the middle class parents, material benefits of children are more real and thus have more salience in the rural setting.[23]

After having briefly investigated the impact of rural residence on education and fertility, it seems important to verify also the validity of the hypothesis whereby, as a result of industrialization and urbanization, the extended family is superseded by the independent nuclear family. According to the most detailed research so far undertaken, S. Timur has proven that family types vary depending upon the types of economy and relations of production and that property ownership (especially land) is an important determinant of the extended household. The proportion of nuclear families is highest among illiterates and the highest educational group, whereas it is lowest among those with middle level education. Nuclear families predominate among farm workers and small farmers in rural areas and among unskilled laborers in urban areas, all of whom are mostly illiterate or poorly educated. The characteristic family type among professionals and civil servants in urban areas who have university education is also nuclear. On the other hand, extended families are prevalent among large land owners and among those who own middle sized farms in rural areas and in urban areas among artisans, retailers, etc. who have a medium level of education.

When the family ceases to be the unit of production, the patriarchally extended family breaks down. Economic limitations prevent all but the fairly well-to-do from actually maintaining such extended households. Extended households, functioning as common production and consumption units, form a small percentage of village households; one of the major factors to sustain the brideprice tradition is the extended family.

Family types thus not only determine the continuation or end of institutionalized traditions such as the brideprice, but also help to define the status and rôles of the family members. It is the family type which determines the power structure in the family and family modernity. In both urban and rural areas, the patriarchally extended families represent the most traditional and nuclear families the least traditional.

Table 1
Degree of Modernity According to Family Type and Settlement Places in Percentages

Degree of Modernity	Nuclear	Family type Transitional	Extended	Total
	Three big cities/ villages	Three big cities/ villages	Three big cities/ villages	Three big cities/ villages
Modern	69-5	59-3	47-22	62-3
Transitional	27-25	32-26	7-13	28-24
Traditional	4-70	9-70	46-85	10-72

Source: Timur, Serim, *Türkiye'de Aile Yapısı*, Hecetteppe Yayını, No. D-15, table 60, p. 111.
Three big cities: İstanbul, İzmir, Ankara.

The table clearly indicates that wherever extended (patriarchal) family relationships prevail, which means even in metropolitan centers, such as İstanbul, İzmir and Ankara, traditional behavior on the part of women is expected. One of the most blatant examples of the impact of family type on the status of women reveals itself in the eating pattern of rural women.

Timur's inquiry on eating patterns in villages according to family types has shown that while in nuclear families living in villages 91 per cent eat together, among the extended families of rural background only 71 per cent eat together. In 23 per cent of these families there is segregation at meal time and with five per cent of them, the daughters-in-law eat separated even from the other female members of the family.[24]

MIGRATION AND EMANCIPATION

Next to education, income level and family structure, both internal and external migration appears to have a strong influence on the modernization of Turkish women. Although internal migration is an old process, its impact, because of little change in family structure, did not affect drastically the left behind family members. However, in the case of external migration, new features produced important changes. First it should be kept in mind that a considerable number of the Turkish female workers employed abroad — that number reached 143,611 in 1975 in West Germany alone—came from rural areas. Furthermore, the left behind family members even in rural areas have in part embraced a different type of living than those dependents left behind in the case of internal migration. The recently carried out Boğazıyan survey has revealed that an important segment of the left behind family members are living in a form of nuclear family and have adopted new, independent forms of conducting family affairs. In other words, the migratory process has changed, among other things, the decision making process, patterns of authority within the family and role expectations among the spouses. This trend is reflected in the following table:

Table 2
Financial and Other Decision Making According to Family Types in Boğazıyan and Villages in Percentages

	Nuclear		Extended		Total	
	Financial	Other	Financial	Other	Financial	Other
Male in household	7	9	34	43	17	22
Male out of household	7	28	2	8	5	21
Elderly female in family	5	6	18	23	10	12
Wife	68	50	28	20	53	39
Others	6	4	11	2	8	4
No answer	7	3	7	7	7	4
	100	100	100	100	100	100

Source: Nermin Abadan-Unat, R. Keles, *et al. Migration and Development, A Study of the Effects of International Labor Migration on Boğazıyan* District, Ajansturk, Ankara, 1976, p. 334.

External migration seems no doubt to have increased orientation predispositions favoring the educational outlook for girls. It causes a substantial amount of marital strain and conflict. High mobility and fragmentation of family induced men to share responsibility with women. Increased income induced women to adopt a conspicuous consumption pattern. Thus, the inclination for working outside the house seems to be rather a corollary function of an industrial society, rather than a consequence of change affecting the status of women. Yet even where external migration seems to have contributed to the reinforcement of traditional values, it still has opened the door for social dynamism.[25]

Finally, the impact of mass media on rural women or inhabitants of squatter houses seems definitely to have increased the political knowledge level of female listeners/viewers as O. Tokgöz has shown. Mass media consumption during electoral periods substantially increases the cognitive level of female voters, even if there seems no open correlation between increased knowledge and increased political participation.[26]

TURKISH WOMEN IN INDUSTRY

The influx of Turkish women to industrial jobs, at home and abroad, is no doubt one of the consequences of rapid urbanization and industrialization. In 1970, 35.8 per cent of the Turkish population was living in urban areas and it is estimated that the last census will round out this figure to 40 per cent. Not only the percentage of urban population, but at the same time the number of cities, namely those settlements of 10,000 and more, increased to a great extent in the last three decades. The number of cities has risen from 98 in 1945 to 264 in 1970 and it is expected to reach 350 in the last census. Since this urbanization is not a healthy one, but a "demographic concentration",[27] the first question to be treated is whether the surplus population pouring out from the villages into the towns due to the mechanization of agriculture is able to find any employment and what is the position of women in this respect?

Legally speaking both urban and rural female citizens enjoy, according to the 1961 Constitution, special protection (Art. 35, 43, 58). However, since most of these women enter the labor market with a minimum level of education, the service sector seems to be their only outlet, which basically does not provide social security privileges. Indeed, there is a remarkable increase within this sector — 75,334 in 1960, 103,968 in 1965.

Those women who, owing to a partial or completed primary school education, are able to find gainful employment in industry, where they can benefit from a multitude of social measures, are in an overwhelming majority concentrated in the category of production workers, craftsmen and repair work. The number of women employed in these occupational groups increased from 136,670 in 1960 to 144,948 in 1965.[28]

While the women active in agriculture so far have not been covered by any substantial social security organization except for sporadically scattered mother and child health centers attached to the Ministry of Health, the Turkish female worker employed in industry is in a much better position in terms of legal protection and social welfare, even if a great amount of it remains so far only on paper.

To begin with, the vital question of equalization of wages between sexes has been settled within the Labor Law, according to Art. 26 which guarantees equal pay for equal work and prohibits any discriminatory provisions in collective bargaining. The same law prohibits the working of female employees six weeks prior to and six weeks after birth (Art. 79). Furthermore, the General Hygiene Act (Art. 177) states that pregnant women may not be employed in any functions which endanger the health of mother and child three months before birth. In addition, mothers who are nursing their babies have to be given permission to go home one hour earlier to nurse their babies or rest at work during the first six months twice every day for a duration of half an hour during working hours (Art. 177). A new decree treating special conditions concerning night work for women workers (Decree No. 7/6909-27/7/73) prohibits extra work at night, classifies the various types of dangerous work unsuited for women, prescribes the obligation for the employer to provide transportation for female workers employed on night shifts, prohibits the employment of women at night within six months of their last birth giving. Another decree, promulgated also in 1973 (No. 7/6821-20/7/73), deals with the obligation of establishing nurseries in work places with 20 female workers and day care centers and kindergartens in establishments with over 100 women workers. The nurseries have to be at a distance not more than 250 meters, the day care centers for children of 0-6 years not further than 1,000 meters (Art. 6) from the place of employment. The financial aid providing agency to the expectant mother in case of delivery, during her nursing period and for regular medical visits are cited under the heading of "Motherhood insurance" (Art. 43-51) in the comprehensive Social Security Law, No. 506 of 17/7/1974.

However, as can be witnessed even in the most advanced countries, legal provisions are by themselves unable to ameliorate or change a given situation. Implementation depends to a large extent on the size of trade union affiliation. In this respect it should be stressed that young female workers especially are increasingly joining trade unions, participating in union seminars and assuming roles in strike organizations, etc.

Looking over Turkey's industrial female manpower, one should not forget that almost the equivalent of the gainfully employed women within Turkish industrial establishments works abroad as migrant workers. It is quite relevant that of the great majority of the women migrant workers in West Germany, 78 per cent are married and of these 88 per cent are together with their husbands. In many cases a complete reversal of the traditional roles can be witnessed.

Independent wage earning wives want to establish separate bank accounts and to decide mutually on joint investments. All these innovations, together with the grave problem of raising children either in alien surroundings as "bilingual" illiterates or deprived of parental care and affection in the home country represents only some of the many problems which Turkish families are facing abroad.[29]

TURKISH WOMEN IN THE PROFESSIONS AND GOVERNMENT SERVICES

As pointed out by many social scientists, the disintegration of a traditional society does not assure modernity. Accordingly change occurs in an unequal, uneven way and affects some groups more than others. This seems to be particularly true in the case of the daughters of urban, middle class parents, who were able to benefit fully from the egalitarian educational reforms introduced by Atatürk in the late 1920s.

Although Turkey of today still has to look for a solution to reduce the rate of 67 per cent illiterates among its total female population, the ratio of enrollment of girls in higher educational institutions is almost equal to industrialized Western countries such as Great Britain. Thus, in 1967 the ratio of girl and boy for every 100 university students was 25:100 in England, 21:100 in Turkey. Since then, this proportion has reached one quarter.[30] In 1974/75, out of 104,304 newly registered university and higher education students, 25,574 were girls. About the same rates prevail among the teaching staff. There were a total of 14,210 academic personnel at the same date, out of which 3,423 were women of various academic ranks.[31]

Actually, there is a steady growth of women in government services as well as in the professions.

Indeed, the percentage of women among administrations related to the general budget has increased from 7.7 per cent in 1938 to 21.6 per cent in 1970. Similarly, in the economic state enterprises their rate has doubled from 10 per cent in 1938 to 19 per cent in 1970. The distribution of women among the various branches of the public sector is also interesting. The highest number of women working in government agencies is in the Ministry of Education (31.6 per cent), followed by the Ministry of Tourism and Information (26.3 per cent), the Ministry of Health and Social Assistance (22.2 per cent) and the Ministry of Labor (19 per cent). It seems that women officials show a tendency to work in increasing proportion in services which are being slowly preempted from men and which generally have a social service content.[32] When trying to find the major reasons which push women to work as public officials, one has to cite, at first hand, economic ones. This economic pressure helps us also to understand the root of conflict many career/home-maker women are facing and which leads some women to discontinue work.[33] In this respect education plays the most important role in keeping the desire for professional activity alert. While only 16.6 per cent of women with higher education wanted to discontinue work, this ratio went up to 47.8 per cent among women with technical education. The decisive factor in continuing or giving up work is not primarily concerned with harmony in marital life, but rather economic necessities. Turkish women by and large are entering gainful employment in public services for financial reasons and are contributing to the family budget. Once relative ease of income is secured, the likelihood of discontinuance depends largely on their professional background. New legislation in the form of an amendment to the pension law affecting public servants (No. 1992-3/7/75) makes it possible for women public servants to retire after the completion of 20 years of active service.

The growth of professional women in Turkey represents certainly one of the most conspicuous steps toward modernization. Not only did Turkish women enter into almost all professions, but they even became a vanguard in certain male dominated fields such as the legal professions. The first woman to be elected to any Supreme Court of Appeals in the world was Turkish (the late Melâhat Ruacan, 1954). In 1973, out of 3,022 judges on the bench in courts throughout the country, five per cent (149) were women. In the case of notaries public in office this percentage reaches 11.2 per cent (266:30). As far as practicing lawyers go, the percentage for women is 14.9 per cent.[34]

Table 3
Women in the Professions (Selected Groups) 1953-1970

	1953	1970
Teachers	15,309	70,553
Doctors	502	1,566
Medical Profession (Midwives, nurses)	4,807	33,967
Legal Profession (Lawyers, judges)	738	3,653
Fine Arts (Literature, music, plastic arts)	2,080	6,050
Engineers, architects	610	8,843
Managers	680	4,513
Saleswomen	4,000	21,259
Accountants	—	18,509

Source: For 1953 *Mesleki ve Taknik Öretim* Müesseseleriyle ilgili rakkamlar—Ankara, 1961; for 1970, 1970 *Genel Nüfus Sayım-sonuçları*.

The most relevant trend seems to be, on one side, the steady, consistent growth in previously male dominated professions such as in the legal and medical fields and, on the other side, the conquest of business related fields such as engineering, architecture, management, accounting, sales, etc. The rapid growth in these areas certainly proves the fast rate of industrialization and its impact on female motivation toward new jobs.

SUMMING UP

During the first half century of the Turkish Republic, Turkey's womanhood has been confronted with important challenges. Legal emancipation permitted Turkish women to free themselves of a legitimized disqualification in favor of men.

The second important challenge, the transition to a multiparty system and the extension of franchise to all citizens over 21, placed upon the shoulders of Turkish women voters a heavy and responsible task.

The third challenge came because of deep rooted structural changes such as rapid urbanization, industrialization, mechanization of agriculture, exposure to mass media, internal and external migration. Reformers believed that education and the removal of discriminatory and seclusive treatment within the family would enable women to develop into better wives and mothers. Increasing entry of women into higher education and the pressure of rising standards of living within the middle class helped to strengthen the illusion of rapid improvement in their conditions and achievements of equality. As a result, the deteriorating situation, particularly of rural women, remained invisible. As Vina Mazumdar rightfully remarked, traditional society, while it certainly did not treat women as equals, did provide meaningful, necessary and guaranteed roles to women. The claim for protection from society rested on the recognition of the value of their contribution. The process of modernization, particularly economic change, has disturbed these roles and the guarantees are fast becoming inoperative. New guarantees are necessary but they cannot come by treating the women's problem as a marginal issue to be dealt with altruistically.

Turkish planners and policy makers have reached the point where they must adopt new approaches and ways of thinking in order to cope with problems of a rapidly modernizing social group: the rural and urban Turkish women of today and tomorrow.

NOTES

1. Pervin Esenkova, *La femme Turque contemporaine, éducation et role sociale.* Extrait de la Revue *IBLA.* (Tunis, 1951), p. 285.
2. Gotthard Jaeschke, "Die Frauenfrage in der Türkei," *Saeculum* X, Heft. 4, p. 361.
3. Halide Edib, *Conflict of East and West in Turkey,* 3rd edition (Lahore: Sh. Muhammad Ashraf, 1963). p. 194.
4. Charlotte Lorenz, "Die Frauenfrage im Osmanischen Reiche mit besonder Berücksichtigung der arbeitenden Klasse," *Die Welt des Islams* 6, (1918), p. 82.
5. Enver Ziya Karal, "Kadın Hâkları Soŕuňu ve Atatürk," *Türk Dili,* Vol. XXXII, No. 290 (Nov., 1975), p. 608.
6. Enver Ziya Karal, ed., *Atatürk'ten Düşünceler,* (Ankara: İş Bankası, 1956), p. 52.
7. Halide Edib, *op.cit.* p. 111.
8. Enver Ziya Karal, ed., *Atutürk'ten Düsünceler,* p. 52.
9. *50 Yıllık Yaşantımız,* 1923-1933, Vol. I., Milliyer Yayını, 1975, p. 115.
10. Dankwart A. Rustow, "Atatürk as Founder of State," *Abadan Armağam,* (Ankara: SBF Yayını, 1969), p. 545. Throughout his career this thought prevailed in Atatürk's decision: "There is a Right, and Right is above Force."
11. Nermin Abadan, "Turkey", in Raphael Patai, ed., *Women in the Modern World.* (Free Press, 1967), pp. 94-95; Paul J. Magnarella, "The reception of Swiss Family Law," *Anthropological Quarterly.* 46, pp. 100-116.
12. Sabine Dirks, *La Famille Musulmane Turque* (Paris and The Hague: Mouton, 1969), pp. 34-40. The French Civil Code as well as the German

were rejected because they attribute a too subjugated role upon the woman within marriage. See Sauser-Hall, *Réception des droits européens en Turquie*. p. 344.

13 Nermin Abadan, *Social Charge and Turkish Women*. (Ankara: SBF Yayını, 1963), pp. 21-23; Kemal Karpat, "L'Etat de la famille Turque," *Çağdas*. (İstanbul, 1946): Ü. Gürkan discusses the legal implications which might occur in case a married woman takes up a renumerated job outside the home without the explicit or tacit consent of the husband and its probability to be grounds for divorce. Ülker Gürkan, "Kadının Emeğinin Değeri ve Evli Kadının Çalısmasının Kocanın İznine Bağlı olmasının yarattığı Sosyal ve Hukuksal Sorunlar," *Hacettepe Sosyal ve Beserî Bılımler Dergisi*, Cilt 8, Sayı 1-2, Mart-Ekim 1976, p. 116ğ132.

14. Nermin Abadan, *op.cit.*, p. 23.

15. A. I. Inan, *Fiilî Birleşmelerle bunlardan doğan çocularm teseiline dair kunun. yönctmolık ve sözleşmeler* (Les lois, l'administration et les conventions concernant l'enregistrement de enfants des unions illégitimes), (Ankara, 1965).

16. Fatima Mernissi, *Beyond the Veil. Male-Female Dynamics in a Modern Muslim Society* (New York: John Wiley and Sons. 1975) p. 81.

17. *Türkiye'de Toplumsal re Ekonomik Gelismenin 50 Yılı*. Devlet İstatistik Enstitüsü, Nr. 683 Ankara, 1973), p. 111.

18. Erol Tümertekin, "Gradual Internal Migration in Turkey," *Review of the Geographical Institute of the University of Istanbul*. 1970-1971, No. 13, pp. 157-169. Nermin Abadan-Unat, *Turkish Workers in Europe 1960-1975. A Socioeconomic Reappraisal* (Leiden: E.J. Brill, 1975) pp. 7-9.

19. Ruşen Keleş, *Urbanization in Turkey*. (New York: Ford Foundation, 1974).

20. Baha Tunalıgil, "Kırsal kesimde kadın," *Pulitika*. 4/11/1975.

21. Serim Timur, *Türkiye'de Aile Yaptst*. (The structure of family in Turkey), Hacettepe Yayını, No. D-15, (Ankara, 1972) p. 176.

22. Serim Timur, *op.cit.*, p. 178.

23. Çiğdem Kâğıtçibaşi, *Value of Children*, paper presented at the Second Turkish Demography Conference, Çeşme, Izmir, Sept. 29-Oct. 1, 1975.

24. Serim Timur, *op.cit.*, pp. 112-113.

25. Nermin Abadan-Unat, "Impact of Migration on Emancipation and Pseudo-Emancipation of Women," *International Migration Review*. 1977, 1, pp. 50-52.

26. Oya Tokgöz, "Televiyonun kadının siyasallaşması üzerindeki etkisi (The impact of TV on the politization of women), (Ankara, 1976, unpublished Doçentlik thesis).

27. Turan Yazgan, *Türkiye'de şebirleşmenin nüfus ve isgücü bünesine tesirleri.* (The impact of urbanization on population and manpower), unpublished Ph.D. dissertation, İstanbul University, Faculty of Economics, 1967.

28. *Statistical Yearbook of Turkey*, 1973 (Ankara: D.I.E.-State Statistic Institute, 1974), Publ. No. 710, p. 48; Gülten Kazgan, "Labour Force Participation. Occupational Distribution, Educational Attainment and the Socio-Economic Status of Women in the Turkish Economy," paper presented at the "Women in Turkish Society" seminar, İstanbul, May 16-19, 1978, pp. 32, Table XIII.

29. Ayşe Kudat, *Stability and Change in the Turkish Family at Home and Abroad: Comparative Perspectives*, International Institute of Comparative Social Studies, Berlin, 1975, Pre-Print, p. 91. Hrsgb. Franz Ronneberger, Türkische Kinder in Deutschland (Turkish Children in Germany) (München: Südosteuropa-Gesellschaft. 1976); Nermin Abadan-Unat, "Educational

Problems of Turkish Migrants' Children," *International Review of Education*. Vol. XXI (1975), pp. 311-322.

30. Hasan Ali Koçer. "Turkiye'de kadın Eğitimi," *A. Ü. Eğitim Fakültesi Dergisi. 1972, p. 116; Ferhunde Özbay, "The* Impact of Education on Women in Rural and Urban Turkey," paper presented at "Women in Turkish Society" seminar, İstanbul, May 16-19, 1978.

31. *Statistical Figures related to Higher Education Enrollment in 1974/75* (Ankara: State Statistical Institute, 1975), p. 119.

32 Mesut Gülmez, "Turk Kamu Görevlilerinin Sayısal Evrimi," *Âmme İdaresi Dergisi,* Vol. 6, No. 3 (September, 1972), p. 44. (The numerical evolution of Turkish Public Servants).

33. Oya Çitçi. "Women at Work," *Turkish Public Administration Annual.* (Ankara, 1975), p. 159.

34. Tezer Taşkiran, *Women in Turkey* (İstanbul: Redhouse Yayıneni, 1976), pp. 94-96.

3

WOMEN IN GOVERNMENT AS POLICY-MAKERS AND BUREAUCRATS: THE TURKISH CASE

INTRODUCTION

When compared to other cultural areas, predominantly Muslim nations have low rates of reported economic activity, low female literacy rates and low female school enrollment at all levels. For women in these countries, seclusion from economic activities and economic dependency are the norm.

Two types of restrictions operate to affect women's status in Muslim societies. The first includes the legal and religious restrictions and inequalities mentioned in the Quran, Hadith, Sunna and Sharia law codes, and the second is that imposed by the practice of purdah or seclusion (White, 1978). Turkey, however, together with the Soviet Republics of Central Asia and Albania, represents those Muslim countries which following major revolutions have eliminated the Muslim inheritance pattern and introduced secular, civil law into all spheres.

Indeed, for the founder of modern Turkey, Kemal Atatürk and his close collaborators, the abolition of women's inferior status had been a major goal from the beginning of the War of Liberation (Abadan-Unat, 1978a). Atatürk strongly believed that the modernization of Turkish women could only be realized by the reform of two major institutions: education and law. Thus, in a series of bold strokes,

---

Reprinted from *Women, Power and Political Systems,* E. Margherita Rendel, ed., 1981, pp. 94-114. London: Croom Helm.

the theocratic edifice of the Ottoman state was destroyed. In 1923 the Ministry of Education took over the administration and control of all religious schools and all their means of support (endowment and funds). The abolition of the Caliphate in 1924 was followed by the closing of all medreses (religious seminars) and other separate schools. In 1928, Article 2 of the first Constitution of the Republic of Turkey, which had made Islam the state religion, was amended to provide for disestablishment and, in 1937, the principle of secularism was incorporated into the Constitution. In the meantime, the jurisdiction of the Shariat courts were taken over by the lay government.

Through the adoption of the Swiss Civil Code in the new Turkish Civil Code in 1926 and the creation of courts modelled on those in Western countries, orthodox Islamic laws and their application were discarded. As a result, a series of reforms affecting women's status, such as the establishment of a minimum marriage age and registration of marriage, prohibition of polygamy, abolition of *talaq* (one-sided divorce, pronounced by the husband), recognition of the right to divorce and the enactment of a secular inheritance law, and a civil code replacing all religious laws were effectively carried out.

Parallel to the adoption of the Swiss Civil Code, Article 6 of the Civil Service Law, no. 788 was amended in 1926, so as to secure women the right to be employed as civil servants. Thus, Turkish women, who had already begun to enter public service in 1880 as teachers, were given a sound legal basis for their employment rights.

Turkish women were granted political rights much earlier than women in many European countries. They were enfranchised for municipal elections in 1930 and four years later were given the right to participate in national elections. Thus, secularization not only meant the adoption of new laws and the sweeping away of the religious elites' traditional power, but it also meant a change in the patterns of authority and in the value system of Turkish society.

The realization of these legal and educational reforms in Turkey has yielded significant results. Female educational achievements have been great. Female school enrollment at all levels in Turkey is far ahead of all other Muslim countries, with the exception of Soviet Central Asia and Albania (White, 1978). Turkey has produced a greater percentage of women lawyers and physicians than the highly industrialized Western countries such as the USA or France. Similarly, government positions related to high-level policy-making have greatly attracted Turkish women. The ratio of female judges, prosecutors and top rank administrators in government in Turkey outnumbers many of the more advanced Western countries (Abadan-Unat, 1978b).

In this light the chapter aims to find some answers to the following questions: can modifications in the superstructure alone, such as reforms in law and education, produce noticeable changes in the mentality and outlook of women? Do they influence the sex-role distribution noticeably and thus produce a different perception of politics and society? Or, does education as a dependent variable merely determine status and class identification, and thus primarily act as an instrument for social mobility? If so, do equality before the law and expanded educational opportunities facilitate only the growth of the middle class? In order to answer these questions the author has attempted to evaluate the impact of the modernization of Turkish women by analysing their role and function in public administration—the sector which has recorded the highest and fastest growth over the past 40 years.

The hypothesis adopted here is that, because no systematic effort has been made in public policy or ideologically to assert the ethical value and social function of work outside the home, the prime motivating factor for women to enter employment is economic need, and only in rare cases the quest for social prestige. Consequently, social institutions such as the family and the powerful mass media, especially television and its consumer oriented advertisements, have become the major framework for value judgments and preferences. This is one of the reasons why women are relatively less interested in training programs which increase chances of promotion.

Since the transition to a multi-party system, no new definitions of women's role in Turkish society have been made. On the contrary, the conservative ideologies of successive governments have caused a tacit elimination of innovative activity such as intensive efforts to expand female literacy and women's rural programs. The most important factors inducing noticeable changes in the outlook and attitudes of Turkey's young female generation have been urbanization, migration and industrialization (Kazgan, forthcoming). In this respect, a striking similarity with Tunisia is to be noted. In contrast to Bourguiba's early efforts in 1956 towards the adoption of the Personnel Status Code, which replaced segments of Quranci laws with new statutes, and his strong support for women's education and political involvement, Tunisian policies of the 1970s marked an increasing tendency to conservatism and a significant reduction in government program for cultural reform and resocialization (Tessler, 1978). Thus, only indirect factors such as urbanization have continued to modernize women.

In order to throw some light on questions specifically pertaining to women in government service, a brief reassessment of women's position in economic life seems pertinent.

WOMEN IN ECONOMIC LIFE

Although Turkey embarked some decades ago on a program of accelerated industrialization, it still retains some of its basic agrarian aspects, indeed the major socio-economic characteristic is one of economic dualism, as defined by Adelman and Morris (1973). Such a dualism is characterized by the coexistence of low productivity, a subsistence agriculture sector, along with high productivity in agri-business and the industrial sector. In this type of sectoral disharmony women suffer more economic hardships than men. Classified by the same authors as a 'moderate dualism country', women's share in economic life in Turkey closely follows the pattern of decreasing employment opportunities with growing urbanization that Boserup so ably described (1970). Table 5.1 gives us a clear picture of the evolution over the last 20 years. It can be seen that no more than 11 per cent of Turkish women are employed outside the agricultural sector. Furthermore, the 1975 census revealed that only 15 per cent of all urban women are employed. More than four-fifths of all urban women are housewives.

Table 5.1
Women in Agriculture, Industry and the Services 1955-75 (%)

Sectors	1955	1960	1965	1970	1975
Agriculture	96.6	95.0	94.1	89.0	88.9
Industry	2.3	2.7	1.5	5.1	3.5
Services	1.6	1.9	2.6	5.0	7.4
Others	0.5	0.4	1.8	0.9	0.2

Source: DIE, censuses of 1955, 1960, 1965, 1970 and 1975.

The overwhelming majority of women working in agriculture are unpaid family members. They represent the major source of 'cheap labor', a significant portion of Marx's labor reserve army. Being lodged and fed free in the parental home, the girls of peasant families secure a sizeable income for their fathers through the 'bride price', which in practice is actually an indemnity paid for the loss of (unpaid) service. In the case of wage-earning female agricultural workers, such as cotton, tobacco and fruit pickers, the discrepancy between male and female wages still persists. Owing to the absence of an effective agrarian trade union organization, and the absence of voluntary payments into social security for the rural sector, this discrepancy has so far not been eliminated.

Within the industrial sector a trend similar to India (ICSSR, 1975) can be registered. Though total employment in factories has been increasing steadily, women's employment in this sector has decreased since 1965, their share being reduced from 11.5 per cent in 1965 to 3.5 per cent in 1975. (Kazgan, 1981). Owing to the absence of comprehensive studies, it could be assumed that this decline is partly attributable to the extent and nature of modernization methods, and partly to external migration. Industries which have adopted a higher capital-intensive technology resulting in the displacement of labor have found it easier to displace women than men. Furthermore, a significant number of female migrant workers have taken industrial jobs. In West Germany alone their absolute number increased from 173 in 1960 to 143,611 in 1975 (Abadan-Unat, 1977). Whether these women would have taken up industrial jobs in their home country remains a debatable issue. In contrast to the general neglect of social policy in the agrarian sector in Turkey, a number of protective labour laws have been adopted in the industrial sector to secure women's social welfare. However, actual implementation of these laws is lacking. Moreover, the number of trade union affiliated female workers is minimal. Only 9 per cent of all women employed in industry in 1977 were covered by social security—a function that is fully dependent on affirmative action by trade unions (Tezgider, 1978). Again as in India (ICSSR, 1975), women have increasingly shown a growing interest and determination to enter government jobs. Since empirical studies dealing with the attitudes and behavior of Turkish women in the executive and judiciary are not available, the author has preferred to make extensive use of the findings of Oya Çitçi's comprehensive survey (1979), embracing a large number of governmental agencies, including all kinds of clerical, administrative, managerial and specialized occupations, and to deduce from these findings some implications applicable to top-ranking women policymakers.

TURKISH WOMEN IN PUBLIC ADMINISTRATION

During 1938-76, the number of female civil servants in Turkey increased 19 times, while the number of male civil servants rose sixfold. In order to assess this growth, a chronological table listing the various types of government agencies is necessary (see Table 5.2). At first glance one significant feature becomes evident: the greatest concentration of female civil servants can be observed in agencies covered by the general budget, while there is a decline in municipal agencies—the reason being that a great number of recently created municipal agencies are located in rural areas where limited educational opportunities have not permitted women access to government jobs.

When measuring the educational level of these women officials, the first fact to be noticed is their higher level of educational attainment compared with men. While 54 per cent of all male civil servants are only primary or secondary school graduates, 68.5 per cent of women are educated to high school (*lycee*) level or beyond. As other authors have noted, women have to be better qualified for particular posts than men. Thus, there seems to be a rather clear relationship between educational level and non-agrarian employment. According to the 1975 statistics, showing the occupational mobility of girls, 5 per cent of Turkey's primary school graduates, 12.5 per cent of its secondary school, 30 per cent of its high school, 56 per cent of its vocational and 70 per cent of its university graduates were able to find a job in the non-agrarian sector (Die, 1976). In addition, the most qualified female labor seems to be concentrated in the service sector—be it private enterprise or government service; 41 per cent of all women working in this sector have some form of higher education. Although university graduates represent only 1.9 per cent of the total active female labor force, they represent 16.6 per cent in public administration.

Another interesting aspect of women's entrance into the civil service is the fact that, unlike the prevailing pattern in Western countries, there is no visible interruption in the pattern of Turkish women's working life. While in industrialized countries there are two peak periods for participating actively in the public domain, namely the 20-25 and 40-60 age-groups, in Turkey entrance into employment is a kind of apprenticeship before marriage. Those women who remain in employment after marriage, make no interruption at all. Partly owing to the unwillingness of the women themselves, and partly from the country's prevailing structural unemployment and the lack of part-time jobs, there is practically no chance of women returning to employment once they have left to raise a family.

Table 5.2

Distribution of Female Civil Servants in Absolute Figures and Percentages, 1938 and 1976

Type of administration	1938	%	1946	%	1963	%	1970	%	1977	%
General budget	4.287	8	12.573	15	47.414	20	80.099	22	190.313	27
Annex budget	824	4	3.813	6	3.487	10	3.748	8	7.783	21
State economic enterprise	731	10	2.502	13	15.623	13	26.116	19	48.380	
Local administration	6.874	18	11.140	21	6.178	10	4.838	8	7.829	12
Total	12.716	9.5	30.046	13.5	72.702	16	123.812	19	244.305	25

Note: General budget covers all ministries and administrative agencies in the provinces representing the central government.
Sources: DIE, *Memurlar İstatisgiği*, no. 149 (DIE, Ankara, 1938); DIE, *Memurlar İstatistiği*, no. 288 (DIE, Ankara, 1946); DIE, *Devlet Personel Sayımı*, vols. 1-3, nos. 473,503,518 (DIE, Ankara, DIE, *Devlet Memurları Sayımı*, no. 664 (DIE, Ankara, 1970); Devlet Personel Dairesi, *Kamu Personeli Anket Reporları*, vol. 1.

51

In 1963, 43.9 per cent of all women employed in the public sector were under the age of 30; in 1976 this percentage rose to 55 per cent for the same age group. The highest percentage of women working in public administration belongs to the 18-24 age group Çitçi, 1979). After the age of 25, a definite decrease can be witnessed. Therefore, it is not erroneous to state that the great majority of women serving in public administration possess little commitment; they do not wholeheartedly embrace a career, but work to obtain an additional source of income. This tendency has been confirmed by the Hacettepe Population Census of 1973 which revealed that among those women who gave up their jobs, 35 per cent gave marriage as the major cause, 18 per cent child-raising and 5 per cent the negative attitude of their husbands (Özbay, forthcoming).

With this in mind, one might ask what kind of positions are occupied by women? This question can be answered by evaluating both the distribution pattern of women among the various agencies as well as their occupational activity. The census taken in 1976 by the State Personnel Directorate reveals that the highest number of women working in the government agencies are located in the Ministry of Education (31.6 per cent), similar again to India with a heavy predominance of pre-school and primary school teachers. The second favored ministry, requiring adequate foreign language knowledge, is the Ministry of Tourism and Information which employs 26.3 per cent of the women. In third place comes the Ministry of Health and Social Assistance with 22.2 per cent, representing once more a government agency with a heavy concentration of 'feminine occupations', such as nursing and midwifery. It is interesting to note that this tendency to work in ministries with specific, female-oriented tasks has increased over the years. Those three ministries were employing 55.7 per cent in 1963, 67.9 per cent in 1970 and 69.1 per cent in 1976 of the women (Ozbay, forthcoming).

Overall it appears that women tend to work in occupations from which men are excluded or which have a general social service content, or which require upper-class multilingual training. As to the jobs, the 1976 census reveals that almost half (44 per cent) of the female employees are performing clerical work. The typists and bureau clerks are the most numerous (70.3 per cent), while 1.5 per cent occupy assistant directorships or higher positions.

With regard to professional women, another trend familiar to studies of Third World countries seems to be the rule in Turkey. It is characterized by the following: (i) the percentage of professional women is relatively higher than in capitalist countries; (ii) women are mainly concentrated in metropolitian and urban centers; and (iii) since they seek security and facilities related to their work rather than quick promotional opportunities, they prefer government employment to private practice. Thus, while the total percentage of female lawyers in Turkey is 18.6 per cent, they are over-represented (with 42.1 per cent) in institutions covered by the general budget or classified as state economic enterprises. Similarly the proportion of women engineers in these enterprises is 7.9 per cent—higher than in most capitalist countries.

The reciprocal relationship between education and employment, however, becomes most evident when the distribution of women according to their educational level and labor force participation is examined. Since the growing participation of Turkish women in public administration is essentially the result of long-range educational policies rather than a specific special element of an egalitarian, democratic, nondiscriminatory public philosophy or political program, its impact has remained instrumental and class-oriented. Apart from the early years of the Republic, when successful, professional *avant-garde* women were presented to the public as model pioneers on the path of the new, Western-inspired civilized society, no political party or government program has committed itself to improving the status of women other than through small legal changes in favor of urban civil servants. Indeed, after the transition to a multi-party regime in 1946, a sizeable number of political parties have publicly reiterated traditional values, constantly praising the function of housewives and mothers. The findings of the first comprehensive empirical research on Turkish women employed in various public agencies, carried out by Oya Çitçi, furnishes convincing evidence that women enter the public domain with an internal set of values based on an ideal housewife model.

SOCIOECONOMIC CHARACTERISTICS OF TURKISH CIVIL SERVANTS AND EMANCIPATORY VALUES

Çitçi's sample consisted of 742 women civil servants out of a total of 14,838, representing 15 administrative agencies in Ankara, the capital, each employing more than 500 women (1979), and 68.5 per cent of the respondents of the survey were high school or university graduates. Most of them were from upper-middle-class families and their fathers were employed in liberal professions, business or bureaucracy. More than half of the respondents (52.1 per cent) were married, two-thirds coming from nuclear families. The majority classified themselves as additional bread-winner—only 8 per cent of the women were heads of families. The average number of children was 1.6. Because of the relatively high percentage of low-age children (70.8 per cent), the question as to who is entrusted to take care of them was very relevant. The survey indicates that 63.1 per cent were entrusting their children to their mothers or mothers-in-law and only 12.1 per cent were using the facilities of day care centers, while another 6 per cent were employing domestic help. Equally important is the fact that 79.2 per cent had no additional household help.

These characteristics determined to some degree the response concerning the function and role of women in society. Although 75.3 per cent consider women's emancipation—here conceived as women's ability to benefit from all legal and educational reforms—quite important, only 5 per cent thought that equality between men and women had actually been achieved. It was felt by 30.2 per cent that men should retain their superiority. This superiority was explained as having been sustained for the following reasons:

(i) The patriarchal character of the Swiss Civil Code, which became the Turkish Civil Code. Article 159 limits the married women's 'actual ability' to take employment by requiring her to seek her husband's permission. In case of refusal, the women may apply to the court, and, there, must furnish convincing proof that her prospective employment will serve 'the genuine interests of her family.'

(ii) The persistence of tradition and mores in favor of male supremacy.

(iii) The fact that by-and-large men are the major breadwinners and heads of the family.

Participation in the public domain can produce profound changes in the mentality of women only if the socialization process for girls places a different emphasis on sex roles. Oya Çitçi's survey furnishes detailed data indicating that granting equal educational opportunities—even for those who make the best use of them—is ineffective for the majority of women in society as long as 'the family, educational institutions, mass media and books are uniformly reinforcing the traditional outlook emphasizing that women primarily have to be good homemakers and mothers.'

This attitude is also reflected in the 1973 Hacettepe Survey, which revealed that only 33 per cent of women would continue to work if they did not need money. Thus, it becomes clear that two-thirds of the married women work to help the family income and tend to stop working as their economic situation improves (Özbay, forthcoming).

All these figures indicate that, by and large, Turkish women in employment acquiesce in the dual role of women (first defined by Alva Myrda) and, without attempting to introduce significant changes into their lives, aspire to return to their traditional functions. On this particular question, the place of residence plays a minor role. Women of rural origins approve of male supremacy by 93.4 per cent and urban ones by 83.6 per cent. Education, however, seems to be a more important factor. Respondents with a primary education approve of this option by 93 per cent and university graduates by only 75 per*cent. Nevertheless, the fact remains that three-quarters of all female civil servants attribute a secondary importance to their own employment and career.

On the other hand, these same women give way to some contradictory thoughts and feelings when confronted with a set of alternatives fitted to delineate the ideal way of life for women. Table 5.3 indicates that a negligible percentage of the respondents considers a career life style as an ideal. The majority would like to achieve self-realization and the best combination of career life and housework. In other words, if society is ready to provide women with various supportive services and build up institutional assistance, there appears to be a readiness to work outside the home in spite of the traditional climate of opinion that has been outlined. Women want to use their innate abilities and talents, but, apparently in the absence of affirmative action and strong organizational support, these women do not find the courage, zest and determination to fight for their rights. The lack of a value system based on a work ethic, encourages many women to make use of the early pension plan. With only partial unwillingness they assume the roles of sex-object and passive homemaker.

This early retirement scheme (Law no. 1992, 3 July 1975) makes it possible for female civil servants to retire after the completion of 20 years of active service. The justification for it has been the stress women have to endure because of their dual role. It is significant that the legislators, instead of introducing unpaid extended maternity leave or broadening various forms of social assistance, have opted for a solution which actually sends women home at an age when they could devote most of their time to work outside the house.

When the Oya Çitçi survey was undertaken the law had not yet been passed, and this early retirement plan was met with great enthusiasm; 80.9 per cent of the respondents indicated their intention to make use of this right. Of the university graduates, 71.9 per cent wanted to give up their careers. However, since the passage of the law, only a very limited number of working women have actually used this option. During the period between July 1975 and July 1977 the number of female civil servants who retired after 20 years of work was 2,058, while 24,114 women officials continued to work (Çitçi, 1979). There is a discrepancy between stated intention and actual behavior which could reflect many factors, particularly the pressure of economic necessity.

Female officials have been conditioned by traditional values to such a degree that, when asked whether they would consider a better job with better opportunities for promotion and higher pay, but requiring longer working hours and absence from home, 74.2 per cent refused to consider such an offer.[1] Oya Çitçi intelligently tried to detect the extent of this 'self imposed' limitation to liberation by gauging the behavior of the respondents with regard to their marriage, use of income, degree of participation and activity in association. With regard to marriage, Çitçi presented a set of alternative solutions almost totally centered around the preponderant role of the family: 60.2 per cent of the respondents declared they had independently chosen their spouse; 11.7 per cent disregarded the choice made by their family and opted for their own choice; 19.5 per cent were married through an intermediary or a 'matchmaker', and another 8.6 per cent concluded a prearranged marriage. Although about 79.6 per cent said that they made their final decision after a harmonious consultation with their family, only one-tenth actually acted totally on their own.

The attachment of economically active women to their family is also reflected in the interesting survey which Kandiyoti carried out on a sample of two generations among urban women in Istanbul (Kandiyoti, forthcoming). Her findings confirm the trend described above. In her conclusion she states that while the education of the daughters is very high (especially when compared with their own mothers) and their level of employment is not negligible, their ways of meeting their future marriage partners have been quite traditional and their definition of the 'successful woman' is one who reconciles the traditional and modern demands. Kandiyoti indicates that in spite of the considerable degree of social change in the mothers' generation, the daughters have not been able to modify their traditional expectations in any fundamental way, but have just taken on some new roles. This might also explain why puritan values related to chastity are still strongly supported, punishment of adultery with imprisonment is upheld, and the double standard in morality not protested against. While some young Turkish women, belonging to leftist political groups may be strongly in favor of radical change in the economic and social order, they consider a strong stand

Table 5.3

Views on the Ideal Way of Life for Women, According to Marital status, Residence and Education (%)

Women in public administration	To be only a good homemaker	To get a professional education and use it eventually	To be a successful career women	To combine the roles of housewife and career woman
Marital status				
Married	17.5	16.2	0.2	65.8
Bachelor	12.5	15.2	0.3	71.7
Widow	16.3	9.1	—	75.5
Residence				
Rural	21.7	17.3	—	60.8
Small town	24.4	16.3	—	50.1
Urban	13.4	19.9	0.3	71.1
Education				
Primary	27.9	6.9	—	65.1
Secondary	16.9	17.1	0.2	65.7
University	5.6	14.6	0.5	79.2

Source: Oya Çitçi, 'Türkiye' de Kadin sorunu ve calisan Kadinlar', mimeographed unpublished Ph.D. dissertation, Ankara, 1979, Tables

against sexism irrelevant, alien to the social structure and distracting from the basic social issues.

The close relationship of working women to their families is likewise reflected in the way they use their income; 60 per cent add all, or the major portion of their income to the family budget. In this respect marital status plays a determining role. While only 17 per cent of married women officials spend more than half of their income for their own needs, this percentage reaches 69.7 per cent for unmarried women. As may be anticipated, the amount of income working women contribute to the family budget is closely related to the general income of the household.

Another important criterion which might help to establish the degree of emancipation of Turkish female employees is their participation in family decision-making matters. Table 5.4 casts light on the major issues in which women actively take part. As would be expected from the idealized dual feminine role, women have the most say in their traditional stronghold, that is, household management. Although the percentage of matters decided jointly is relatively high, there is a kind of tutelage in settling professional matters solely concerning women. In this domain 7.8 per cent of men are taking the decisive steps.

A slightly higher degree of individual freedom prevails in political matters, although there, too, 12.8 per cent unconditionally accept the political choice of the men they live with (husband, father and brother). With regard to the political participation, namely voting, a number of surveys have shown a definite pattern wherein Turkish women's voting participation is lower than men's—married women are less inclined to vote than unmarried girls or widows, while working women show a greater interest in politics than housewives (Tekeli, forthcoming). Çitçi's survey confirms these findings. Only 64.2 per cent of her respondents admitted to having voted in the last election. Differentiated according to their marital status, 72.9 per cent of the married, 50 per cent of the unmarried and 81.6 per cent of the widows went to the polls. This means that bearing responsibility as 'head of the family' leads to increased civic interest and political participation. As can be expected, education plays the most important differentiating role. While 88.7 per cent of the university graduates voted, only 56.3 per cent of the primary school graduates made use of their citizenship rights.

Finally a few words on the attitudes of women civil servants towards membership of associations. Only 23 per cent of the respondents admitted belonging to any kind of association. Here, membership in a professional association seems to dominate (77.1 per cent). Thus, a

Table 5.4

Distribution of Sex-ratio in Decision-making Within Families (%)

Subject	Female	Male	Both sexes
Food expenses	25.7	8.1	66.1
Clothing	18.6	5.7	75.5
Furniture	6.5	4.7	88.7
Social problems concerning women's professional life	34.9	7.8	57.2
Special problems concerning mens' professional life	—	57.9	41.9
Family size, family planning	3.9	3.9	92.1
Education of children	11.2	2.3	86.3
Household chores	67.7	0.7	31.4
Invitation of guests	9.1	9.4	81.3
Holiday, travel	2.8	5.5	91.6
Political behavior of women	39.1	12.8	48.0
Political behavior of men	—	52.0	48.0
Selection of newspaper subscribed at home	10.2	25.7	64.0

Source: Oya Çitçi, 'Türkiye' de Kadin soruna ve calisan Kadinlar, p. 242, Table 100.

number of general tendencies can be summarized:

(i) Irrespective of the positions occupied, both women officials and professional women with higher education adopt a conciliatory, dependent, passive role in the public domain. Their readiness to fight for greater equality and wider liberties for women at large is relatively weak with the exception of those who have a strong political or ideological commitment.

(ii) The importance attached to emancipation is determined by education and place of residence as well as by class affiliation. The urban middle-class families seem to place the greatest importance on emancipatory values.

(iii) Ambivalence towards continuing a career while assuming the role of housewife and mother is the rule rather than the exception.

(iv) The beginning, duration and termination of active participation in government service is more dependent on special conditions (economic needs or child-raising) than on personal feelings and preferences. The highest level of motivation to continue work outside the home seems to prevail among those jobs outside the country, namely among blue-collar and white-collar workers abroad. The dominant climate of opinion in favor of high productivity and a high standard of living in those highly industrialized countries seems to play a determining role for these migrant workers.

(v) Where there is conflict arising from the clash of loyalties, solutions favoring the smooth functioning of family life are preferred.

(vi) The job status of women officials does not automatically increase democracy within the family or political participation. Here again educational level, marital status and class affiliation produce diversified patterns.

WOMEN IN THE JUDICIARY AND EXECUTIVE POSITIONS

Can the findings of Çitçi's survey covering a broad range of women civil servants be equally applied to the women elite in the executive and the judiciary? In the absence of empirical findings, we are forced to do some speculative thinking. Law and medicine have traditionally been exclusively male professions. In Western industrial societies very few women have been able to penetrate these strongholds until recently (Epstein, 1970). Yet in Turkey both of these professions have attracted a surprisingly large number of women. One in every five practising lawyers in Turkey is a woman. Again, one in every six practising physicians is a woman. This surprisingly high ratio has not been confined to the middle-range positions, but has also produced as significant number of women in higher positions. In fact, the very first woman judge in the highest court of appeal was a Turk, the late Melahat Ruacan, whose nomination in 1954 attracted worldwide attention and praise. Similarly female judges have been elected as chairmen of sections in the highest administrative court of Turkey, the State Council, for over 20 years. Not only have women been eager to enroll in law schools, but with equal enthusiasm they have tried to be active within the judiciary, as reflected in Table 5.5

The sex-ratio distribution within the Ministry of Justice reflects a strong male dominance with a slight inclination to admit a few women into top position. A similar trend can be observed in another traditionally male-oriented ministry, the Ministry of Foreign Affairs. Women became eligible for diplomatic posts only after the promulgation of the new Constitution in 1961, in which Article 12 categorically prohibits all

Table 5.5

Sex-ratio Distribution According to Occupations Within the Ministry of Justice (as of 3 February 1978)

Position	Female	%	Male	%	Total	%
Júdges	102	3.1	3,172	96.9	3,172	100
Prosecutors	13	0.6	1,891	99.4	1,904	100
Other women employees with non-juridical background	2,525	11.3	19,800	88.7	22,325	100

Source: State Personnel Directorate, unpublished data.

forms of discrimination based on sex, although previously they were not legally prohibited from entering such posts. Here, as in the other ministries, only a few top positions are occupied by women.

Table 5.6

Sex-ratio Distribution According to Occupation Within the Ministry of Foreign Affairs (as of 11 May 1977)

Position	No. of females	No. of males	Total
Head of section	5	63	68
Second secretary	5	20	25
Second secretary (abroad)	6	45	51
Counsellor	1	100	101
Consul	8	48	56
Expert	1	30	31
Administrative asst	49	130	179
Total	75 (14.6%)	436 (85.4%)	511 (100%)

Source: State Personnel Directorate, unpublished data.

The significant difference in male/female recruitment within two traditionally conservative ministries obviously lies in a class-determined educational requirement. Diplomatic service, as well as service in the Ministry of Information and Tourism, requires fluency in a foreign language. These skills are acquired in expensive, foreign-sponsored and financed private schools, available only to the daughters of the upper-middle-class families whose parents consider this kind of education the best investment for a desirable marriage. It is usually these girls, who are not taught the value and gratification of work, that are able to compete with men and get easy access to these positions. However, after the first stage of apprenticeship in the home country, when the time comes for appointment abroad, a surprisingly large number of diplomatic candidates resign. This results from the policy adopted by the Ministry of Foreign Affairs which prohibits the appointment of married couples together in one embassy or consulate. To be a liberated woman, ready to face the many difficulties of professional life alone, requires a new mentality. If this mentality has not been acquired, only a temporary solution such as the appointment of the spouses to nearby cities may be tried, or resignations occur.

By analysing the sex-ratio in the key positions of two other central administrative agencies, namely the Ministry of Commerce and the State Planning Organization, interesting differences can be observed. The Ministry of Commerce is one of the major administrative units dealing with the male-dominated business world. Thus, the women who work in this ministry function are engaged chiefly in research (that is, securing foreign and domestic statistics, summarizing reports and making diplomatic contacts) as well as in the usual clerical domain. In the key positions, as in the Ministry of Foreign Affairs, young women with fluency in foreign languages are able to compete with men—once again proving the importance of the connection between education and class affiliation.

In the most recently created central administrative unit, the State Planning Organization, the situation has improved a great deal in. favor of women. Planning is a future-oriented activity requiring constant fact finding, compilation of statistics and the carrying out of predominantly advisory and coordinating functions; it seems to appeal more to women than to men. Here, too, some sort of imbalance is evident—the secondary positions related to expertise and specialized planning are fairly well staffed with women, while the strategy-determining positions are still preponderantly occupied by men. This agency appears to be the only one where there is remarkable balance in the ratio between men and women in positions higher than clerical.

Table 5.7

Sex-ratio Distribution According to Positions in the Ministry of Commerce, 1977

Position	No. of females	No. of males	Total
Asst commerical adviser	2	15	17
Asst commercial attaché	1	8	9
Commercial attaché	1	35	36
Asst rapporteur	6	18	24
Rapporteur	16	89	105
Head rapporteur	1	9	10
Head of section	10	86	96
Adviser	4	18	22
Total	41 (13.2%)	268 (86.8%)	309 (100%)
Other positions	295 (19.6%)	1,180 (80.4%)	1,505 (100%)

Source: State Personnel Directorate, unpublished data.

It is interesting to note that in those ministries where the heaviest concentration of women in lower positions is to be found—such as Education, Health and Social Assistance—promotional opportunities for women have been very limited. Only 3 out of 27 general directors in the Ministry of Education are women. In the Ministry of Finance, the general director of the treasury is a woman, but other senior positions are heavily occupied by men.

Can one expect that the relatively high number of professional women active in public service will continue, and is it possible to assume that their value judgments differ essentially from the values of their sisters in the middle and low ranks? In view of an overall climate of opinion favoring the traditional social function of women, it would be erroneous to answer in the affirmative. The basic difference between women officials in the higher and lower ranks lies in the nature of their informal activities. The choices of those in higher ranks will be heavily determined by the choices of the upper class, and include especially

Table 5.8
Sex-ratio Distribution According to Positions in the
State Planning Organization (as of 3 February 1978)

Position	No. of females	No. of males	Total
Head of section	2	10	12
Planning expert	27	58	85
Asst expert	24	44	68
Total	53 (32.1%)	112 (67.9%)	165 (100%)
Other positions	129 (30.3%)	296 (64.7%)	425 (100%)

Source: State Personnel Directorate, unpublished data.

leisure activities such as sports, card games, attendance at fashion shows as well as charity work and voluntary association affiliation. As pointed out by Vida Tomsiç, a Yugoslav social scientist, the influence of traditional values and ideas concerning the role of man and woman in the family and society has its own obstinate persistence long after the circumstances in which a certain value or prejudice originated have disappeared. This is especially true when the living conditions cannot be changed as quickly and profoundly as legal regulations (for example educational and employment possibilities). Research on the attitudes towards the new status of women in a socialist society shows that people have changed more in theory than in practice. One cannot help but get the impression that some of the new values accepted during the National War of Liberation in Turkey—when women's emancipation was one of the objectives as well as one of the reasons for women's active participation in the revolutionary movement—have been lost in today's practical life. Fighting tradition is a long and complex process (Tomsiç, 1975).

CONCLUSION

I return to the question posed at the beginning of this chapter: what has been the impact of legal and educational reform in Turkey with regard to women? It can be said that among all Muslim countries, Turkey has definitely been able to achieve remarkable results. But, as underlined by Özbay, class privileges in education particularly affect the female population. Furthermore, education by itself is incapable of equipping women or men with a new outlook on society and its social and economic structure. Education may eventually help to develop a stronger personality, but it does not contribute directly to a new consciousness. The presence of the relatively large number of professional women in the various government agencies has not been sufficient to open up new avenues towards a strong movement for a more egalitarian society. The modernization of women through education has primarily enlarged the ranks of the middle classes. The increasing interest of women in politics, mostly observed during largescale meetings and political rallies, has so far remained rather emotional. Women in responsible executive positions have done little or nothing to channel these growing aspirations into new activities, where the female work force could have had a positive effect on production.

Women in the executive and the judiciary are really freed in the public domain from all sex-defined stereotypes. Their performance can be summarized as asexual and totally adjusted to the standard male behavior rules. Only in the realm of private life does one encounter the traditional, conformist way of life. The degree of self-assurance, gained through work outside the home, permits these women to shoulder this ambivalent way of life.

The number of women participating in public administration could be a misleading indicator of equality, as they are predominantly assuming secondary roles with limited reponsibilities. Systematic efforts and specially designed policies have induced women to appear satisfied with non-demanding jobs and slight responsibilities. The fact that the general right to strike has so far not been granted to civil servants, men and women, has reduced the potential for pressure for specific demands concerning women officials. Justified claims for better working conditions, longer maternity leave, paid maternity leave and the creation of part-time jobs are all demands which have not been expressed through the activities of the associations, but rather through non-governmental organizations with limited influence.

No doubt the most significant progress has taken place in the level of participation in the professions. In this respect Turkey is displaying the characteristics of 'developing' Third World countries, where women enjoy access to the prestigious professions despite the low rates of participation in the non-agricultural labor market. As Öncü correctly stated, the ready availability of lower-class women as domestics in private homes has significantly contributed to the 'emancipation' of upper-class women to pursue professional careers. Furthermore, the need for qualified personnel has so far encouraged women from elite backgrounds to enter the prestigious professions. Thus, this process is to some extent historically specific.

Looking to the future, it may be expected that the growth in number of both Turkish civil servants and professionals will steadily continue, noticeably in regions with fast rates of urbanization and industrialization. But unless the question of female employment in general is treated as a subject on its own merits, and specific policies and programs developed for urban and rural women, women's role and impact on government affairs will not produce effective changes in society. The essence of efforts to advance the social position of women and their complete integration in development goes beyond the problem of legal and educational equal opportunities. It requires a deep structural transformation of society, a growing awareness of the need to use human resources fully and a strong ideological commitment to fight all forms of discrimination between the sexes.

NOTE

1. A recent survey of Turkish civil servants shows that fewer women than men move between departments and that a smaller proportion of women than of men are fully satisfied with their jobs. See Omer Bozkhurt, *Türkiye' de kamu* büroknasisinin sosyolojik görünumü(*Sociological Portrait of the Turkish Civil Service*) (Memurlar, Ankara, 1980), pp. 214 and 215.

PART 2
ECONOMIC DIMENSIONS

4

THE EFFECT OF INTERNATIONAL LABOR MIGRATION ON WOMEN'S ROLES: THE TURKISH CASE

INTERNATIONAL MIGRATION: A BRIEF HISTORICAL PERSPECTIVE

Over the course of history, migrations of various kinds have been nearly universal. Three main patterns of migration can be discerned: group migration, free individual migration, and restricted migration (Thomlinson, 1976).

Group migration, or large scale population displacements, may spring from various causes, including invasion, conquest, forced labor, colonization, war, etc. In recent centuries (with some exceptions), migration has tended to be in smaller units: a single person or a nuclear family unit, sometimes accompanied by other relatives. This free individual migration has been defined as "a spontaneous movement of individuals, relatively free . . . from legal restrictions, sometimes aided by the land policies of some leading countries of immigration" (Fairchild, 1925, quoted in Thomlinson, 1976, pp. 285-86).

Especially after World War II, however, rules regulating external migration increased in number and restrictiveness, resulting in the present pattern of restricted migration. The migratory movements of today take place within the framework of carefully designed bilateral agreements, as governments adopt deliberate policies toward migration, even embedding such policies in their development plans. Rather than individual decisions, migration is now a function of government plans

Reprinted from *Sex Roles, Family and Community in Turkey*, C. Kağıtçıbası, ed., 1982, pp. 207-36.

for "manpower import" or "export of excessive manpower." Thus migration has become an inherent element of the prevailing economic system, supplying a new army of reserve labor.

INTERNATIONAL MIGRATION:
CURRENT AND FUTURE PERSPECTIVES

Today, international migration flows mainly towards the highly industrialized countries—to Europe, the U.S. and Canada, and the oil-rich countries of the Middle East. There are regional movements as well to the more developed countries of Africa and Latin America. All of these migratory movements have been subjected to policies based on one or another of three models: a) the immigrant or integration model; b) the guest worker or rotation model; or c) the selective migration model. As the Turkish case has been subjected, at different times, to all three types of policies, a short analysis is in order.

The first model has been adopted by countries which are or have been underpopulated, or have experienced a sharp demographic decline, so that foreigners are invited for both economic and demographic reasons. Thus, countries such as the U.S., Canada and Australia, and more recently, France and the Federal Republic of Germany, have accepted foreigners not only as economically productive manpower, but also as potential citizens, and have, therefore, made efforts to integrate immigrants and their families into their own economy and society. These countries, however, have been quite selective, often on cultural or racial grounds. Most recently the criteria for selecting immigrants have focused on both the qualities of the immigrants (level of skill, education) and the country of origin.

The guest worker or rotation model is basically a product of the economic expansionism of the highly industrialized countries of post-World War II Europe. Most important in spearheading this model were Switzerland, West Germany, and the Netherlands, but in the second half of the 1960s, it was generally accepted by almost all the EEC countries. During this time, essential structural changes affecting the Common Market countries, such as the attainment of a high level of concentration and centralization of capital, the internalization of capital, and the tendency of this capital to move to peripheral areas, led to the invitation of foreign workers for primarily economic (not demographic) reasons, as cheap imported labor fed economic growth by holding down or at least stabilizing wages and maintaining high rates of profit, investment and expansion (Abadan-Unat, 1976; Paine, 1974).

The migrants of the new "European South" (at first predominantly male, later increasingly also female) from the Mediterranean countries such as Portugal, Spain, Italy, Greece, Yugoslavia, Turkey and the Maghreb, permitted the worker class of the host country to move up into skilled or semi-skilled jobs (Nikolinakos, 1973). Given the fact that these foreign workers were considered to be employed for a limited period of time and potentially dischargeable in periods of recession, efforts towards integration were not undertaken. The host countries were much less selective as to the occupational, national and racial backgrounds of the foreign workers.

The Turkish external migration concept was built upon this model. The Turkish economists and administrators who designed the first Five Year Development Plan assumed that Turkish migrant workers would sign contracts of one year's duration, acquire during this period new skills and experiences, gain the possibility of saving and sending home remittances and, after the completion of their turn, return home in order to make room for a second group. The spirit of the Turkish-German bilateral agreement of October 31, 1961 reflects these ideas. However, events took another course. The demand for additional manpower in Europe was so acute and intensive in the 1960s that very soon the duration of the working contracts was prolonged, first for two years, later for an indefinite period of time. Furthermore, many migrant workers bluntly refused to return home. Employers, too, were reluctant to undertake new efforts and expenses and to lose time in order to receive replacements for their work force. Finally, arguments based on human rights began to exert pressure on public opinion, labelling the rotation model as unjust and unfair. These developments prepared the ground for the transition to the third model, which became dominant after the energy crisis of 1973 (Abadan-Unat, 1976; Weber, 1970).

In the third model, called *mixed or selective integration*, some foreigners are invited for demographic and economic reasons and are encouraged to become citizens of the host country, while others are invited only for economic reasons and are encouraged to return to their home countries after a given number of years. This policy was developed by France, followed by Belgium. France, for instance, encourages Portuguese and Spanish migrants to settle, but attempts to induce North Africans to return home.

Following the energy crisis of 1973, all European countries totally stopped any further recruitment, thus bringing the remnants of any rotation practice *de facto* to an end, and replaced it with the model of selective integration. This significant change of policy had most important consequences with regard to family reunion, employment of women migrants and education of the second generation. It affected not only the Turkish migrant population in Europe, but indirectly also the demographic structure of some regions within Turkey with a high rate of external migration, such as Yozgat, Sivas, Şereflikoçhisar, Denizli, etc.

In addition to these three major types of post war migration, a new form of selective migration, applied mainly in the Middle East, deserves special attention. Migratory workers in this area are exclusively male and handled as "package deals" between governments and entrepreneurs of large projects (Choucri, 1977; Adler, 1975). Thus, instead of granting migrant workers the right to work for a given period of time, the work permit is only given for the duration of the project.

In all cases of present day migration, the major "pull" factors have been: economic expansion, unfavorable demographic situations in both the sending and receiving countries, and a steady upward mobility of indigenous workers. On the other side, the major "push" factors in the sending countries have been unemployment, poverty, economic underdevelopment, and retarded industrialization (Castles and Kossack, 1973).

These processes lead, as Galtung rightly points out, to asymmetrical interaction relations between nations and create a new form of dependency (Galtung, 1971). Thus "center nations" tend to require a higher level of skill and education, knowledge and research, whereas "periphery nations" continue to supply raw materials, markets, and surplus labor force.

Since the abrupt halt in recruitment to all EEC countries in 1973, new forms of illegal migration have emerged as a logical consequence of the asymmetrical dependency. So-called "tourist" workers from Turkey continue to intrude into West European and oil-rich countries, hoping to find some employment. Furthermore, increasing requests for asylum for alleged political persecutions are creating new political conflicts, since most of these demands are actually economically motivated. This desperate search for new job opportunities has resulted in further restrictive policies, such as the decision of West Germany, followed by other European countries, to require entrance visas from citizens of Turkey, Pakistan and Sri Lanka.

To sum up, Turkish migration has undergone four major phases. Each of these phases has affected both these migrant women who went abroad as well as those who were left behind. The first phase represents "predominantly single exodus, husbands leaving wives at home."

The second phase contains "family reunion under special conditions," implying a minimum term of two-year employment abroad. During the third phase, which coincides approximately with the recession of 1966-67, "priority in recruitment of women workers" is accorded. This phase marks the sudden rush of Turkish migrant workers to Europe. The fourth phase, which follows the energy crisis of 1973, is marked by "consolidation of the numbers of existing migrant workers, encouraged family reunion, opening of work possibilities to women migrants, and acceleration of male migration to oil-rich Arab countries."

During all these phases, migration has posed problems very different from those arising from internal movements; problems such as longer absences, greater distances, uncertainty of remittances, significant wage differentials, the necessity of mastering a new language, difficulties in communication with authorities, longer separation of family members, and cross-cultural conflicts. It is in the light of these special problems that we endeavor to analyze the impact of international migration on women with special reference to Turkish empirical data.

WOMEN IN INTERNATIONAL MIGRATION

Contrary to prevalent opinion, significant numbers of women join the international labor migration movements autonomously, though they also accompany their families and join the labor force in the receiving country. Between 1960 and 1974 in the U.S., 53% of the 1,977,400 immigrants from Latin America, 56% of the 933,800 immigrants from Asia and 56% of the 1,753,300 immigrants from Europe were women. In Africa in 1973, 43% of all the emigrants leaving for residence in another country were women (Youssef, Buvinic and Kudat, 1979). In 1978 there were about 215,000 Turkish migrant women employed in Europe. Their distribution was as follows: Austria, 31,800; Federal Republic of Germany, 134,342; Switzerland, 12,979; Belgium, 5,175; the rest being scattered over France, Holland, and the Scandinavian countries (OECD, 1979).

During the initial phases of the labor movement from one country to another, female participation is often low. It increases during subsequent phases, owing both to autonomous and to dependent female immigration, but is predominantly controlled by explicit migratory policies of the host country. The sudden flux of Mediterranean excessive population was at the beginning almost exclusively male.

However, due to economic factors such as the continued usage of out-dated industrial equipment, lower wages, and technical need for manual dexterity, etc. right after the recovery from the recession of 1966-67, there has been a growing demand for the employment of female migrant workers (Abadan-Unat, 1977). This situation produced a brand new challenge not only to Turkish women, but even more so to Turkish men. Due to the fact that at that period over one million Turkish men were registered for work permits and contracts at the Turkish Labor and Employment Office, the possibility of sending one's wife or daughter ahead, thus creating the legal ground for family reunion, created in the mentality of a great number of traditional-minded Turkish men revolutionary concepts. Women of rural background, traditionally socialized, totally unprepared mentally and to a considerable extent unwilling, were strongly urged by their fathers, husbands or other relatives to take up industrial or service jobs in foreign countries in order to secure for their male relatives the possibility of obtaining lucrative jobs with higher income possibilities in the near future. Thus, a great number of Turkish women entered industrial jobs with no knowledge of city life, highly disciplined working hours or production norms.

Meanwhile, new recruitment has come to an end, and most of the European receiving countries are elaborating comprehensive sets of policies in order to smooth family reunion. The only exception to this trend is the position of the immigration countries in the Middle East. At present, Libya, Saudi Arabia and the Gulf States have adopted very restrictive immigration policies. Accordingly, Saudi Arabia permits only professionals, experts and the staff people of those corporations with a minimum of 300 million dollars capital to bring their families with them.

TYPOLOGIES OF MIGRANT WOMEN

Because there are so many different types of international migration (seasonal, temporary, permanent), an attempt to develop some criteria for classifying migrant women may be useful.

One classification may be based on the type of instigation to leave the home country. Three basic types may be distinguished. a) *Accompanying migration:* in this case the woman or girl leaves her country of origin together with the male head of the family. b) *Induced migration:* in this case the woman's migration is imposed by a husband or father in order to facilitate his own exodus or that of other male members of the family. c) *Autonomous migration:* In this case the woman's migration represents an individual decision and should be

74

counted as the product of an emancipatory process.

A second classification may be based on degree of experience in urban settings in the home country. Again, three categories may be distinguished. a) *Urban background:* in this case, the woman was born in the city, or has lived in the city for an extended time prior to migration. b) *Transitory urban background:* in this case, the woman has spent time in the city only as the first step in a two-phase out-migration process. Here familiarity with urban structures remains extremely limited, and there is little change in the rural life style. c) *Rural background:* in this case the woman has no urban experience in the home country prior to migration. This situation represents the most abrupt transition from peasant culture to Western urban culture.

A third typology, based on the duration of stay abroad or at home, may be suggested. Once again, three groups may be differentiated: a) migrant women, who after a period of waiting join their husbands and take up permanent *residence abroad;* b) migrant women or girls, who after a lengthy stay abroad, are *repatriated;* and c) female members of migrant workers' families who *stay behind in the home country.*

Depending on the nature of the questions to be analyzed, one or all of these three typologies may be of relevance.

CHARACTERISTICS OF TURKISH MIGRANT WOMEN

- Turkish migrant women represent a relatively young population group; more than half (56%) are in the age group of 25-30. Similar to other migrant women in Europe, 76% of the Turkish migrant women are less than 35 years old.
- More than two thirds of the employed Turkish women are married (64%), 58% live with their husbands in Europe.
- The highest fertility rate belongs to Turkish families, the lowest to Greeks. Generally 50% of the Turkish workers have 2 children, 21% have 3-5, and 10% have more than 5 children.
- The educational level of migrant women reflects two distinct groups. Those who have not attended school at all are slightly more numerous than among the male migrants (10% vs. 7%). The same difference is also reflected among the groups that only attended primary school: while 70% of the men attended 3-5 years in primary school, this percentage is 61% for women. The second group of women represents those who attended secondary or professional schools. Among this group the ratio is opposite. More women have a higher educational level than men (38% vs. 21%).

- The occupational training of women is considerably less than that of men. In 1974 there were 16% of women versus 34% of men who benefitted from school or enterprise-furnished occupational training. Even so, Turkish women abroad are more skilled than their counterparts in Turkey (Maehrlaender, 1974).
- Most are employed in jobs requiring no qualification (50%). Out of 81% engaged in production jobs, 26% are employed in the metal branch, 19% in textiles, 9% in the food industry, and another 9% in the chemical industry; the remainder work in the service sector, in which 11% work in cleaning jobs. In Scandinavian countries the majority of Turkish migrant women are employed only in part-time jobs.
- As their primary motivation for migrating abroad, 55% of the women surveyed indicated the desire to join their families, while another 45% indicated the desire to save money.
- Turkish women workers are receiving noticeably lower wages than men. In 1977, 66% of the women workers in Germany were receiving a monthly net income between 500 and 800 DM, while 63% of the men received an income of 900-1500 DM or more.[1]

ECONOMIC ACTIVITY, OCCUPATIONAL ROLES, AND OUTLOOK FOR FUTURE EMPLOYMENT

Migration has a more positive effect on men than it does on women. Female migrants experience lower occupational status, longer working hours, lower earnings and worse living conditions. Discriminatory practices are bound to affect women migrants because they are restricted from the outset in terms of opportunities, types of work, and work conditions available to them.

Although migrant women in general are aware of the lower wage scale they are paid and the limited opportunities for promotion they are given, their adjustment to industrial life is totally negative. This is partly due to the fact that while "female" occupations are underpaid, work in sectors with heavy female employment such as textile, clothing, and food packaging is not exhausting. Although the nature of the work is relatively simple, repetitive and monotonous, it is not particularly hazardous.

The basic source of dissatisfaction among migrant women workers seems to be the open discrepancy of wages. According to Abadan's 1963 survey, only 36% were satisfied, the dissatisfaction rising with increased education. While only 44% of primary school graduates expressed critical attitudes, the rate went up to 58% among secondary school graduates (Abadan, 1964). This tendency has been confirmed in another comparative survey (Maehrlaender, 1974), in which 64% of the Italian, 64% of the Turkish, 68% of the Greek, 54% of the Yugoslav and 41% of the Spanish women workers evaluated their wages in regard to meeting the cost of living as "bad."

On the subject of chances for promotion, a significant proportion (48%) of migrant women had no opinion. This reflects the failure to inform migrant workers about the possibilities of social mobility. Among those who saw no chances (20%), 32% cited as the major obstacle ignorance of the language, 15% lack of professional training, and 14% prejudices and discrimination on the part of Germans (Maehrlaender, 1974).

Lack of previous working experience, belonging to different social strata together with unaccustomed spatial arrangements in dormitories seem to be factors contributing to a high degree of isolation and alienation among migrant women, preventing the development of an "esprit de corps." This reflects itself in situations requiring mutual assistance and group integration. In the Abadan survey of 1963, while 25% of the migrant women claimed not to be able to receive any help during working hours, this proportion reached only 15% for men. Similarly, 80% of the men rated group cohesion as highly favorable while 65% of the women expressed the same degree of satisfaction (Abadan, 1960).

The frustration encountered during working hours due to isolation seems, however, to be compensated for by increased friendship ties after work hours. While only 41% of the men met their colleagues outside of work, this rate went up to 60% for the women. Especially among women with vocational education there seems to be a higher degree of communication. Fifty percent of the workers with such backgrounds meet their work colleagues also outside the factory.

Another interesting point is related to preferences for fraternization with other contingents. While both men and women seem to prefer the citizens of their host countries for friendship forming, men cited in second place Italians (9%), while women preferred Greeks (6%). This preference shows that negative stereotypes are losing their effectiveness if similar social conditions of the respondents help to create common frames of reference. This observation was reconfirmed by a recent study in West Germany, in which migrant women emphasized the same preferences (Abadan, 1964; compare also Teber, 1980).

It is possible to conclude that the entrance of foreign women workers into complex industrial enterprises of developed countries should not be looked upon as an unsuccessful venture. In spite of migrant women's difficulties in terms of adjustment, industrial jobs and even menial ones expose migrant women to factory work, discipline, awareness of time, punctuality, trade union activity, and access to social security, all of which were unknown to most of them prior to their departure from their home country. In addition, environmental conditions in satisfactory housing, life in big cities, and increased exposure to mass media prepare the ground for emancipatory actions. This process also explains why unemployed migrant housewives in West Germany are eagerly waiting for an opportunity to work outside their homes (Table 1).

Table 1
**Intention of Foreign Housewives to Enter
the Labor Market (%)**

Nationality	Yes	No	Perhaps
Greeks	52	36	12
Italians	48	36	16
Yugoslavs	72	16	12
Turks	80	08	12
Age			
Under 25	90	10	—
25-35	48	35	17
35 and over	66	18	16

Source: Bundesministerium für Jugend, Familie u. Gesundheit, Situationsanalyse nichterwerbstaetigen Ehefrauen auslaendischer Arbeitnehmer in der BDR, 1977, Tabelle: 11.

OCCUPATIONAL OPPORTUNITIES FOR MIGRANT WOMEN

One of the fundamental characteristics of the labor market in all industrialized countries is the marked degree of segregation by sex: women are concentrated in a limited range of occupations and industries. Occupation or industry thus divides the male and female labor force effectively into two different and relatively noncompeting labor markets. Hence labor market segregation has important implications for adjustment to technological change.

The labor market is also segmented, with a primary sector employing so-called "advantaged workers" and a secondary sector employing "disadvantaged workers." Disadvantaged workers are employed in enterprises where wages are low, working conditions poor, employment often unstable, and opportunities for further on-the-job training limited. A great many of the "female" occupations referred to above are in the so-called "secondary sector." Technological changes are worsening this situation.

As reported by ILO and other UN specialized agencies, the decline in female employment in particular industries such as the metal trades, clothing, leather footwear, food and beverages may be attributed in large part to the extent and nature of modernization methods. Industries which have adopted a higher capital-intensive technology resulting in displacement of labor have found it easier to displace women than men. They have justified this on the ground that women lack skills, are illiterate, and are unwilling to learn new processes. This argument hits mostly migrant women workers, who fit in these categories and due to language barriers are unable to improve their qualifications (Beneria, 1978; Tadesse, 1979; UN Decade for Women Conference, 1980).

In textile industries, ILO found that when new machines were installed, the tendency was to substitute male workers for women workers and to keep women workers on the older, non-automatic machinery. In postal and telecommunication services too, new technical equipment resulted in the abolition of temporary or part-time jobs. Such posts were frequently occupied by women and it was the female staff who were most affected by the adoption of new techniques (ILO, 1977).

A recent report of the UN stresses that "in the absence of full employment, rapid and thoughtless technological change can only exacerbate social problems, especially through the displacement of workers—particularly minorities and women who are just beginning to achieve job levels which permit them to enjoy the benefits of technology" (UN Decade of Women Conference, 1980).

The estimation of employment chances for women in the 1980s indicates that automation of manufacturing processes has tended to diminish much of the routine work typically done by women (light assembly, conveyor belt work and packing). The general pattern in such technical developments seems to be to reduce or downgrade the openings for routine work, but to enlarge the opportunities for more highly qualified people (UN Seminar, 1969).

This tendency obviously leaves only domestic service as a future outlet for female employment (aside from low status industrial jobs). This is especially well documented in Latin America and France for those migrants who are young and have arrived recently in the capital city areas. In 1970 in Buenos Aires, 62% of migrants coming in from neighboring countries found employment in domestic service (Jelin, 1977). In France, of 210,000 active migrant workers, 76,000 were employed in industry, and 73,000 in domestic services (Secretariat d'Etat, 1975). In the case of Turkish women workers, those who enter domestic jobs are opting for such an occupation as a supplementary income source. They usually perform domestic work on weekends and are predominantly widows or divorced women with heavy family charges. However, looking closer at the salaried work, a great number of Turkish women are performing in the service sector; we may detect that a great majority are cleaning jobs, especially with municipal institutions in large cities.

Many employed migrant women are not only confronted with the problem of handling the double burden of work and housework, but, in order to secure an additional source of income, are shouldering a third type of work, the illegal "black work." This accumulation of stress due to overwork, of course, results in physical exhaustion. In 1976, 44% of Turkish women (versus 38% of men) were ill longer than 10 days (Nolkensmeier, 1976).

SPENDING, SAVING AND INVESTMENT TENDENCIES

For migrant women, the basic motivation in taking up any type of work is economic. The tendency of migrant women to spend more and remit less money than men is quite sharp. A Turkish survey on spending and saving habits of Turkish migrant workers revealed that 47% of women are not sending any money back. Lack of confidence in complex organizations and inadequate information on banking facilities seem to induce women to keep large sums at their temporary homes. While men are more eager to invest in agricultural enterprises or land, women prefer houses or flats in the home country. Women seem to prefer safe, riskless and passive investment forms. The irresistible impact of advertisements, mass media, and especially TV, encourage Turkish women migrants towards excessive purchase of clothing and durable household goods. A belief in the superiority of commodities produced abroad leads them to pronounced conspicuous consumption (Abadan-Unat, 1977).

However, freedom for consumption does not necessarily mean the liberty of choosing a different way of living. If one looks at many of the houses built in Anatolia by migrant workers who have returned or are still working abroad, one may see that in these brightly painted, large (five or six room) houses, most of the rooms are left unused. Thus we may ask whether economic affluence and the cult of foreign consumer goods can serve as a criterion for emancipation. It seems that these new habits represent more pseudo-emancipation than deep and lasting change in mentality (Yenisey, 1976). Marginalization as a minority group in an alien society at large probably leads to compensation by means of showing off. Women in this respect appear to be especially vulnerable and open to consumerism-oriented advertisement.

In Turkey, as in other Mediterranean countries, among the urban, lower income groups, husbands are as a rule the principal breadwinners. Even in rural areas, where women bear an equal share with men in terms of participating in agricultural production, the husband is the sole middleman between the household and the market. This unchallenged position becomes shaky if women are the first to migrate. This sudden role reversal became particularly visible during the third phase of Turkish migration to West Germany, when women workers were preferred over men and large contingents of psychologically unprepared rural women were, so to speak, catapulted abroad when they entered a world they were unable to comprehend (Abadan-Unat, 1977).

Thus, one of the most important sources of dispute among working spouses has been and still continues to be the allocation and control of household income, the establishment of separate bank accounts and the authority to decide on these subjects. Dispute also arises very frequently over the use of joint savings and the type of investment (Kudat, 1975).

Whether or not migrant women will be willing to make greater use of educational opportunities in order to be able to compete in the face of dwindling work opportunities depends to a large extent on the attitude of the husbands. The likelihood that more free time will be made available to women through a kind of partnership marriage arrangement is not very high, due to the overwhelmingly traditional orientation of the Turkish migrant group abroad. This strong social control prevents the growth of belief in internal control of reinforcement, meaning a tendency to assume full responsibility for one's actions. The existence of large ethnic groups in foreign countries generally means that the individuals there, especially the women, are more "other-oriented" and less prepared to develop an autonomous, self-reliant, active behavior tendency (Akpınar, 1977).

PSYCHOLOGICAL CONSEQUENCES OF MIGRATION

At first glance the entrance of migrant women without industrial work experience into the labor market, or their joining their husbands abroad, seems to take place without particular friction or conflict. Since a great number of migrant women have been brought up in a traditional way, the assumption is that in their childhood they were already prepared to adjust themselves at any time to totally different environments (e.g., Kıray, 1979). Yet very soon it becomes evident that confrontation with a highly different environment and the resultant steadily growing nostalgia create much psychological change and stress which may lead eventually to behavioral disturbances. The effects are as follows:

- Multifaceted abruptness

  Women who for the first time in their lives have to undertake a long journey alone or are obliged to commute to their work place by themselves are prey to serious frustrations. Similarly, unexperienced women are suddenly introduced into a complex industrial system where they work for wages with an intricate tax deduction scale on the payroll, which needs detailed explanation to be understood. Some of these examples clearly indicate the unpreparedness to which many migrant women are exposed. The crucial point in this process is that when all this exposure occurs simultaneously, it creates among an important segment of the migrant population acute anxiety and alienation.

- Discontinuity

  For many migrant women the change of work participation appears to be limited to their stay abroad. Since they consider their new occupational role to be temporary and assume that they will have little or no chance of using their working experience, they are not very highly motivated to learn new skills or the indigenous language.

  A significant change occurs also in their self-image. Women suddenly measure almost all their actions from the point of view of being a breadwinner, a money maker, a capital accumulator. Thus the entrance of migrant women into the labor market means generally not to become an "industrial worker," but to "make money, and accumulate savings." This monetary orientation has a deep effect both on the wives and children who accompany their husbands and those who are left behind (Gürel and Kudat, 1978).

- Easing Up of Social Control

  The total change of environment means generally that migrants from rural or small town origins are no longer subject to the permanent control of the family, especially the father, relatives of the father, and later the husband. Migration causes changes in the composition of the family structure and the acceptance of new frames of reference. Instead of submission, passivity and lack of initiative, migrant women are psychologically ready to accept new patterns of behavior. This is a healthy development if it is also supported by the environment, which is often not the case.

- Impact of Migration on Mental Health
The extraordinarily fast transition from traditional to industrial life has produced mental disorders. A recent survey of migrant women workers in the Rühr region of West Germany indicates that particularly migrant women workers from rural areas who were obliged to move directly from their home villages to large cities abroad and to be separated from their husbands and/or children without any knowledge of a foreign language were subject to psychosomatic diseases. Out of 77 female patients, 53 were treated for conditions such as "uprootedness syndrome," "atypical depression," "neurosis," "depressive reaction" and "nostalgia reaction." The most common symptoms of these patients were intense anxiety accompanied by heart or chest pains, stomach ulcers, sleeplessness, lack of appetite, physical deficiency, sexual problems, and head and back aches. These symptoms generally appeared after an incident such as a traffic accident, discharge from work, or bad news from home. The average age of these 53 Turkish women patients was 30; their duration of stay abroad, 6.2 years. A second important group of disorders were of a more serious nature, such as schizophrenia, paranoid syndrome and fatal melancholy. Among this group, too, women were in the majority. These recurrent patterns have resulted in the acknowledgement in medical circles of a new type of disorder, labeled the "guestworker syndrome" (Teber, 1980; Benhert, Florn and Fraistein, 1974; Melon and Timsit, 1971; Özek, 1971). In general women migrants, once faced with serious challenges, seem to be less able than men to overcome unfavorable conditions.

IMPACT OF MIGRATION ON FAMILIAL ROLES: INSTABILITY OF FAMILY STRUCTURES

Important changes take place in the composition of migrant households as a result of out-migration and settlement in urban areas. In contrast to the relative stability of rural or small town households, the make-up of the migrant urban household tends to be more temporary in nature.

Migrants often need to exercise not only paternal bonds, but also those of kinship, neighborhood, fellow townmanship, friendship and affinity. According to T. Parsons the isolated nuclear family is a response to the demands of an industrial economy. However, much of the recent sociological research on urban social organizations in Western societies has demonstrated the significance of extra-household kinship ties and the supportive functions of the kin group. Litwak, Sussman and Leske (1965) assert that among industrial urban groups, modified extended family structure consists of a coalition of nuclear families in a state of partial dependence. This interaction is situational and takes place according to the needs of the moment.

This general observation is particularly true for the family structure of migrants. Although the basic rule is to have a nuclear family, important changes may take place as a result of out-migration and settlement in urban areas. This is equally true for families left behind. As Kıray correctly states (1976), the major characteristic of the migrant family is the change in its composition. The migrant family may split itself into various parts and compose itself in many ways with other kin as the conditions and possibilities of job, money and accommodation change for the migrant himself during his stay abroad. Thus the choices for migrants are quite varied. They may live as married or single residents in dormitories (Heim); with their wives, some or all of their children, and/or with paternal or maternal relatives; they also may share flats with previously unrelated couples or several singles. Any given household of migrants throughout its existence abroad or at home may assume multiple configurations as each arrival and departure affects the network of relationships. Its temporary nature is attributable to the over-all high turnover rate among the migrant population. Even in cases of prolonged stay abroad or definite settlement, the unbroken ties with the home country due to intensive physical mobility, maintain this structural instability (Kıray, 1976).

FRAGMENTATION

The families involved in the migratory movement are eager to accept employment abroad; try to secure employment also for the marriage partner if possible; and for financial, cultural or personal reasons to leave dependents in the home country. As a result, family fragmentation becomes almost a rule. It has become normatively acceptable for a family unit to remain separated for years. In Turkey such a practice was traditionally widely accepted for men, while wives and children would be entrusted to the care of relatives. The big change has been triggered by external migration. Not only unmarried and married women without their families were permitted in recent years to leave in order to secure jobs abroad, but women heading households also became acceptable for the families left behind (Abadan-Unat, 1977). These families could choose between joining either spouses' families or leading an independent existence in their own homes. Kıray considers heading the separate house in the village to be one of the most important functional changes in the role of women brought about by migration in Turkey, a change which no law of the republican era could have brought on such a scale (1976).

Thus one may conclude that a temporary, independent lifestyle due to migration might eventually reinforce emancipatory efforts at home or abroad, yet fragmentation of family life produces a great number of serious inconveniences too. The most essential ones are as follows: separation of spouses may result in very long absences, causing alienation within marital life. This might be especially detrimental to women, considering the "machismo" value judgments or the "double standard" accorded to men. Furthermore, due to various reasons such as the desire to educate children in the home country, unemployment, bad housing, or maladjustment, women are more likely to return to their home country. Fragmentation in such cases increases mistrust among partners, fears of divorce, neglect of children, and deprivation of affection.

FAMILIAL RESPONSIBILITIES AND DIVISION OF WORK

Migration provokes a rapid change with regard to familial responsibilities and work division. The degree of change strongly depends on whether the man or the women has migrated first, in what kind of milieu the migrant family settles, and to what extent their social network acts as a buffer mechanism to overcome the hardships of adjustment. Generally, even in cases of family reunion in countries placing a strong emphasis on egalitarian values and norms between marital partners, the married migrant woman worker remains attached to the values of her traditional upbringing. The pressure of the in-group tends to reinforce this attachment. Thus, working wives are expected to carry a "double burden," which may become extraordinarily heavy under tiresome work conditions in industrial settings, household chores and poor housing conditions. Even in cases where the woman acted as vanguard and was the first to obtain a work permit, thus acting as the head of the family and being the main breadwinner, reunion seldom produces an equal sharing of tasks. On the contrary, the economic independence achieved by migrant women almost inevitably leads to sharp conflicts.

Another factor which influences women's independence in decision making is the social and economic status occupied by the migrants in their home country previous to migration. An anthropological study of Turkish migrants of rural background in Sweden indicates that the social background of the migrants influences decision making (Engelbrektsson, 1978). Thus the social networks which link migrants at home and abroad has an impact on their capacity for making independent decisions and determines whether they can become "architects of their own destinies" (Magnarella, 1979). This last item is crucial in regard to whether or not women of rural background are permitted to take up employment outside the home.

For those migrant women who by choice or legal restriction are confined at home, other problems gain relevance. For women from cultures where the daily life of the sexes is well separated, such as in many Mediterranean countries, the only way to overcome loneliness is in groups of the same sex. Thus, for instance, the much-criticized Turkish residential ghettos like Kreuzberg and Wedding in West Berlin, Rijkoberg in Stockholm, Feijenoord in Rotterdam, etc., actually provide a tightly structured community life, which represents the only means to escape total isolation. Integration in such communities decreases problems of daily life; however, by reinforcing traditional behavior, the chances for an emancipatory process within the family are blocked. (See Baumgartner-Karabak and Landesberger, 1978; although the picture this book presents of Turkish migrant women is grossly exaggerated, it nevertheless gives some insight into the social control exercised in these ghetto districts.) Taking into consideration the fact that migrant women—employed or not—are confronted with serious handicaps such as uprootedness, lack of language, isolation, and prohibitions against going out alone, the interaction of the micro-community they belong to and the macro-community they live in affects basically only their behavior as consumers. While daily shopping is more or less acceptable, any further exploration in community life becomes an absolute taboo, especially for housewives. As revealed by a comparative study with a group of Greek, Italian, Yugoslav and Turkish housewives, 80% never went to a swimming pool, 63% to a movie, 55% to a restaurant, or 51% to a coffeehouse by themselves (Johansen). This prohibitive code of behavior explains the relatively weak usage of the adult educational opportunities offered. Aside from radio and weekly TV programs in their respective national languages, very few modernizers seem to be able to touch the non-employed migrant women living abroad. To sum up, the change of intra-familial roles takes a longer time than the change of the individual migrant women abroad or the females left behind at home.

DECISION MAKING AND AUTHORITY

The growth in size of fragmented families due to migration affects authority patterns and decision making within the family both abroad and left behind in Turkey and almost forces women to act independently. Those who are abroad have their own bank accounts, and feel free to invite their own relatives or friends to their homes for lengthy periods, sometimes without even consulting their husbands. In the home country, wherever women act as head of the family in the absence of their husbands who are migrant workers abroad they are obliged to carry on a number of previously unknown transactions such as cashing remittances from the post office or bank, requesting credit for crops or building, choosing the place and type of schools for their children, organizing social functions such as engagements, weddings, etc.

Generally speaking, women migrants who have acquired economic independence abroad or those who are leading an independent life at home in Turkey increasingly handle their income, savings and investments more autonomously.

In nuclear or transient extended families abroad where the migrant woman's authority is not strongly challenged by the husband or other relatives, the new role assumed makes the woman more aware of the importance of literacy, schooling and family planning.

However, migration does not inevitably enlarge the horizons of women in terms of participating more in decision making and sharing authority with the husband. The dominant pattern for husbands and fathers still seems to be to retain as long as possible their traditional privileges based upon inequality within the family and to attempt to transmit these values through socialization. Nevertheless, migration imbues participants with an increased awareness of change. The reaction against these drastic changes depends much on the environment, the background of the family and no doubt to an important degree on the type of personality.

In this context, dominant values cherished by the public opinion of the Turkish community abroad also play a decisive role. Liberalizing tendencies are deliberately counterbalanced by fundamentalist, traditional moral values diffused through various socializing institutions such as Koran courses, cultural programs, films and some press organs. A review of a considerable number of Turkish films shown in West Germany indicates that in 90.5% of them traditional male-female roles continue to be depicted. Women in all these films were subordinate to men and women were shown either as housewives or in less than flattering occupations, such as prostitutes, belly dancers, etc. In every instance, decision-making roles were in the hands of men. As the author of this content analysis points out, sexism persists in contemporary Turkey (Suzuki).

The least consulted persons in migrant families are daughters of marriageable age. Those who were born abroad or who joined their parents at an early age may have enjoyed professional training. However, the family head, under the influence of the social control exercised by the ethnic group to which they belong, particularly in urban centers of high concentration, may advocate abrupt cessation of school attendance and force upon the girls the acceptance of pre-arranged marriages, many times in exchange for bride prices. Torn between two cultures, not strong enough to resist, not old enough to achieve economic independence, these girls face grave problems. They tend easily to become drop-outs, to acquiesce in the choices of their families, or sometimes to desert them.

Contrary to expectations, migration does not affect the fertility pattern of migrants, especially among the families left behind in rural areas. No matter how much they may be the mistresses of their own homes, the wives left behind do feel lonely because of long years of separation from their husbands. Reunion is the only hope for both sides. One solution is to have children with great frequency. To be pregnant or to be breastfeeding infants helps to keep the women emotionally satisfied (Kıray, 1976).

An interview carried out with a midwife within the Boğazlıyan survey in the village of Çalapverdi revealed that although as a rule there are one or two births each month, in March there is an abundance of births, because the migrant workers who come back on vacation in July almost invariably impregnate their wives. In 1975, as many as 30 women in the village were expecting babies in that month. According to this midwife, these women were not at all interested in birth control methods. The most common reason for childbearing is that they have enough money and property to feed their children, so why not? Reconsidering that according to the Boğazlıyan survey, 65% of the family members left behind were illiterate, 11% were only able to read and write, 7% had attended primary school and only 3% had completed primary school, it is not surprising that in an underdeveloped rural setting a proper evaluation of the nature of the husband's employment abroad and its estimated duration cannot be expected from these women. Here only age seems to be relevant. Among newly married couples since 1970 on, there is some interest in family planning, particularly the pill. There are some 40-50 women in the village in this category. However, they have difficulty in sticking to a daily schedule (Yenisey, 1976).

Turkish migrant women employed abroad are less eager to raise a large family. As far back as 1963, 57.3% of the migrant workers did not want a family larger than three children. The preference of women for no more than two children (38.7%) was slightly higher than that of men (31.5%). Similarly, readiness to make use of family planning methods was quite high (65%). However, important factors may cause an almost total rejection of these intentions. The decision of the government of West Germany to extend the maternity leave up to eight months and support it through financial incentives in order to overcome the steady decline in the growth of West Germany's population, exercised its most important effect on migrant workers. Turkish families especially did not hesitate to take advantage of this new right and to produce larger families despite the crowded and unfavorable housing conditions a great majority have to endure (Seidel, 1979).

Migration obviously has also brought about some significant changes in the relations between men and women. Although the majority of Turkish migrants, being aware of their minority position, are generally strongly committed to projecting a profile of strict puritan values, there are many who lean toward the more permissive rules of conduct of Western countries. It should not be forgotten that migration by its very nature leads to a lengthy separation within the family. This very fact produces a consequent exposure to a more liberal social environment. There are quite a few reports in the Turkish press testifying about migrant heads of families who bring with them during their yearly leave their "German wives," even requesting that their legal wives serve and entertain these important "guests." In other cases, local rumors or letters from local informants about the alleged misdemeanor or unfaithfulness of a female family member (wife, sister or daughter) have induced some Turkish migrants to return home in order to save the "honor" of the family by divorce or homicide.

It can be assumed that even in the future, as the incidence of separation may be reduced and the sex composition of the population adjusted, the drift to a more liberal social environment and the changing economic status of women will perpetuate a higher rate of adultery and even bigamy (Kudat, 1975). Parallel to this tendency, the number of children born out of wedlock may continue to increase.

EDUCATION OF CHILDREN, CHILD-RAISING FUNCTION OF FEMALE TEENAGERS

The most crucial issue for fragmented families is the problem of the children either left in their home countries or raised abroad. The decision of how many children should remain abroad depends largely on the migratory policy of the host country. Although Turkish families in West Germany had the largest proportion of large families in 1971 (18% two children, 29% three children, 16% four children, 10% five children, 6% six or more children), they kept the least number of children with them abroad (Maehrlaender, 1974, p. 206). In 1971 only 5% of Turkish migrant workers had three and 3% had four children living with them. This situation changed drastically when West Germany implemented a revised tax law and entitled for family allocation only those families, both German and foreign, who kept their children living with them. This legislative amendment provoked a "child rush." Another legislative amendment mentioned above concerning a prolongation of maternity leave with financial assistance also resulted in the growth of family size. Thus it seems realistic to state that decisions in regard to family reunion are taken more on the basis of regulatory policies than individual preferences.

In those cases where all or most of the children are brought into the country of immigration a special role falls upon the shoulders of the eldest daughter of the family, who becomes a surrogate mother, although she is not emotionally ready for the task of raising small children. In addition, these girls—usually in their their teenage years— are deprived of school attendance and left deliberately without formal education and professional training (Abadan-Unat, 1977; Meister, 1975; GED, 1979; Berger and Mohr, 1975).

In those families where the mother remains at home, the language barrier prevents these migrant women from helping their children with their homework, and similarly they are unable to establish any contact with school authorities. Neither are they able to transmit adequately to their children the culture, customs, religious values or language of the home country. Wherever bilingual education has not become a part of the immigration policy of the host country, the problem of severe inter-generational cultural gaps and conflicts preoccupies educators and social workers.

The socialization process within migrant families as contrasted with the institutionally guided socialization efforts shows important differences. In regard to child discipline, for instance, there are diametrically opposed values between German and Turkish families. In Turkish families it is predominantly the father who disciplines the children, while in German families discipline problems and educational matters are considered to be the province of the mother. In almost all Turkish families, the father also acts as mediator between the outside world and the family. Thus one can say that within the Turkish family, as in other southern Mediterranean families, the power structure leans more toward patriarchal attitudes, while in about two-thirds of German families, a model of equal partnership is more dominant.

Another important source of differences of opinion is related to the anticipated goals of education. A comparative survey among the major migrant groups living in Germany yielded a juxtaposed picture. For German families the most important goal for their children was to help them become more self-sufficient, independent and responsible, and to develop an autonomous personality, while for the Turks learning aspiration for achievement, obedience and adherence to order occupied the first place (Holtbrügge, 1975).

Another relevant trend seems to be the high importance placed by Turkish migrant families on loyalty toward the state and identification with religious and national identity. Parents attempt to transmit these goals through a patriarchal value system, which very often is rejected by the adolescent second generation. Young boys, especially, in order to achieve full integration, conform to the dominant ideas of their indigenous peers (Neumann, 1977; Ronneberger, 1976; Wilpert, 1976; CIME, 1979).

The temporary migration syndrome in Europe thus compels people to belong to two worlds. Wherever a pluralistic cultural approach towards the migrant child is provided—at present West Berlin has started such a curriculum in districts with heavy concentrations of Turkish children—a balance can be achieved between the culture of the receiving society and that of the country of origin. However, where such a compromise school model is not pursued, institutions performing an "ersatz" (support) function are appearing, such as the numerous Koran schools in West Germany. These private schools escape any public control. They emphasize recitation and memorization, and they practice physical punishment. Such schools no doubt represent serious obstacles to the child's development and to its integration into the receiving society. Yet almost all of the pupils of such schools attend them under the strong pressure of their parents (Abadan-Unat, 1975, 1979).

The ambivalent position of parents toward their children in migrant families is very important. The clash between different civilizations, cultures and religions creates in the minds of these youngsters confusing pictures. Having grown up in family settings where little importance is placed on personal communication and where mass media takes up the majority of free time available, youngsters are practically deprived of linguistic means of expression. The pattern of communication is reduced to simple conversation focused on errands of daily life. On the other hand, second generation children are often ostracized by their peer groups in the indigenous population. Since they have little affinity with their home country, they do not feel themselves at ease anywhere and become obsessed by the norms of the affluent society, which all tend towards conspicuous consumption.

With regard to the position of migrant women as mothers, two different models seem to emerge. Women of predominantly rural background with very little or no education, whether employed or not employed, are virtually unable to fulfill their maternal roles after their children outgrow babyhood. Not knowing any foreign language, they are dependent on their children for any communication. This situation often causes children to look down upon their mothers, considering them useless and ineffective.

This first category represents a rather large group. The acute isolation to which these women are subject not only severs them from the accustomed network of their neighbors, relatives and peers, but also undermines their emotional relationships within the family, shaking their personal and psychic stability, contributing to an increasing alienation between mother and children.

The various types of assistance offered by social services exercise only a limited influence. Initiatives taken in favor of women migrants usually originate from voluntary, non-governmental associations, which, instead of helping the growth of awareness and consciousness, reinforce the traditional roles of women by offering courses in tailoring, sewing, cooking, etc. Thus, for these women migration does not necessarily mean emancipation, understood as individual independence, self-realization, and liberation from repressive social influences. However, women migrants with slightly higher educationalevels or satisfactory professional training, who display an eagerness to learn the local language and are aware of the benefits of social security, may improve their status in regard to equality and responsibility.

The second group of women, representing the family members left behind, should be evaluated in two categories. The first one embraces those women who have been entrusted by their husbands/fathers to stay at home within the family of the male migrant. Living with parents-in-law in the patriarchal and patrilocal extended household seems to delay the process of a bride's establishing herself as second-in-command to her husband. This becomes particularly relevant when the husband is out of the country. In the second category, representing semi-complete nuclear households, where the wife left behind is acting as plenipotentiary head of family, the long separation and deprivation of marital companionship may create some problems. But by and large those women belonging to the second category seem to handle the situation with greater vigor and energy. As a result of the challenge, they are obliged to deal autonomously with many questions previously left to the discretion of the male head of the family. This situation permits them to develop in a relatively short period a strong, independent, self-reliant character. Female heads of migrant families are showing—as in the survey of Boğazlıyan—that migration can play a decisive role in accelerating emancipation.

CONCLUSIONS

Present day migration represents a planned exchange of manpower subject to complex governmental policies and bilateral agreements. This situation plays an important role in decisions concerning the choice of working place, family reunion, family size, children's education, etc. The alternatives adopted by migrant women at home or abroad are not exclusively taken on the basis of individual preferences, but as by-products of the policies shaping the international migration process. Structural changes within migrant families have to be evaluated also under the light of rotation, integration or selective integration policies.

Problems of adjustment depend largely on the type of migration such as accompanying, induced or autonomous. Other criteria related to residential background, duration of stay in various settings, and interaction between networks connecting the home country to the migrant's living place, as well as the prevailing family structure (fragmented, reunited or repatriated), also influence the status of migrant women workers and the structure of their families.

Turkish migrant women are generally employed in "feminine" industrial jobs and the service sector. Considerably lower wages than those of their male counterparts, little or no opportunity for acquiring new skills, lack of awareness of existing labor legislation and limited participation in trade-union activity are the dominant traits of Turkish migrant women employed abroad. Their economic participation substantially changes the family pattern of saving, investing and spending. Conflicts due to financial questions are frequent. A strong move toward conspicuous consumption is noticeable.

The psychological impact of migration on migrant women both at home and abroad is noticeable. Abroad, alienation and isolation create significant psychic disturbances. Stress situations deeply affect sex roles within the family, often leading to psychosomatic diseases. Monetary concerns overshadow traditional loyalties.

Structural changes within the migrant's family are characterized by constantly changing dimensions of fragmentation. Migration causes intrinsic changes in decision making and authority, ambivalence in fertility patterns, and polarization in regard to heterosexual relationships, ranging from archconservative traditional behavior to permissive, liberal attitudes.

Major inter-generational conflicts due to clashing value systems in the socialization of migrant children create a permanent source of serious conflicts. The "surrogate mother" function, imposed upon a great number of teenage girls, along with prearranged marriages leading to forced repatriation, increases stress situations within the family. The school attendance of girls both abroad and at home remains a serious problem, closely related to the educational level of the parents, especially the mother, the impact of social control, life in ghettos, religious indoctrination and duration of stay abroad.

Migration does not logically lead to emancipation of women, understood as liberation from social pressures hindering individual independence and self-realization. Emancipation requires increased redistribution of roles and role-sharing within the family and during leisure time. It also requires a grasp of the interrelationship of structures related to production, power structures, social norms, and value judgments. Looking ahead, one might wonder whether the rigid policies concerning visa requirements for Turkish citizens with migrant relatives abroad will not lead to an increasing fragmentation of the migrant family or the family left behind.

NOTE

1. Data in this section are drawn mainly from empirical research material of the author (see Abadan, 1964); data relevant to the 1970s are drawn from a comprehensive German survey and another comparative survey carried out in West Germany on behalf of the Friedrich Ebert Foundation by U. Maehrlaender (Maehrlaender, 1974).

5

IMPLICATIONS OF MIGRATION ON EMANCIPATION AND PSEUDO-EMANCIPATION OF TURKISH WOMEN

In many underdeveloped Mediterranean countries with few occupational opportunities, external migration during the two decades from 1955-1975 became a matter of governmental policy, frequently regulated by international bilateral agreements. As such, external migration began at this time to represent a typical future of the post-war development. This migration was distinguished, however, by a predominantly non-individually motivated, yet highly administratively organized character.

The highly industrialized West European countries were the main targets for these migrant workers. These countries exercised full employment policies and extended vocational training, which resulted in a more facile upward mobility and in a large number of employment vacancies in the socially undesirable, tiresome and dirty jobs. Initially, these employment factors led to the export of a significant portion of the male population. Later, however, as industry continued to employ out-of-date industrial equipment and lower wages, there was a rising demand for the employment of female migrant workers, particularly in the manufacturing, iron and metal industries. More specifically, female workers were concentrated in the sector of electronics, automotive industry, textile, chemical production, food processing and packaging as well as cleaning services.

Reprinted from *International Migration Review* Vol. 11, No. 37:31-57. Spring 1977.

In West Germany, after the recession of 1966-1967, there actually appeared a limitation of new job offerings for men, in which the demand for female workers continued. This produced a situation whereby traditionally trained, non-migratory motivated women were strongly urged by their fathers, husbands, or other relatives to take up industrial jobs in foreign countries by which they could secure lucrative positions with higher income possibilities for their male relatives. Thus, countless Turkish women entered urban jobs without knowing what constituted city life, highly disciplined working hours, or production norms.

This chapter, then, endeavors to sketch briefly the status of Turkish women workers employed abroad in the industrial and informal sectors. It shall contrast the intended and the unintended migratory moves of women in an effort to discern the link between the migrant workers who have taken up semi-permanent residence abroad and their impact on the female family members left behind in terms of the latter's emancipation or pseudo-emancipation. As such, the entrance of women workers into new jobs, will be received as a contribution to the far reaching social and economic changes in the home region of the migrants in rural and urban areas.

GROWTH OF TURKISH MIGRATION

Turkey, unlike many of the Mediterranean countries, has maintained no continuing migratory tradition. This tendency is reflected in Dr. Lerner's analysis on the empathy among citizens of Middle Eastern countries. This antipathy toward geographical mobility has changed drastically in the last two decades. The primary cause for this change may be found in the structural change taking place in the Turkish economy. Since the early 1950's, the introduction of modern technology, cash cropping and increased indebtedness for transportation and marketing, have resulted in a rapid de-peasantization of this rural population forcing the peasant to turn to non-agriculturally based income sources. In urban areas, the sudden surge of the informal sector also induced a large number of employed people to seek their livelihoods abroad. These elements, when coupled with the impact of rising expectations and the desire for better educational opportunities, led to the constant growth in the number of potential candidates for external migration. The proportion of women workers at the beginning of the large-scale Turkish exodus, that is, during the first decade of 1956-1966, was relatively low. After 1966-1967 statistics indicated that while new offerings were limited for men, a continuous demand for women workers was registered. This date also marks the heavier migration of women directly from rural areas. After 1966, many employers preferred the recruitment of women workers, who were earning relatively low wages and who were predominantly inactive in trade union activities.

These women, mostly of peasant origin and frequently unwilling to migrate, were coaxed by their husbands or fathers to take up industrial jobs in foreign countries. For most, this trip was equivalent to a military service which, from the beginning appeared to be temporary. The major reason for this insistence on behalf of the men, was that the legal provisions applicable to foreign manpower in Europe, according to almost all bilateral agreements, authorized family reunions and issued legal working permits according to the employment of one of the spouses. This economically justifiable option totally reversed the role of the breadwinner. Women, even if they were personally and mentally unprepared for a new life in an alien environment, were catapulted into urban jobs with the assumption that their entrance into a foreign labor market would be temporary and simply designed to obtain lasting employment for the male spouse. Women, however, who did undertake new urban jobs remained with their new employment while deep structural changes affected their family life. Before analyzing these changes in terms of emancipation, a brief statistical assessment must be presented.

Table 1 indicates the growth in the number of women workers in West Germany, the major recruiting country for Turkish women. Table 2 embraces all other foreign countries, including Australia, where Turkish women have been officially placed through the Turkish Employment Service.

During the period of 1961-1975: 1) There has been a large rise in the proportion of women in official migrant departures, 2) There was a marked cyclical variation in the proportion of female departures, which rose sharply during the 1967 slump and declined as the cycle picked up again, 3) The proportion of female migrant workers was still disproportionately low in view of their share in the economically active population, which amounted to 38% in 1965 and 37% in 1970 and the proportion of female migrant workers when compared with the share of women in Turkish non-agricultural employment, which was 8% in 1965 and 11% in 1970 still greatly exceeded the domestically employed labor force. Particularly significant is the high proportion of skilled female migrant workers. This tendency clearly reveals itself in Table 2.

Table 1
Growth of Turkish Female Migrant Workers in Federal Germany, 1960-1975

Years	Absolute Figures of Women	Absolute Figures of Men	Percentage of Women %
1960	173	2,527	6.8
1961	430	6,370	6.7
1962	1,563	17,283	9
1963	3,569	29,395	12.1
1964	8,045	77,127	10.4
1965	17,759	115,018	15.4
1966	27,215	133,735	13.4
1967	25,456	105,853	16.9
1968	34,257	118,648	19.4
1969	53,573	190,762	22.4
1970	77,405	276,493	21.9
1971	97,358	355,787	21.5
1972	100,763	348,913	20.2
1973	128,808	399,606	20.4
1974	159,984	457,547	25.9
1975	143,611	409,606	26

Source: *Auslaendische Arbeitnehmer 1971,* Nünnberg 1972, p. 19; *Auslaendische Arbeitnehmer 72/73,* Nürnberg 1974, p. 70-71; *Amtliche Nachrichten der Bundesanstalt für Arbeit,* March 1976, p. 227-278.

In order to assess the role played by women workers abroad, it seems useful to distinguish between the first wave of women workers, recruited prior to 1966 and the second wave, which represents the larger bulk. While at the beginning, the educational level of the women was notably higher than that of the men—the Abadan survey carried out in 1963 indicates 57% primary school graduates among men against 33% among women, 14% secondary school graduates among men against 24% among women, 3% senior high school graduates among men against 10% among women—this situation changed in the second period, where not only some kind of parallelism between the two sexes in terms of educational level became noticeable, but there was a significant entrance of female workers from predominantly rural and less developed areas. A recent survey conducted in West Berlin, where there is a

Table 2
Number of Women Workers, Officially Sent Abroad By the Turkish Employment Service According to Skill Level and Selected Occupations, 1967-1974 all Foreign Countries

	1967	1968	1969	1970	1971	1972	1973	1974
Total number of women work.	3,533	11,341	20,765	20,776	14,200	18,651	27,035	1,330
% of women workers out of the total figure of workers sent abroad	39	26	19	16	16	21	19	6
Unskilled women workers in total figures	3,254	9,915	17,942	18,628	11,924	15,838	23,461	1,119
% of unskilled women workers out of the total figure of women workers sent abroad	52	31	22	19	20	16	29	8
Skilled women workers in total figures	279	1,426	2,823	2,148	2,276	2,816	3,571	211
% of skilled women workers out of the total figure of women workers sent abroad	10	11	11	6	7	9	6	2
Textile women workers in absolute figures	39	261	708	891	246	226	398	10
% of women textile workers	10	16	27	51	15	14	7	2
Women tailors in absolute figures	233	1,141	2,096	904	1,759	1,802	1,339	3
% of women tailors sent abroad	77	64	69	82	75	72	69	3

Source: *Work and Manpower Bulletin*, No. 163, July 1974.

high percentage of Turkish workers, reveals that 70% of the women had never worked before. When broken down according to the level of development of the different regions of origin, 58% came from highly developed, 72% from fairly developed, 80% of less developed and 79% from under developed regions. This same survey indicated that contrary to the first phase, the educational level of workers went down, 7.5% had a schooling period of 1-5 years.

EMANCIPATION AS A RESULT OF MODERNIZING PROCESSES: UBRANIZATION,[1] INDUSTRIALIZATION, MIGRATION

Emancipation of any kind is closely related to the process of modernization. Modernization refers to change both in the socio-demographic aspects of societies as well as the structural changes of social organization. In order to develop a set of criteria to evaluate emancipation[2] it would seem necessary to scrutinize briefly the impact of major modernizing processes on the status of women.

Industrialization leads to 1) increased participation of women in economic life and in economic life external to family enterprise, 2) disappearance of the family as a unit of labor (Goode, 1963), 3) increased geographical mobility to industrial areas, 4) occupational mobility, 5) family fragmentation. Physical segregation of women from the rest of the society becomes more and more difficult, and women are more directly affected by social events and political decisions.

Urbanization under given circumstances exercises its greatest impact on family life. The changing nature of the social environment and social control mechanisms, the opening and intensification of relationships of family members with the society at large and the decline in the degree of economic dependence of family members, the changing patterns of settlement, the new structure of services and the communication in urban setting all affect intra and interfamilial relationships. The development of the concept of companionship between husband and wife or man and woman, unless certain city dwellers are still urban villagers (Lewis and Hauser, 1965), is associated with urbanization (Barie, 1967). Of course urbanization has to be dealt in its own proportion in terms of emancipation. As Allan Schaniberg suggests, the primary determinant of modernism remains to be socio-economic attainment, urbanism is a less proximate factor.

Migration too appears to be an independent factor affecting both family life and the status of women: spatial mobility tears the social matrix of the family and permanent location changes disintegrate its inner unity and consensus. Migrant families become more egalitarian, their family relations become more open, more emphasis is placed on achievement and independence of children. Women also come to exert more influence in decision making (Rosen, 1973). At the same time, however, instability and divorce are increased and the authority of the parents over their children decreases. (Gonzales, 1961). The culture contact, culture shock, acculturation greatly influences the value judgments of men and women.

By combining the impact of the above enumerated factors, a given set of criteria enabling us to measure the degree of emancipation, can be developed as follows: 1) Decline of extended family relations; 2) Adoption on nuclear family role patterns; 3) Fragmentation of family structure; 4) Entrance into a wage earning production process; 5) Increased mass media exposure; 6) Decline of religious practices; 7) Increasing belief in egalitarian opportunities of girls and boys in terms of education; 8) Adoption of consumption oriented behavior and norms.

However, temporary adjustment to all or some of these changes as well as intensive focusing on consumption-oriented behavior may also indicate the existence of pseudo-emancipatory processes. Since broadening of emancipation is closely linked together with the socialization process during early childhood, special attention has to be devoted to the first generation of international commuters. Since undecidedness about the length of stay abroad happens to be one of the most relevant characteristics of postwar intra-European migration, it can be assumed that the degree of emancipation will increase with the duration of stay of family members abroad.

WORK CONDITIONS AND PROBLEMS RELATED TO THE POSITION OF TURKISH WOMEN EMPLOYED ABROAD

Adjustment to industrial work

Considering the short span of time in which a relatively high number of unexperienced women entered a number of industrial enterprises, this totally different environment would necessarily create major difficulties. The results, however, were just the opposite. The nature of prevailing, repetitive, relatively simple, monotonous jobs have not created any significant disturbances. Turkish women are concentrated in certain fields such as textile, tailoring, electronics, and food packaging. Working conditions in these industries are not physically exhaustive.

The Abadan survey demonstrated that 74.5% of the women employed in FRG in 1963 were seated during production hours. The rate of industrial accidents was significantly lower for women than for men: one accident among women per three accidents among men.

The basic source of dissatisfaction among women workers seemed to be the open discrepancy of wages. According to Abadan's survey, only 36% were satisfied with their wages, the dissatisfaction climbing up with increased exposure to education. While only 44% of primary school graduates adopted critical attitudes, the rate went up to 58% among secondary school graduates. Similarly, women were slightly more critical toward their superiors, 18% of the women cited only negative attributes about the supervisors, while this percentage reached only 11% for men.

This high degree of adjustment can be partially explained by the female socialization process specifically in rural areas of Turkey. Fatma Mansur notes that a young girl is called a "guest" in popular parlance, meaning that she will eventually leave the home of her parents. She is taught discretion, chastity and obedience and is constantly encouraged to become mentally ready for situations requiring a high degree of adjustment.

However, the female migrant workers' lack of previous working experience, personal conflict within the different social strata, together with spatial arrangements contribute to a higher degree of isolation among women. This is reflected in situations requiring mutual assistance and group integration. While 25% of the women claimed to be unable to furnish any assistance to co-workers during working hours, this proportion declined to 15% for men. Similarly, 80% of the men rated group cohesion as highly favorable, while only 65% of the women expressed the same degree of satisfaction.

The frustration encountered during working hours due to isolation is compensated by the women by increased friendship ties after work hours. While only 41% of the men met their colleagues outside of work, this rate went up to 60% for the women. Women with vocational education seem to face a higher degree of exchange of ideas and communication. Fifty percent of the workers with such a background meet their work colleagues also outside the factory.

Another interesting point is related to preferences of fraternization with other national contingents. While both men and women seem to prefer the citizens of their host countries for friendship forging, men cited Italians (9%) as their second choice, while women preferred those of Greek extraction (6%). This preference once more proves that negative stereotypes are losing their effectiveness as similar social conditions of the respondents help to create a common frame of reference.

The fact that Turkish workers are more subject to psychological than physical strain reveals itself in all situations dealing with isolation. Almost twice as many women than men (43% versus 22%) express their desire to be able to talk and exchange views with their superiors. Evidence collected, indicates that the exposure to industrial work has been instrumental for women's acquiring a given amount of new knowledge. This reflects itself predominantly on the subject of learning a foreign language, where twice as many women as men attended language courses. However, the formation of large ghettos in many big cities of Europe, where almost all contacts can be established in the mother tongue, seem to have slowed down the willingness for this learning process.

It would seem then that the work performed by women without any industrial experience, especially by those coming from rural areas, does not generally equip them with new versatile skills. Thus, upon return, whenever this might take place, their reintegration in home industries does not occur. Often, such industrial enterprises do not even exist. Therefore, entrance of migrant workers to new urban jobs is usually not leading to new centers of employment at home. This is particularly true for transitional societies, where women are relatively more discriminated both in terms of recruitment and in terms of social control. Nevertheless, the undetermined period of time during which these women are utilized in industrial jobs, even if menial ones, exposes them to factory work, discipline, time sense, punctuality, social security and trade unions all of which were unknown to them heretofore. Environmental conditions such as partial integration into the host country such as living in densely populated workers' districts, being more exposed to mass media, etc. increases the degree of acceptance and understanding of these institutions. Furthermore the possibility of independent earnings, satisfactory income and the possibility of saving are all emancipation promoting factors. The most difficult aspect of adjustment to new urban jobs for migrant workers stems from the family and the reversal of role patterns as well as the solution of problems related to children's education.

Structural changes in family and degree of emancipation abroad
Although the model for Middle Eastern countries has always claimed to be the extended family, various studies (Stirling, 1965; Timur, 1972) have shown that more than 60% of the families have nuclear family households. This is a natural variation of the master model of the

extended family and the influential role played by the male members of the older age groups can always be seen. Until migration made its impact on Turkish society, family patterns always operated in favor of males, furnishing them with greater property rights. Even today, a considerable number of the peasant women, despite their full participation in productive activities, are excluded from market transactions and therefore from the control of revenues and expenditures. (Erdentug 1959, 1963; Helling, 1966; Stirling, 1966). It is their exclusion from this aspect of home economics and their disadvantageous stand vis-a-vis property rights that make the peasant women low in social status and less influential in decision making. (Kudat, 1975; Timur, 1972).

Migration, because of its deep penetrating impact on family life, has contributed to an extension of women's emancipation while at the same time putting greater strain on both women abroad and those at home. Recent empirical research on structural change within family life indicates that migration has led to a variety of fragmented family types. Twelve combinations can be deducted from three basic situations—namely: a) Father working abroad, b) Mother working abroad, c) Both parents working abroad. (A. Kudat, 1975)

The two major reasons for disintegration have been 1) regulatory policies of European host countries, which in order to reduce the strain on social infrastructure, have discouraged family reunions in many ways, and 2) the desire to increase savings. Thus, one of the cited reasons is endogamous while the other exogamous. Given these, the families involved in the migratory movement: a) accepted employment abroad, b) tried to secure employment also for the marriage partner and c) tended to leave dependents in the home country. As a result, family disintegration or fragmentation predominates. In other words, it has normatively become acceptable for a family unit to remain separated for years. In the Turkish case, this acceptance is, no doubt, a partial extension of existing traditional norms and practices. In Turkey, it is a widespread practice to entrust one's wife and children to relatives during the periods of military service or seasonal migration or even during the initial phase of permanent migration. Thus, it is not unusual for a family unit to remain temporarily separated. Until recently, however, in such cases, mother and children would remain behind and live together or at a location very close to relatives. The big turn, which has been triggered by external migration, has been the acceptance that unmarried and married women without their families would be permitted to leave in order to secure jobs abroad.

Reversal of role patterns

In all cases where the wife has gone abroad first and the husband joins her later, the husband submits to his wife's protection and teaching for a long time. By the time he has also learned what to do and what not to do, their relations have changed so much that it is never the same again. In such cases where wives have migrated prior to their husbands, the wife becomes the principal breadwinner and the husband the primary childcarer.

It is interesting to note that at the start of Turkey's large external migration, constant requests addressed by Turkish workers to government representatives were focussed on the demand of prohibiting women to leave their countries for work. Such attitudes today, whenever they find expression, are rather the product of fundamentalist, traditionalist political party propaganda rather than individual spontaneous reactions.

It is obvious that the concepts of women both in cities and in the countryside have changed tremendously and will keep changing. This fast change can be detected as far back as 1963. Turkish women employed abroad looked at that time upon German families as enviable in terms of status, equal rights among spouses, equal chance to work, etc. They also considered children to be better educated because of the wife's higher educational level (38.7%), while more than one fourth of the men regarded family structure in the FRG as decadent and worthy of utter condemnation. (27%) Those women who admired more the relationships in German families clearly realized that this superiority is due to the higher degree of emancipation of German women. Even women originally coming from small towns (29.5%) and villages (25.4%) have realized that better child care, harmonious life between men and women is linked up with the status of women within the family. It seems that, generally speaking, Turkish women adjust faster and better to unusual circumstances and hostile environments, because their traditional upbringing in the family is geared to prepare them to adjust to totally different environments.

Women's economic participation and budget control

Besides a receptivity for new values and norms, women's increased economic participation too seems to affect the household composition. While in traditional families the invitation for a short or longer stay to any person is determined predominantly by the husband, it becomes more and more accepted, that working women, with or without their husband's permission, complete the legal requirements of an invitation and bring their own parents and/or siblings to Europe. In addition, they may decide to admit different categories of people into the house in order to share rental and other costs, thus changing uncontested rules of conduct. In these cases, too, the head of the family seems to be the woman.

In Turkey among the urban, lower income groups as a rule, husbands are the principal bread-winners. Although wives are expected to participate in the production process in rural areas, the husband is the sole middleman between the household and the market. This unchallenged position becomes shaky once women migrate. A. Kudat reports that two of the major sources of dispute among working spouses are the allocation of household income, and the establishment of separate bank accounts. When employees, following the requests of the women, deposit their earnings in separate accounts, the husband's authority is shaken. The adjustment of both men and women to this change in the balance of powers does not occur easily. Disputes also arise over the use of joint savings. When husbands, following the traditional pattern, register the acquired property only in their own name, although joint remittances have been used, disputes arise.

All of these various forms of conflict lead to marital realignments. When reorganization occurs, a new type of family is created in which the woman's emancipation has contributed considerably to the increase of the wife's share in the conduct of all common matters.

Premarital and extramarital relationships

Since migration by its very nature leads to a lengthy separation within the family there is a consequent exposure to a more liberal social environment and a change in the economic status of women and estrangement of the marriage partners and family members seems at first sight to be a highly probable eventuality. Already in 1963. Abadan reports that the majority of women seemed inclined to evaluate mixed friendships as acceptable and natural, while almost two thirds of the men objected to such an idea.

Kudat reports that in West Berlin, out of 15 randomly selected days in 1973, a daily average of 37 "social problems" were brought to one of the offices dealing solely with Turkish workers, 19% of which were divorce attempts grounded on adultery. Two contradicting tendencies seem to have developed towards both men and women while on the other hand adultery is no more excused when commited by men. In other words the widely accepted Mediterranean double standard operating in favor of males, seems to have lost ground.

The problem of alienation is evaluated under different approaches: while Kudat considers even the desirable changes observed among workers such as liberalization of the women, greater equality in family relations as harmful in the long run, M. Kiray does not evaluate the human tragedy of migration in terms of alienation to be as great as one would imagine.

Child-raising function of teenagers

The most crucial issue of fragmented families concerns the problem of the children left either in their home countries with relatives, in foster homes or childcare centers or in the care of the eldest daughter of the family abroad. Actually the situation of large families where both parents are working results usually to the detriment of the eldest daughter, who is of school age and who due to the presence of younger sisters and brothers, is "de facto" deprived of any educational opportunities. In cases where the mother takes employment abroad or when the migrant father ceases to remit, girls over age twelve, and sometimes younger, are frequently expected to assume many of the duties previously performed by the mother. Thus, the eldest daughter of the family fulfills the "mother ersatz" function although she is neither physiologically nor emotionally ready for the task of raising children in an alien environment, which deprives her of all kinds of assistance that neighborhoods normally would provide in her home country.

U. Mehrlaender reports that among the various foreign contingents, Turkish families have the highest proportion of large families: 18% two children, 29% three children, 16% four children, 10% five children, 6% six and more children. However, until 1973, Turkish families again in comparison to other foreign manpower contingents, kept the least number of children with them abroad. In 1971 only 5% of Turkish migrant workers had three and 3% had four children living with them. This situation changed drastically, when the West German parliament adopted a revised tax law and entitled for family allocation only those families, both German and foreign, who kept their children living with them in FRG. This legislative amendment provoked a "childrush" especially to West Germany; together with the abrupt stop of foreign manpower recruitment following the energy crisis, the number of family reunions increʳsed considerably. This means that more school age girls are entrusted with the task of childcare, thus subjected to parental discrimination. The fact that even at a time when fewer children were living with their parents abroad, Turks were the least interested group to obtain vacancies in childcare centers and kindergartens (only 19% of Turkish workers applied in FRG for their children), may serve as an index for the assertion that the prevailing pattern is childcare through minor girls, deprived of school attendance. Here, the emancipatory process of the mother, hits mostly her own daughter.

It has to be added that the existence of strictly differentiated norms concerning the working of young girls outside of the family have noticeably changed. While in Turkey, low income families prefer to have the mother perform household cleaning jobs or factory work and retain the unmarried girl at home—predominantly in order not to jeopardize her reputation (chastity) by any means, this rule was quickly pushed aside from the very day gainful employment abroad became lucrative for young women workers. Although this category of young girls/women, usually between the age of 18 and 25, is not identical with the teenagers left at home to look after small children, the important point to notice is the same: economic reasons both lead to the deprivation of schooling even in a highly literate, industrial setting and contribute to the breakdown of the rule keeping unmarried girls at home.

Since the savings of such young girls are by no means negligible many Anatolian rural families in recent years have strongly approved of the departure of their daughters abroad. Considering that some of these young women at home were almost never allowed to move around unchaperoned (the transition from a strictly controlled social environment to an anonymous one), it is not difficult to imagine that highly organized industrial setting created a great number of problems. Since almost all unmarried young foreign women workers are lodged in the "Heim" (worker's dormitory with rather strict rules concerning closing hours and men visitors), the expectation of an individual liberation leading to a more independent character seems to be too optimistic. Collective housing and participation in industrial production no doubt changes the setting of such young women, but certainly could not, in a short period, produce a full scale emancipatory mental process.

In the case of both teenagers and young adults, basic changes in social norms are more easily accepted and validated, when open discussion channels with the family members are provided. The clash between generations, which gains in volume in sexually segregated societies becomes even greater wherever normal intrafamilial communication breaks down, because of the inability of sharing a common language. The fact, that a large number of teenagers left at home are unable to express themselves in either language—Turkish and the prevailing language of the host country—leads to severe mental blocks and psychological frustrations, even where as a rule during leisure time there could be an exchange of opinion between the family members. Migration here creates an additional obstacle concerned with personal interaction, or better said blocking stones, within the intrafamilial communication channels.

Saving and investment tendencies

The foregoing explanations have helped indicate that almost all actions in favor of greater independence and emancipation have been motivated by the desire to accrue more savings and to acquire the ability of undertaking individual investment. The empirical data in this direction confirms this tendency and shows, that in the case of women, their foremost concern is related with self-determined spending and investment forms.

In 1970 the Turkish State Planning Organization (SPO) undertook an extensive survey on this subject, which permits the evaluation of the particular options women have preferred to take. Using three categories—men of rural and urban background as well as urban women—the trend in the form of savings appeared: according to sexes, the lowest propensity to save is found among women (37%); then come urban men (50%) and rural men (57%). When considered in terms of marital status, less married women than men are saving. (40% women, 55% men). Considering age categories, women over 35 are more likely to save than women under 25. (Over 35: 53%, under 25: 32%). Interestingly the highest level of savings occurs at the lowest level of education. (Illiterate 56%, primary school graduates 53%, university graduates 30%). The tendency of women to spend more and remit less money is quite sharp: 47% women are not sending any money back home. This group is represented among men only with 18%. Lack of confidence towards complex organizations and inadequate information on banking facilities seem to have caused situations where these people are keeping high sums of savings at their temporary home. (Of the women, 43% are preserving their savings with their personal belongings, while this percentage is only 31% with urban men and 17% with rural men.) Women workers are spending 38% of their savings abroad on cars, while among men this percentage reaches only 13% in rural, 29% in urban areas. It would, however, be erroneous to assume that women are more eager to drive. Most probably their preference for automobiles lies in the relative facility to sell these cars and make considerable profits.

Scrutinizing the field of expenditure once returned home, contrary to the preference of men to invest in agricultural enterprises (25%) and transportation means (34%), women invest in the safest field, which is housing (10%). Their interest in obtaining quick and riskless return reveals itself in their preference to lend money against high interests provided that sufficient guarantees are shown (8%). All these patterns of behavior indicate that women, although they are independent wage earners and theoretically capable of undertaking all kinds of investment forms, prefer to emulate safe, riskless and passive investment forms.

This tendency is reaffirmed in their utter disinterest about any joint investment into cooperatives or worker's shareholder companies. In 1970, 94% of the workers did not invest in any one of them. Among the reasons justifying this negative attitude of women workers the following were cited: lack of confidence (38%), lack of information (8%).

From the cited data, one may deduct that by and large women are more now-oriented and more egocentric. They attempt to achieve upward mobility by conspicuous consumption, which can be deducted from the relatively low amount of savings while abroad. It appears that women not only look upon a stay abroad as a better opportunity to work, or better said, the only permissible place to work and save, but also to enjoy a different life style. This is traceable in their outspoken preference for traveling as fun, a tendency not noticeable among men. Independent income seems to detach women more than men from their family obligations. However, this move toward more independent behavior could not be interpreted as a cutting off of dependency relations, but rather as a means to increase self-confidence. Basically women's knowledge about complex organizations, such as banks, trade unions, cooperatives, etc. appears to be much lower than even men of rural background. A fact which is not surprising for women who are raised in a segregated society. Thus, one could claim that their financial emancipation so far is not conducive to further steps of social liberation, but rather axed on an imitative pattern. Provided that more extensive social institutions would guide these women toward more differentiated forms of societal participation, the experience accumulated during their stay abroad would certainly enable them to a larger degree of independence.

IMPACT OF MIGRATION ON THE LEFT BEHIND FAMILY MEMBERS, ESPECIALLY THE WOMEN

Migration, internal as well as external, is a consequence of a basic structural change in any given society. Especially in underdeveloped agrarian societies, the main reason for external migration is the rapid change in the pre-modern agricultural system. Thus, as noted by M. Kiray, migration today is not simply an accidental movement to gain cash for a single expenditure such as buying an ox, or saving enough for bride price; it is, rather, to start a new form of life and even those who within this irreversible process are still left behind in villages and small towns are equally affected by this sharp challenge. Considered in the host country as members of a given marginal group, these migrants at home are looked upon as successful social climbers, who succeeded to change their status. According to a survey carried out in 1975 in Boğazliyan, Yozgat, Turkey, and its surrounding villages, out of 127 returnees, 18% considered themselves to belong to the upper low, 44% to the middle and 18% to the upper middle strata, thus indicating that only 16% evaluated on a subjective scale their chances for mobility as nil after their exodus from the home country. No doubt that the consciousness of a changed social status affects equally well those family members, whose family is still abroad. One of the women, interviewed in the survey whose two sons were employed in Holland, remarked: "Previously the grocer of our village did not even let me enter his shop. Now, if I wish, I could buy out all his stapled merchandise!"

Current intra-European and even intercontinental migration carries an important characteristic: it denies to cut off links with the past similar to the thousands of uprooted immigrants of the past century. On the contrary, postwar immigrants, mostly due to increased mobility (A. Toffler, 1970) exposure to mass media and rapid communication, maintain close links with their home country. Out of 113 returnees, who stayed 7 years or more abroad and returned to Boğazliyan, 84 had taken a yearly home leave more than five times. This confirms the observation that the family of these immigrants, those new international commuters, emerge to be the most stable anchorage in society. Given this close relationship, the impact of such an exodus can easily be traced down at home, especially in small communities. Thus, it is not exaggerated to state, that in all villages and small towns with a high quota of migration, a new social division has been established: the *alamanyali* (families with members being employed out of Turkey) and the rest of the community. The former ones can even be physically detected by their relatively large houses, usually erected on the outskirts of the villages with each wall painted in a different color (pink, yellow, blue, green) and with the symbol of newly acquired property: iron fences and window bars.

Given that these new houses and a considerable number of old ones are inhabitated by fragmented families, it seems again imperative to repeat our previous questions. Who lives with whom? Whose roles have changed? What is the impact of migration of fertility, child rearing, consumption, authority and decision making, emancipation?

Type of household of fragmented families in Turkey
Social scientists dealing with the composition of the Turkish rural family based either on national survey (Timur, 1972) or case studies of

individual villages (Yasa, 1955; Stirling, 1965; Erdentuğ, 1959; Kiray, 1964) have shown that more than 60% of the families have nuclear households. The explanations these scholars are furnishing, however, are by no means concomitant. According to Stirling, "The reason why such households (joint extended) are in a minority are far more psychological and ecological than social." Timur, on the other hand, shows on a national basis that the extended household can stay together only so long as its land or other wealth can support it and can offer adequate opportunities to the younger generation. In rural areas, the farmers—especially those who own more land—live constantly in extended families, whereas the landless farmworkers have the largest proportion of nuclear families (28).

Analyzing the Boğazliyan data, where 32% of the migrants decided to move elsewhere because they did not own any land, the data confirm the above cited tendency. Fifty six percent of those family members left behind are living in a fragmented nuclear family (spouse and children) and 29% in an extended family (spouse, children and members of the husband's family). This distribution is not permanent and it may change almost every season. As Kiray suggests, migration rejects every rule and pattern about the family and shows that the dispersal and composition is really a kaleidoscope, where the pattern may change every year or with every vacation the man has. Yet, one significant phenomenon deserves attention. More and more independent households are established for wife and children in spite of the fact that the parents of either the wife or the husband are living in the same village or town. This practice seems also to be prevalent in large cities although no empirical data are available thus far. No doubt the growth in size of fragmented families due to migration affects authority patterns and decision making within the family and almost forces women to act independently. Interestingly, it does not affect the fertility rate, especially in rural areas. No matter how much the mistress of her own home, the left behind wife does feel lonely because of long years of separation from her husband. Reunion is the only hope for both sides. One solution meanwhile is to have children with great frequency. To be pregnant or having breast-fed infants keeps women emotionally satisfied.

An interview conducted by L. Yenisey in the village Çalapverdi, Boğazlivan district, with a newly graduated, 21-year old midwife, revealed that although as a rule there are one or two births each month; particularly in March, there is an abundance of births. These are the wives of the migrant workers, who come back on vacation in July and almost invariably impregnate their wives. In 1975, as many as thirty women were expecting babies in that month. According to this midwife, these women were not at all interested in birth control methods. The most common excuse for expecting children is that they have enough money and property to feed the children, so why not. Reconsidering that according to the Boğazliyan survey 65% of the left behind family members were illiterate, 11% knew only how to read and write, 7% had attended primary school and only 13% had completed primary school, it is not surprising that in an underdeveloped rural setting a proper evaluation of the nature of employment abroad and its estimated duration cannot be expected from these women. Here only age seems to be relevant. Among newly married couples since 1970 on, there is some interest in birth control, particularly the pill. There are some 40 to 50 women in the village belonging to this category. However, they have a problem sticking to a daily schedule.

Thus, by and large, unlike the situation of the working wife abroad, who due to her economic independence was feeling free to invite relatives and friends or even tenants to join the household, the size of the household at home appears to be determined by the husband, even in those cases where the family continues to live on a fragmented nuclear basis. Nevertheless the insistence of left behind wives to be permitted to lead a semi-independent life by not joining the other relatives of the family may serve as an illustration of a process which can be defined as pseudo-emancipation.

Decision-making and authority

Decision-making in villages usually concerns a well defined set of topics: cultivation, livestock, cash expenditure and marriage. In towns and cities educational matters are increasing in importance. Tradition until recently demanded in all types of Turkish peasant families—nuclear and extended—that the husband be granted the final word. This supremacy, which is the expression of a hierarchic order, enhances the next oldest man in the family, a first born son with the same authority in case the father is absent and this goes down the line. Migration seems to have induced a major change in this respect. Women, even if uneducated, were, so to speak, catapulted in a new world, they had not previously entered.

Women have become the major persons to whom cash income is sent by mail or bank service. Money is sent to the left behind head of the family (in nuclear families, the mother) at regular intervals or left in the bank to be drawn as needs arise. Here starts a new cycle of important interactions for the women. It consists of dealing with institutions of the society where the relationships are anonymous; such as banks, post offices, trips to town to government agencies to have documents sent abroad such as birth cerificate, etc. All types of new and unforeseen activities, definitely non-existent previously, are now encountered by the wife. Furthermore, whenever there is some land left, it is the woman who decides what work is going to be done, when and by whom. In nuclear families her authority on her children is also not challenged by others, such as mother-in-law or husband. All such new roles for wives in the family have made her understand the importance of literacy and schooling. While in extended families with no direct connection to the outside world, literacy might still appear as disfunctional to women; today in all communities which are confronted with the challenge of the absentee family heads, the desire for increased learning for girls becomes evident. The most recent data collected in Boğazlıyan may serve as an illustration.

Table 3
Decision-making Patterns on Money Sent from Migrants Abroad in Percentage by Household Type

	Financial decisions		Other important decisions (Education, marriage)	
	Nuclear	Extended	Nuclear	Extended
Male in household	7	34	9	43
Male out of household	7	2	29	8
Wife	68	28	50	20
Elderly female in family	5	18	6	23
Others	6	11	4	3
No answer	7	7	2	3
Total	100	100	100	100

As already emphasized, the size of household plays a determinant role in the management of income and decisions related to changes in family life. Interestingly, wives are acting more independently on purely financial issues and comply more to consultation with other family members in cases where mutual discussion seems appropriate and conventional such as for engagements, marriages and education. Thus, once more, economic factors such as independent income seem to serve as the triggering mechanisms for more liberated behavior.

Observations of field worker L. Yenisey confirm that some capable women enjoy the freedom of movement and action in such a way, that they even do not particularly look forward to their husband's return. They complain that the men disturb the division of tasks so well organized without them.

Another important index of independent behavior is the way of shopping. Since in all "gemeinschaft" type communities tight social control strongly inhibits the free circulation of women, the degree of flexibility to go shopping irrespective of the pattern of consumption, deserves special attention. By itself, it becomes again an index of greater or less freedom.

Predictably, the freedom of movement depends largely upon age and place of settlement. Sexual mores are strictest in small towns. Shopping is done in small towns ranging between 2,000-10,000 generally by the

Table 4
Shopping Patterns of Migrant Wives According to Family Type and Age in Percentage

Family type		Shop	Market	Both	Neither
Nuclear family		86	50	76	46
Wife with husband's family		14	50	16	46
Wife with own family		0	0	8	8
Total		100	100	100	100
Age					
19-25	100	5	2	19	74
26-30	100	4	2	48	46
31-35	100	9	0	59	32
36-40	100	4	3	71	22
41-45	100	5	5	70	20

husbands; usually married women may not buy their own clothes, but must fashion them from materials bought by their husbands. They are taken to the doctor or dentist by their husbands. What happens now if they lead an independent existence? A clearcut polarization can be observed. For those who, in spite of living independently, are not even venturing to the shops or market, it is common practice to entrust the sons of the family—a boy of seven or more—to cope with daily commands. For more elaborated shopping, resort to some trusted chaperone might be customary.

On the other side, especially with increasing age, a remarkable shift to independent action may be observed. As table 4 indicates, a clearcut growth of independence appears with a given age limit. The critical point seems to be 35, an age when many married women are about to become themselves mothers-in-law, thus acquiring respect within the community. It remains an undeniable fact, that in societies with great emphasis on sexual segregation, age plays the role of breaking the ice. One could assume that the daughters of the modernizers of today might adopt in the future a more emancipated behavior, provided that socio-economic development sustains them.

Other important areas of decision-making such as choosing the proper school, voting, etc. seem to pass over to the exclusive discretion of the wives left behind. Given the fact that out of 737 family members of the Boğazliyan area who were left behind, 293 (78%) were women, it is quite remarkable to note that only 16% turned to other relatives or neighbors for assistance in registering their children in school. Similarly the educational preferences for girls in this same group where the partly literate mothers dominate, are quite revealing:

Table 5
Preferences for Educational Levels of Daughters by Left Behind Family Members in Percentage

Only primary school	23
Only Koran teaching	—
High school and vocational schools	13
University	18
As long as the daughters wish	23
Girls don't need to go to school	1
	100

Source: Boğazliyan Survey, 1975, unpublished data

118

re responsibility and decision-making with women. This trend
Equally interesting is the fact that only 7% of the migrant husbands send their political instructions by mail at election time while 84% of the wives decide independently which political party to back.

Consumption patterns of the left behind

Economists have been repeatedly stressing that the foreign currency accumulated abroad tends to be used, wherever there is no strict control of imports to pay for imports of foreign consumer goods by the non-migrant population and by recipients of remittances. According to an ILO report. "There is an increasing familiarisation with foreign consumer goods brought about by the publicity surrounding migration and by the migrants themselves. It leads in effect to a widespread disdain for domestic products and a higher value placed on foreign goods."

Actually the most visible effect of external migration in rural and urban Turkey is the high value placed on conspicuous consumption. As T. Veblen so currectly stated, "No class of society, not even the most abjectly poor, foregoes all customary conspicuous consumption." One even may be tempted to state that for a given group of women the ability to dispose independently over remittance represents for them the most relevant aspect of a new freedom. It is predominantly in this sense, that the concept of pseudo-emancipation is used here, a freedom which actually does not liberate women but serves rather as an escape mechanism. This tendency is closely related to social mobility. Migrants and their family members are extremely anxious to acquire within their communities an image reflecting their affluence and prestige. This involves purchasing new styles of furniture, which results in simulated city rooms in village houses (TV's, electrical appliances, even where electricity is so far only anticipated). Together with insistence on show pieces comes a bad taste for low-price manufactured furniture and rugs. Traditional handicrafts such as rug and kilim weaving have almost completely vanished. Instead, tapestries brought from Europe are decorating the walls. One can even find a woven Last Supper tapestry in some Muslim homes.

Iron beds are among the first things that migrant families buy after money becomes more abundant. Again, only household heads sleep there. During the survey in Boğazliyan, Yozgat, L. Yenisey encountered in a village household a guestroom looking rather like a shop: two electric blankets, two lamps, an electric juice maker, an electric knife, two refrigerators, one in the other room, five or six clocks, and a vacuum cleaner.

Together with conspicuous consumption there is also a tendency to avoid more work and time consuming activities, such as the upkeep and care of sheep. Again, girls of marriageable age are still preparing their trousseaus, however handicrafts have surrendered their place to synthetic fibers and manufactured goods.

Interestingly, almost identical tendencies are traceable in the change of life styles created by internal migration. D. Kandiyoti, who studied newly emerging workers' settlement, notes that their family structure and life style keep pace with the slower process of urban assimilation. This creates a rather unique blend of functions and habits such as the refrigerator, being a valued exhibit much in evidence in the living room; the traditional coffee house being used to watch television; the guest room full of the better belongings of the family being closed to the daily usage of household members in an already congested environment. In this context it is specialized space for children that becomes sacrificed. They sleep with parents, with other relatives, do their homework in a crowded sitting room. Oddly enough even in the new four-color painted houses of migrants, usually erected at the edge of the village or town, where five or six large rooms are available, the life style has changed very little. Most of these rooms are left unused. Freedom for consumption does not always mean the liberty of choosing a different way of living.

Attitudes toward women's employment at home
One of the significant criteria enabling us to make a distinction between real and superficial emancipation, seems to be the readiness of the left behind women toward the possibility of taking up a job outside of the family. Here still traditional values and attitudes seem to prevail both in terms of the husband's willingness as well as the inclination of the women themselves.

Table 6
Attitude of Husbands and Wives Toward Employment Outside of the Home in Percentage

	Husbands	Wives
Nowhere	48	51
Everywhere	11	26
Under certain conditions	3	12
Only in the fields	27	—
No answer	11	11
Total	100	100

There seem to be more women clinging to mores in terms of seeking employment outside the home than men. The paternalistic, exploitory role which condemns women to unpaid home workers, however, is not accepted by women at all. None of them is anxious to toil in the fields. There is a problem which waits for solution if agricultural production is not to be neglected.

This trend confirms the general observation, that similar to other countries with predominant Moslem culture, the "dialogue within the family can only start on an egalitarian basis if it is preceded by an efficient dialogue in the working place." As long as entrenching socioeconomic measures are not substantially resulting in structural changes, G. Tillion's remark that in Moslem countries progressive women have first to break the hostility of their own sex seems to remain partly true.

CONCLUSION

Accelerated external migration of women workers from developing countries such as the mediterranean exodus to Western Europe has definitely created a chain reaction, affecting both the women workers abroad and those women, employed or unemployed, who belong to the close family of the migrants. The major consequences of this process are here outlined.

The entrance of women workers from countries with chronic unemployment into urban jobs located in highly industrialized countries may not always produce anticipated symptoms of gradual emancipation. As long as this type of employment is regarded as an undefinable temporary status and the jobs occupied are not desired and sought after, many of the natural consequences of urban occupation might fall short.

External migration of women workers leads to a noticeable decrease of extended families and an increase of nuclear family role structures. This sharp reversal affects primarily the division of tasks concerning breadwinning, establishment. of bank account, saving, investing, spending, etc. This change, due to environmental orientation predispositions favors the educational outlook for girls. It also causes a substantial amount of marital strain and conflict and quite frequently ends up with the breaking up of the family. The most handicapped actors within this framework are the elder girls of the family, who have to shoulder heavy responsibilities in order· to substitute the mother's functions.

High mobility and fragmentation of family members induces men to share responsibility and decision-making with women. This trend usually comes to an end after return to the home country.

Increased income induces women to take up crass conspicuous consumption patterns. Promotion for equality in educational opportunities seems to be the rule, yet readiness for jobs outside of the home seems not to be widespread. This inclination for working outside the house seems to be rather a corollary function of an industrial society, rather than a consequence of change affecting the status of women.

Implementation of conventionally trained women in industry and services, especially of rural background, may under certain circumstances lead to isolation and the reinforcement of traditional values and attitudes. Age and opportunity for male companionship seem to play in this instance determining roles. In order to grasp modernism, socioeconomic attainment has to be given priority. Urbanism is a less proximate factor and produces with its complementary processes, such as migration, only limited innovation.

Migration as a component of modernization is exercizing a double function: promoting emancipation of women as well as creating a false climate of liberation, which actually does not surpass increased purchasing power, thus resulting only in pseudo-emancipation.

NOTES

1. An excellent list of items to be included in the modernism indices has been compiled under the headings such as mass media, extended family relations, nuclear family role, structure, religiosity and environmental orientation in the article of A. Schniaberg, "The Modernizing Impact of Urbanization: A Causal Analysis," *Economic Development and Cultural Change,* Oct. 1971, p. 103.

2. A. Schaniberg has used four measures in order to evaluate the impact of urbanism: place of longest residence (1) before the age of ten, (2) between age ten and the time of marriage, (3) between the time of marriage and interview and (4) the place of current residence. A. Schaniberg, "The Modernizing Impact of Urbanization: A Causal Analysis," *Economic Development and Cultural Change,* Oct. 1971, p. 82.

PART 3
SOCIAL DIMENSIONS

6

SOCIAL CHANGE AND TURKISH WOMEN

To radically change the status of Turkish women and transform them into responsible, self-confident citizens was one of the main aspirations of the founder of the Turkish Republic, Kemal Atatürk. He cherished the ideals of equality between the sexes, equal opportunity for education, and family life not based upon a lifelong tie of one-sided bondage. These ideals led Atatürk to focus his attention mainly on the elimination of polygamy, sex-differentiated legislation and traditional Islamic ethical norms. Even though he didn't interfere in the inner sphere of women's private lives, by prohibiting the veil, for example, he devoted most of his time and energy to the introduction of a series of legal and administrative reforms including the right to vote. According to Atatürk, the emancipation of women would come about of itself with the help of egalitarian legislation.

However, a balance sheet of the last fifty years clearly indicates that revolutionary efforts through law have only resulted in partial changes in both the status and role of women in Turkish society. Republican reform has not been able to remove essentially wide national disparities. Visible discrepancies between town and country, class and region persist. Due to traditional socialization patterns, attitudinal changes of women are slow and resistance is frequently encountered in terms of spouse selection, marriage, and inheritance. Accordingly, a bride price is still demanded in many parts of the country. Yet, a comparison of Turkey with other Middle Eastern countries in terms of women's place in society and their economic and social influence shows that this

---

Reprinted from *Women in Turkish Society,* N. Abadan-Unat, ed., 1981, pp. 5-31. Leiden: E. J. Brill.

country no doubt represents a vanguard. The policy to make full use of educational facilities, which has been systematically followed, has led to a sizeable women elite, especially visible in academia, the liberal professions, art and literature as well as in the different echelons of managerial and clerical activities.

The scope of this chapter is to briefly assess the major areas of change and resistance over the last fifty years and to point out Turkey's major contemporary problem areas. In order to fully assess the results of the planned as well as the spontaneous changes, a quick historical overview, sketching the various phases of this development, appears timely and necessary.

1. The awakening—Evolution of the status of women in Ottoman society during the 19th century

Initiatives to promote the emancipation of women began within the Ottoman Empire as far back as the first half of the 19th century. Those in favor of a radical Westernization of Turkish society asked for the introduction of monogamy into the imperial household and the elimination of the Sultan's odalik (concubine); free choice of feminine garments; noninterference of the police in women's private lives; greater consideration toward women in general; freedom of choice in matters of marriage; the suppression of intermediaries in marriage arrangements; the creation of a medical school for girls; the adoption of a European civil code; the abolition of polygamy in general and the outlawing of repudiation, that is arbitrary and summary divorce.[1]

Another group of intellectuals of that period who were deeply imbued with the idea of Turkish nationalism and who categorized the call for European education as nothing but Montmartrian immorality deplored polygamy, repudiation and the veil.

Even the Islamic traditionalists, who advocated segregation, were ready to concede to women the right to dispose of their own property, to walk alone in the streets, to frequent women's organizations and to attend primary and secondary schools.

Although women's life in the Ottoman Empire was hampered by innumerable restrictions, it would be erroneous to assume that they were completely passive sufferers. Initiatives to encourage more and better education for women were carried out vigorously during the last half of the 19th century. For example, in 1863[2] Sultan Abdul-Aziz ordered the opening of a teacher's training college for girls. In the beginning, the education given to girls in this and similar institutions to follow consisted solely of the memorization of the Koran, but later the curriculum was changed to be more secular. Abdulhamit, who curiously enough prohibited the wearing of the çarşaf (veil) instead of the ferace (dustcoat), in 1883[3] announced that he was in principle in favor of educating women. He wanted to see women trained in a way that would make them helpful to their husbands.[4] However being hostile to non-Islamic ideas, in a 1901 decree, he forbade the employment of Christian governesses in schools and private households.[5]

A logical consequence of these sporadic innovative actions was that only a small Ottoman bourgeoisie could emerge; thus, these emancipatory movements were strictly class-bound. Only the girls of wealthy families, who were educated privately by European governesses, began to aspire to more freedom as a result of their exposure to French and English literature. Another elite group of young girls from the same stratum were nourished on new ideas and different principles by being permitted to attend foreign schools such as the American College for Girls in İstanbul which was founded in 1875. Only they suffered from the prevailing impact of polygamy, the way Halide Edip, the novelist, described her frustration first vis-a-vis her father and later toward her husband.[6]

Bolder steps became noticeable after the return to constitutional rule in 1908, following the dethronement of abdulhamit. The first women's club, "Red-White" (the color of the Young Turks) was founded in 1908 in 1908, following the dethronement of Abdulhamit. The first women's education enlarged their activities. The "Association for the Betterment of Women," especially under the presidency of Halide Edip, was involved in various issues and problems. The secretary of the "Ottoman Society of Women", Kadriye İhsan, in 1910 allowed her photograph to be taken for publication.[7] Educated women from the upper-class started to discard their veils or to use very thin ones. In 1912, unveiled Turkish women attended a reception at the American Embassy. Obviously, all these innovations were only practiced by upperclass Ottoman women.

The most radical women's association was the "Ottoman Association for the Defence of Women's Rights". In 1913 the President of the Association, Nuriye Ulviye Mevlan, started a journal entitled "Women's World" (Kadınlar Dünyası), where, beginning in November, 1913, photos of women were printed. During the Balkan War, the women's branch of the Red Crescent began to train Turkish nurses. The most relevant cultural association of the Young Turks, namely the "Türk Ocagı," started in November, 1913, to organize lectures for women; there, Turkish women, predominantly of Russian origin, made important suggestions and proposals.[8]

2. World War I and the entrance of Turkish urban women into public life

The real impetus for a more comprehensive change came during World War I. Due to the crisis of war, large numbers of veiled and secluded women were catapulted into public life. Suddenly jobs were offered to women in ammunition and food factories thus enlarging the number of working class women. A law was prepared by the Ottoman Ministry of Trade to allow for the creation of a kind of "female labor force." In the stocking factory of Urfa alone 1,000 women were employed. In Izmir, Sivas, Ankara and Konya about 4,780 women were employed in rug production. In Aydın about 11,000 and in Kütahya, Eskişehir and Karahisar about 1,550 were involved in textile manufacture.[9].

Parallel to this growth, banks, postal services, central and municipal administrations, and hospitals opened their doors to women as well. In 1915 Enver Pasha's wife, princess Emine Naciye, created an association to promote the employment of women in various sectors of industry. During the same year an imperial decree *irade* permitted discarding the veil during office hours. However, these changes, accelerated by the demands of the war machine, did not meet general approval. Despite the fact that women had begun to contribute to the functioning of public offices, they were often forced by the police to return home if their skirts were shorter than the officially prescribed length.[10]

The large scale military involvement of the Ottoman Empire not only introduced women into Turkey's urban public life, but it also contributed to the challenge of the supremacy of the sharia. The leader of this fight became Ziya Gökalp, "the father of Turkish nationalism," who was appointed to teach sociology at İstanbul University from 1915 on. In his poems as well as in his essay on the "Foundations of Turkish Nationalism," he openly demands equal rights for women with regard to marriage, divorce and succession. No doubt his ideas, even if not fully, greatly inspired the lawmakers in their draft proposal pertaining to the Family Law of October 25, 1917.[11] While the draft proposal still did not fully repudiate polygamy as such, it included special clauses for a monogamic marriage.

3. Turkish women as militants and soldiers (1918—1923)

Surprisingly, the collapse of the Ottoman Empire and its after effects only slightly slowed down the ongoing struggle for emancipation, Thus on March 19, the Minister of Education Ali Kemal, opened courses for women at the Faculty of Philosophy in İstanbul. In 1921, coeducational classrooms were created, where girl students were permitted to lift their veils only during the lectures. In 1922, Dr. Safiye Ali, Turkey's first female physician, opened her clinic in İstanbul.[12]

In addition to increased education among upper-class women, other subjects began to attract attention. The landing of Greek soldiers in Izmir on May 15, 1919 and the occupation of İstanbul by British soldiers, followed by similar actions of French and Italian armed troops in the south of Anatolia, aroused violent outrage and protest throughout all strata of the population.[13] These events provoked, among other things, a growing political activism among Turkish women. Not only did large numbers of women participate in open-air meetings in İstanbul where speakers, such as writer Halide Edip, Nakiye Elgün, the chairman of the teacher's association and Münevver Sami, a student representative, addressed huge crowds, but a number of bold young women also joined Mustafa Kemal's forces in Anatolia, where the War of Independence was about to start.[14]

Another interesting change took place during this period. Contrary to the past, women not only mobilized themselves for special warfare purposes, but also attempted to directly influence politics. On September 9, 1919 the newspaper, "İrade-i Milliye," announced the foundation of the "Anatolian Women's Association for Patriotic Defence" in Sivas. This association established branches in Amasya, Kayseri, Niğde, Erzincan, Burdur, Konya, Denizli, Kastamonu and Kangal. The Niğde branch alone reported in 1920 to have 1,090 registered members,[15] the majority of whom were the wives and daughters of civil servants and teachers as well as of local merchants. In a short time they became the female counterpart of the core group of Mustafa Kemal's bureaucrats, soldiers and merchants.[16] The major aim of these associations was to show the European public that the whole Turkish nation was united and determined to fight for its independence.

4. The status of Turkish women as reflected in parliamentary debate
From the beginning of his political struggle, Mustafa Kemal, a fierce opponent of autocratic rule, attached great importance to representative government. This explains why he successfully struggled to re-establish the dissolved Ottoman parliament under a new name, the Turkish Grand National Assembly, during the War of Independence on April 23, 1920. The relatively short and concise constitution of this pre-republican interim period was based on the principle of a union of powers; the country being governed by an assembly government. This assembly was the arena for sharp political fights. Although officially there were no political parties, two competing fractions constantly clashed. These quarrels occurred most often on issues relating to women. Further, once the arguments ended, no more action to modify the exploited status

of women was taken. Although Mustafa Kemal publicly acknowledged the heroic deeds of Anatolian women in his speech of February 3, 1923 and promised that "Turkish women shall be free, enjoy education and occupy a position equal to that of men as they are entitled to it,"[17] the divisive composition of the first Turkish Grand National Assembly obliged him to postpone most of his reformist plans. Society at that point was not ready to look upon its women as equals to men. Speakers for the progressive wing, such as Tunlı Hilmi bey, attempted several times to translate Turkish women's longing for equality into legal measures, but the conservative majority of clerks and small town merchants succeeded in blocking them.

Two parliamentary debates in particular further illustrate this negative attitude. The first, a bill concerning syphilis control (Session 122, 1921),[18] and the second, dealing with electoral law,[19] led to violent discussions. Defenders of women's rights (Emin bey and Tunalı Hilimi bey) were not granted the floor; they were grossly insulted and the sessions were suspended. Proposals such as these compelling women to have medical control and including the female population into calculations for the size of voting districts were bluntly refused. The decision of the Ministry of Education to invite the female teacher corps to the National Convention on Education led to a general investigation and finally ended with the resignation of the incumbent minister.[20]

However, Mustafa Kemal, during his various visits to the countryside, continued to declare himself in favor of egalitarian measures. He argued, for instance, in Konya (March 21, 1923), about six months before the proclamation of the Republic, that "the fact that our women, who are subject to much less encouraging conditions, have been able to march along with men, sometimes even ahead of them, is clear proof of their equality and outstanding ability." Thus, Mustafa Kemal, faithful to his farsighted strategy, kept on preparing public opinion for deepseated changes, the culmination of which was the adoption of the Swiss Civil Code in 1926.

5. Legal equality for Turkish women

One of the contradictory aspects of Turkey's stand on women's rights lies in its ambivalence on the improvement of the status of women. Almost all major progressive measures were given, rather than fought for. For this reason the situation shortly before the adoption of the Swiss Civil Code deserves some attention. During the second term of the Turkish Grand Assembly, an attempt was made to codify the 1917 Family Law. The commission in charge approved of marriages at the age of 9 for girls and 10 for boys and of polygamy. It furthermore gave women the right to divorce their husbands only under certain conditions, but it upheld the right of men to repudiate their wives. The very mild, almost unnoticeable reaction of educated women to such measures became a matter of criticism in the Turkish press—Necmettin Sadak in "Aksam"[21] denounced the passive attitude of women. Even feminists, such as Halide Edip Adıvar expressed their criticism, not from the point of view of women's rights, but rather from the angle of conditions favoring a harmonious married life.

How can such passivity be explained? According to Sirin Tekeli, once the extraordinary conditions of war had passed, a country with almost no industry was unable to develop and sustain jobs for its women outside the household. Thus, the perennial glorification of the ideal women being "good housewives, mothers and companions" was bound to continue[22].

How then, can we explain the sudden transition to a European civil law system?

The reasons should be sought within the general setting of the political forces inside and outside parliament, rather than from within the movement for women's rights, itself.

Atatürk, anxious to present to the world a "modern face," began to encourage significant initiatives to eliminate the obvious inequalities in public life, thereby diminishing the political weight of conservatives. An interesting example of such an action was the decision of the İstanbul police chief to order the removal of a curtain separating men and women passengers in public transportation.[23] This decision became a matter of discussion in parliament, where it was asked whether or not it was contrary to the principles of a "Moslem Republic."

Atatürk, determined to fight against the conservative forces gathered around the Ministry of the sharia, succeeded in passing legislation, definitely changing the ideological scope of public life. The first law was the abolition of the Caliphate and the second was the promulgation of the Law for Unification of Instruction, both on the same day, March 3, 1924. The second law brought all religious schools and minority schools under unified control, thus enabling the leaders of the young Republic to extend the right to an education to both sexes.

Determined not to wait for long-term evolutionary processes, Atatürk proceeded from there to use codification as an accelerator for social change. On February 17, 1926, a slightly modified version of the Swiss Civil Code, which was found by the commission to be the most suited to the principle of secularism, was adopted at one session where only speeches in favor were made. For Atatürk and his supporters the granting of equality before law for men and women was the realization of a promise given long before, but even more than that, it was a symbol to the world that the new Turkey was adamant about "reaching a level of contemporary civilization."[24] Arguments in favor of the law also reflected this way of thinking: "The new law incorporates such principles as monogamy and the right to divorce—principles, which are required for a *civilized world*."[25] Thus, all the major rights conferred on Turkish women were much more the result of the unrelenting efforts of a small "revolutionary elite," rather than the product of large-scale demands by Turkey's female population.

The Turkish Civil Code, which became effective on October 4, 1926, made polygamy illegal and gave equal rights of divorce; thus formally insuring the freedom and equality of women. Custody of the children, unlike in the past, was given to both parents (Art. 262). In case of death, custody was entrusted to the surviving spouse. In case of divorce, a judge would decide which parent should have custody (Art. 264).

Equality in inheritance was granted: unlike the old law where women were granted one-half, one-quarter, one-seventh, or even one-eighth depending on their relation to the deceased (Art. 439). Marriage, in order to be valid, had to take place in the presence of the bride, which meant the abolition of marriage by proxy. Equality with regard to testimony was accepted. In the old court procedure, the testimonies of two women were equal to that of a man. Finally, the new civil code prescribed a minimum age for marriage that was slightly different from that in the Swiss Civil Code. At first, the age limit was 18 for men and 17 for women, but later, in 1938, the legal minimum age limits were reduced to 17 and 15 respectively, while the absolute minimum age in special circumstances was kept at 15 for men, but lowered to 14 for women (Art. 85).

How egalitarian is the Turkish Civil Code? The Swiss Civil Code itself reflects the traditional point of view. For example, it does not contain a principle of absolute equality between husbands and wives. Accordingly, the husband is the head of the family. The wife does not have the prerogative to represent the marital union (Art. 154). She must follow the husband, who alone is entitled to choose a domicile (Art. 152, II). The wife is required to participate in the expenses of the household, be it by contributing in financial matters or by assuming tasks in the household (Art. 190). In case the wife wants to assume a profession or work outside the household, she must obtain the consent of the husband (Art. 159), which may be tacit approval as well. However, the wife may freely dispose of her material goods; the rule in marriage—unlike, for instance, the Napoleonic code—is separation of property and goods; and the wife has an unlimited right of acquisition.

How did such a legal transplantation function? Although Turkey's choice in favor of the adoption of a Western legal code provided a favorable climate for change in the status of women, even without the accompanying major socio-economic structural changes, much of the content of the Civil Code has remained dead letter, especially in rural areas with a strong feudal character. However, the Civil Code takes on a more functional character with the increase in urbanization, migration, and industrialization. It also becomes more functional as education levels rise and as more and more women participate in the industrial and service sectors of the economy.

Among the demands proclaimed by 27 women's associations on the occasion of the Women's Year Ankara Congress (5—8 December, 1975), the following major legal demands were set forth:[26]

1. The status of family head should not be confined solely to the husband.
2. The wife should not be obliged to adopt the husband's family name.
3. The prerogative of a husband to forbid his wife the practice of a profession or employment should be abolished.
4 Legal, educational and administrative measures to abolish the "bride price" (Başlık) should be implemented.
5. The prohibition of a religious ceremony before a civil marriage has been registered should be reinforced.
6. In order to equalize tax obligations, individual income tax declarations for husband and wife should be required.
7. The right to join the armed forces should be granted again.
8. Women civil servants and workers should be able to take one paid year leave of absence after childbirth.
9. The agricultural social insurance bill should be passed in order to assure peasant women social security rights.
10. The living conditions of prostitutes should be improved so as to discourage traffic of women.
11. Legal provisions should be enacted in order to prevent the exploitation of female children, who have been apparently "adopted," but in fact are employed in domestic service (besleme).

As one can easily detect, most of the demands cited represent imperfections in a functioning legal system, based in principle on the equality of sexes. However, some of these points are of a more serious nature.

There is no doubt that the most critical point lies in the nature of institutionalized prostitution. According to Law No. 1593, the Ministry of Health and Social Welfare and the Ministry of the Interior are jointly responsible for determining the location and the administration of brothels. Art. 129 of this same law mentions a category of women, "Who are performing prostitution as a profession and as a means of subsistence." This article is in direct contradiction to Arts. 435—36 of the Turkish Penal Code, which strongly forbids activities which encourage prostitution. Prostitution is a social problem deeply related to socioeconomic factors. Thus, it is impossible to prevent solely by applying deterrent measures. In the absence of adequate employment opportunities, poor families, sometimes even middle class ones, are compelled to permit prostitution of their women. As rightly pointed out in the "Report on the Status of Women in India," if women are to become equals of men in society, society must ensure economic, social and psychological security for them and protect them from this form of exploitation. Yet, in Turkey the fact that the woman in question is a prostitute is still seen as a criteria for attenuating circumstances, leading to a reduction by two-thirds of the sentence in cases of rape and kidnapping (Art. 438). This article has recently been abolished in Italy, the place where Turkish Lawmakers received their inspiration for it. Unfortunately however, Turkish public opinion has not yet focused its attention on this topic.

The secularized legal conventions have been adhered to in those places where the economic structure has changed substantially. Legally, religious marriages are not recognized; yet, they in fact exist. They prevail in the present day, small, semi-isolated settlements as the norm, enjoying the consent and tacit approval of the community. Further, they were encouraged both in the 1950s during the Democratic Party government as well as by the Justice Party and the National Salvation Party in the 1960s and 1970s, as this was one way of making use of religion for political ends. The prevalence of these unions is confirmed when one takes into consideration the paucity of registered marriages (Table 1) or when one looks at the number of children who, by legal definition, were born out of wedlock. In 1950 alone, 7,724,419 children were registered under various laws to legitimize such births.[27]

The close relationship between registered marriages and divorces and the developmental level of Turkey's regions, as well as their distribution pattern between the urban and rural population, is quite evident (Tables 1 and 2).

The high number of civil marriages and divorces registered in the major metropolitan areas such as İstanbul, Izmir and Ankara, clearly indicates their higher level of development as opposed to that found in regions with a semi-feudal structure (the southeastern regions), where socioeconomic backwardness is additionally accompanied by a distinctly different cultural framework.

Nevertheless, it must be stressed that the idealistic, modernized society envisioned by Atatürk has provided Turkey's increasingly aware women with an excellent point of departure for further emancipation, freedom and social participation. Turkey still represents the only Muslim country in the entire Middle East where, aside from secondary legal problems, the major goals for the enfranchisement of women as individuals and citizens have been realized.

Table 1
Urban—Marriages in Absolute Figures in Selected Provinces, 1950—1974

Provinces	1950	1960	1974
Ankara	3,019	5,236	10,461
Istanbul	10,057	12,323	26,445
İzmir	3,599	4,666	10,269
Afyon	746	912	2,056
Aydın	942	1,260	2,451
Burdur	331	398	935
Ağri	42	123	132
Bingöl	35	34	86
Van	96	224	413

Source: For 1950 and 1960, T.C. Evlenme İstatistikleri, 1932—1960, Nr. 418. For 1974, T.C. Evlenme İstatistikleri, 1974, Nr. 787.
Ankara, Istanbul and Izmir represent the three metropolitan provinces, Afyon, Aydın and Burdur are provinces located in Çentral Anatolia and the Aegean region.
Ağri, Bingöl Hakkâri and Van are provinces in Eastern Anatolia.

Table 2
Urban—Divorces in Absolute Figures in Selected Provinces 1950—1974

Provinces	1950	1960	1974
Istanbul	929	1,129	1,501
Ankara	—	727	1,057
İzmir	—	806	595
Afyon	208	187	158
Aydın	208	398	410
Burdur		110	139
Ağri		10	10
Bingöl		4	13
Van	5	13	29
Hakkâri		1	3

Source: For 1950 and 1960, T.C. Boşanma İstatistikleri,1932—1960, Nr. 419. For 1974, T.C. Boşanma İstatistikleri, 1974, Nr. 775.

6. Turkish women as voters (1934—)

It is no wonder that, because of valid historical reasons such as their being excluded from active economic participation due to the Ottoman Empire's semi-colonial status in the 19th century and their exclusion from public life due to Islam's ideological definition of second class subjects, Turkish women have never developed a genuine and effective women's suffrage movement. Demands to be "permitted" to participate in election activities were first expressed hesitantly, then neglected for some time, and then finally granted. Relevant sources on this subject furnish opposing explanations. According to Tezer Taşkıran, the driving forces for political rights were the publicly articulated demands of the Women's League in 1927 and growing pressure from public opinion.[28] Afet İnan gives a different explanation. According to İnan, difficulties in teaching democratic rules as a part of civics education, as long as women were deprived of political rights, gave way to serious discussions within Atatürk's inner circle and thereby led to a constitutional amendment.[29]

The hypothesis of Ş. Tekeli, a young political sociologist, is based on an overall evaluation of the Western powers' attitude, reflected by their press, toward Atatürk's transitional one-party rule. Her hypothesis seems to be correct if one considers that, in spite of repeated demands,

Atatürk waited until 1930 then suddenly decided to have a constitutional amendment proposed by Ş. Kaya, which opened the door for political representation and participation of women in municipal elections.[30] According to Tekeli, the real reasons for the 1930 move, and later the one in 1934, lie within the prevailing political forces of the time. In 1930, some European newspapers attempted to draw parallels between the one-party systems of the period, especially Mussolini's in Italy. Atatürk, extremely anxious to differ from any kind of fascist movement, gave an interview to the "Vossische Zeitung" in which he stressed "revolution and dictatorship, even if necessary, can only be used for a short time."[31] In order to prove his genuine belief in a true democratic system—even while continuing to implement a tutelary democracy—Atatürk granted political rights to Turkish women, and in doing so, moved his country ahead of some Western democracies. That same year, an abortive attempt to move over to a multiparty system was carried out in Turkey too.

Thus, Turkish women, who were given political rights in municipal elections in 1931, first used their prerogatives in 1933 and were elected both in İstanbul and elsewhere to municipal and eldermen councils.

During this same year, Hilter's Nazi Party rose to power and confined its women to "Kind, Küche, Kirche." Atatürk, a staunch nationalist but extremely sensitive about not being classified in the same order as Europe's power hungry dictators, realized that democracy was closely related to the active role played by citizens.[32] Thus, on December 5, 1934, the Grand National Assembly adopted a proposal presented by İsmet İnönü and 191 deputies, which conferred on all Turkish citizens having reached the age of 22, the right to vote in national elections. In addition, all citizens 30 years of age, men and women, were given the right to be elected. It is worthwhile to note that one of the speakers in favor of this bill, Sadri Maksudi, stated, "Today there are countries which have undemocratic regimes, where women are deprived of political rights. The granting of political rights to Turkish women is a natural consequence of Turkey's evolution toward a true democratic system."[33]

Assuming that Ş. Tekeli's thesis is correct, the electoral results are self-evident. As long as female political representation was regarded for its independent "symbolic value," the number of female representatives was high. It declined after Atatürk's death and the transition to a multiparty system. For example, when first elected to the parliament, 18 seats (4.5%) were held by women; this number fell in 1946 to 9 (2%), in 1950 to 3 (0.6%) and, after 1960, they never again reached the 1965 level of 11 (1.8%).[34]

For a number of writers (Afet İnan, 1965; T. Taşkıran, 1976) the entrance of Turkish women into politics completes the necessary framework of their more active participation in society. The underlying assumption is that, with increasing educational opportunities and comprehensive social security measures, Turkish women will be able to make full use of their new legal status. This approach, however, has been increasingly challenged. For most of Turkey's post-war social scientists and young writers, the status of women is determined by their role in production and their economic participation (M. Kıray, 1963, S. Timur, 1972, D. Kandiyoti, 1971). Women's subjugation or dependence is the outcome of their socioeconomic position. Accordingly, increased awareness, commitment and involvement in politics and autonomy in political action and behavior are not instilled by persuasive means; but rather, they emerge from such deep-seated changes in the social structure, as internal and external migration, urbanization and industrialization. Since Turkey's transition to a multiparty system coincides with the end of Turkey's self-imposed economic autarchy, the position of Turkish women should be evaluated in light of these major challenges.[35].

7. Turkey's changing social structure and its impact on women's status

Atatürk and İnönü, adopting an elitist approach, firmly believed that the exploitation of women could be remedied by placing great emphasis on all levels of education and that women's new legal status would lead to their increased participation in public life. This attitude was reinforced by the importance attached to the principle of secularism, the separation of religious from state affairs. With the transition to the multiparty system in 1946, and the growing influence of a new middle class, the character of Turkey's mixed economy changed greatly. Instead of etatism, private enterprise received manifold support. As a consequence, new technologies were introduced; mechanization of agriculture was followed by fast internal migration, urbanization and unbalanced industrialization. In addition after 1960, government-regulated exports of excess labor resulted in a massive exodus to Europe.

All these deep-seated changes in Turkey's social fabric no doubt affected its women too. The least touched group, of course, has been the nomadic group, predominantly located in eastern Anatolia, who are practically situated outside the economic and political system of the country.

According to D. Kandiyoti, Turkey's newly emerging pattern can be divided into six basic types: (a) nomadic, (b) traditional, rural (c) changing rural, (d) small town, (e) newly urbanized-squatter (gecekondu) and (f) urban, middle class, professionally employed or housewife.

(a) *Nomadic women:* In nomadic tribes, scattered in eastern and southeastern Anatolia, women's contributions to production are very high and their procreative roles are much esteemed. However, due to the asymmetric division of labor, males dominate all activities having to do with the public sphere. Male authority is obvious in all walks of life. Women's authority can only be detected within the family—a natural consequence of the heavy bride price—and even then, only after they have produced sons and acquired a prestigious position within the family. Inheritance rights for girls are not admitted.[36].

(b) *Traditional—rural:* Whereas nomadic tribal life represents a closed world of its own, the rural setting has been subject to significant changes in Turkey. In villages dependent on the cultivation of some form of subsistence crop, the traditional life style of peasant culture is quite conservative, in that women are not admitted into the male world. However, depending on the geographic and economic conditions these peasant women are: (1) totally involved in home production, (2) additionally involved in traditional crafts such as carpet-weaving, (3) working full time in the fields, or (4) because of external migration, entirely in charge of agriculture. More often than not, their labor input determines the type and volume of production. Their status in these traditional, closed-up rural communities is defined by a male dominated hierarchy. This constant predominance can be seen in Table 3.

Table 3
Distribution of Turkey's Population According to Sex and Activity in Agriculture in Percentage

Sex	1955	1960	1965	1970
Men	63.1	60.9	58.1	53.1
Women	96.1	94.9	94.1	88.7

Source: DPT, Toplumsal Yapı Araştırmast, 1977, pp. 36-37

In traditional villages, the female status determinants are also constant, namely, child bearing and advancing age. Whatever their place in production may be, their labor goes largely unrecognized, the specialized areas and public dealings remaining within the male sphere. Although in 1969, 497 out of 1,000 active persons in agriculture were female, they were economically defined as "unpaid workers of family enterprises."[37]

(c) *Women in changing rural setting:* The big turn in rural areas coincides with the introduction of new technologies, the mechanization of farming and its consequently fast internal migration. The absorption of villages into the national market economy, along with the exceedingly high exodus of excess labor to foreign industrial centers, has turned some members of peasant families, at the beginning solely males and later predominantly females, into wage earners. With the changing economic function of fathers and brothers, women's status has been redefined. The ultimate domain of male authority has decreased. Free choice of marriage partners, self-determined consumption patterns and independent investment by younger women have become noticeable (Abadan-Unat, 1976).[38] Along with these changes a new life style, largely dependent on remittances from abroad has developed. In this setting consumption tends to be conspicuous. These women, having been pushed out of agricultural production and no more preoccupied with home-produced food and clothes, have started to emulate small town ways with increased afternoon visits, use hair-dressers and cosmetics, and generally urban patterns of consumption.

Briefly, rural change has meant a redefinition of male authority relations. This ranges from greater loyalty to the daughter as well as to the female head of the migrant workers' family. There, the wife/mother, living most of the years alone, shapes the life of her dependents almost completely by herself.

(d) *Women in small towns:* Although the attitudes toward veiling, segregation and mixing with male visitors are more relaxed, women in small towns, because of the greater emphasis on the public sphere and the absolute disappearance of female labor, are rather confined to their residential neighborhoods. In these settings, as pointed out by P. Benedict, M. Kıray and F. Mansur,[39] female leisure, which is almost non-existent in rural areas, has resulted in larger social networks—which have been facilitated by the institution of "kabul Gün," reception day. In short, the determinants of status among women in the small town are more directly related to their husbands' positions.

It might be said that the entrance of new values and life styles into the villages of rapidly economically changing rural settlements, such as in the Marmara and Aegean regions, represent a faster process of change than that in small towns.

(e) *Women in newly urbanized settings (squatters):* Turkey's astonishingly rapid rate of urbanization, which in fact preceded industrialization, ushered in a unique housing phenomenon, the Gecekonda (over night houses); and out of these areas came a quite distinct type of woman. In Turkey, as in many developing countries,[40] the transition from traditional agriculture and household industry to modern organized industry and services demands new skills. Women, handicapped by the lack of opportunities to acquire these new skills, find themselves unwanted by the economy. Kemal H. Karpat, in his study on gecekondu life, shows that, while 93% of the newly settled men were employed, only 30% of the women could find employment, out of which 59% were only temporarily employed, their status being predominantly domestic servants.[41] The high degree of mobility, which is inherent in gecekondu women, reveals itself in their aspiration: 23% female versus 12% male wanted to have factory work.[42] However, jobs in industry for women are not abundant. The total female population over 12 years of age employed in industrial enterprises in 1943 was 78,767. A quarter century later this figure has only risen to 143,400, while the same figure for men increased fivefold.[43] Nevertheless, it is quite accurate to assume that the workers—men and women—in the projected massive industrialization program for the 1980s will come from these squatter quarters.

Gecekondu women tend to have an astonishingly high degree of self-confidence—69% of the women versus 59% of the men consider themselves to be the most trustworthy and reliable persons.[44] This can be partially explained by the large percentage of nuclear families in these areas (62.5% in Izmir, 72% in Ankara).[45] In line with their confident way of thinking, gecekondu women insist on having a say in the choice of their future husband (47%). The people in the gecekondu's aspirations for their children and their desire to become more integrated into city life are indicative of the deep changes which have taken place.

Although gecekondu women certainly encounter major difficulties in integrating themselves in urban life by retaining a number of the elements of village culture, they still represent some of the most dynamic innovators in Turkey's modernization process. Their strong motivation will surely have a decisive impact on the socialization process for generations to come.

(f) Urban middle class women (housewife/employed): Unlike traditional rural women, more than three quarters of the economically active urban women are not gainfully employed; 81% qualify as housewives.[46] Nevertheless, the number of female wage earners is increasing; needless to say, in a way reflective of Turkey's uneven

industralization and employment patterns. Certain regions, such as Marmara and the Aegean, as well as the three provinces with metropolitan cities, show the most rapid growth (Table 4).

Table 4
Female Wage Earners by Year and Region in Percentage

Year	Central Anatolia	Black Sea	Aegean and Marmara	Mediterranean	Eastern Anatolia	Three big provinces
1955	1.2	1.2	4.7	4.4	2.0	18.9
1960	4.6	1.4	5.8	3.8	1.4	25.0
1970	6.0	5.3	11.0	10.7	4.0	40.8

Source: Gül Ergil, op. cit., Table 13, p. 47

Indeed, the female working class is growing rather slowly (78,767 in 1943—143,000 in 1968).[47] In this area, the big explosion has taken place outside of Turkey: in W. Germany alone, there were 173 women workers in 1960 versus 143,611 workers in 175.[48] There was a marked cyclical variation in the proportion of female departures, which rose sharply during the 1967 slump and declined as the cycle picked up again.

Within Turkey the more impressive growth lies, not in the industrial sector, but rather within the service sector, where the public services have especially attracted a high number of women. While in 1938 there were only 12,716 female civil servants, this figure rose in 1970 to 123,812 (18,9% in this sector). Thus, one can easily state that a visible bureaucratization of qualified female manpower has taken place in Turkey.[49] The penetration of women into the civil service is more noticeable in the lower and middle level positions. More precisely, 31.6% are in the fields of education, 26.3% in tourism, 22.2% in health and 19% in labor relations. These areas, generally defined as "service sectors oriented towards social goals," have been slowly abandoned by men. Of course, labor relations are still considered to be male domain.

Basically, what motivates women to enter public life? Two empirical studies, conducted over a 20-year period, reveal quite interesting similarities.[50]

For the great majority, economic needs force women to secure for the family a "second source of income," although for many professional women work is a primary tool for self-expression. Thus, whenever a role conflict situation between work and family life arises, retreat from work has been the preference. This is even true for women with higher education belonging to liberal professions (H. Topçuoglu, 1957: O. Çitçi, 1974).

These individual preferences are undoubtedly the by-products of a rather anti-feminist climate that has been reinforced by mass-media campaigns and television programs such as "Five Minutes," Thus, urban women are caught up in two opposing currents of thought. One current continually drives into society's head the idea that women's primary function is to be a good wife and mother, while the other current argues that women should take advantage of all opportunities that give them a chance for self-expression and more freedom. Perhaps at this point we should ask if Ş. Tekeli's class-oriented conclusion is true that "work is a necessity for women of the peasant and industrial classes whereas it is denied to the members of the bourgeoisie."[51]

Even given the above conflicts, one important fact should be remembered. Of all the muslim countries, Turkey has so far produced the highest number of educated women on all levels. In Turkish universities, women's share of the academic personnel, long before the women's lib movements, was far ahead of Europe.[52] This observation is equally true for women occupying high posts in the judiciary.[53]

Nevertheless, all these achievements since 1926 should not result in unjustified euphoria. Because of the deep changes taking place in the socioeconomic structure, the great majority of Turkish women, like women in all developing countries, are seriously handicapped. Their handicap does not come from legal restrictions, but rather from structural inequalities. Their access to education depends greatly upon urbanization and the realization that schooling has functional value. Although the composition in urban primary schools is almost fifty/fifty for girls and boys, only one-third of these girls enter secondary schools. This rate declines to one-fifth in higher educational institutions.

Due to constant and decisive influence of advertising, particularly in the women's pages of the press, women of all classes, especially those living in urban areas, have acquired a growing tendency to spend for the purpose of conspicuous consumption. These women, indeed, display a false consciousness about priorities. These tendencies, instead of moving urban women towards a greater understanding of public issues, are diminishing their interest in politics. Nevertheless, as everywhere, small, articulate groups of women, determined to have their say in politics, are getting stronger. Partly backed by the charismatic personality of political leaders such as B. Ecevit and his party's efforts to involve women in the political process, these small bands have become strong political forces. For the time being it would not be erroneous to say that given the weak class consciousness of employed women, their interests in public issues are ambivalent. During exceptional periods, such as electoral campaigns, it is high, during normal periods rather low. Again, this is not surprising since their rights were bestowed upon them and not fought for.

Even so, the path toward a freer, more independent, responsible and politically aware type of woman is widening. Turkish women are becoming increasingly aware of their subservient role as unpaid household labor. For some, the remedy lies within a general change of the political system; for others, human will power is the answer.

The impact of the changing structure of production and the changing determinants of what women do, how they do it, and how they are recognized or not recognized for it has created a great deal of conflict in women's attitudes and values. The resulting inconsistencies are reflected more and more in contemporary literary works. Recently, women writers, such as Nezihe Meriç, Füruzan, Adalet Ağaoğlu and Sevgi Soysal, have successfully described and analysed the superficial "pseudo modernism" of new urbanities, the clash between traditional and progressive value judgements, and the deliberate adoption of the "feminine mystique" so cleverly disguised behind a systematic campaign for increased mass consumption.

Which of the following factors, urbanization, industrialization, or migration has affected Turkish women most? Does Boserup's observation concerning rural change also apply to Turkey by widening the productive gap and leaving women the performance of simple manual tasks? As D. Kandiyoti rightly indicates, in Turkey, rural change did not intensify the already existing asymmetry between sexes, but rather the social stratification of males. Those who controlled the new agricultural technology and land resources consolidated their economic positions; the rest were pushed into a marginal category.[54] In other words, the changes for women merely complemented the changing relationships in the male world. Similarly, urbanization has not unconditionally led all city dwellers to the nuclear family pattern. As S. Timur has shown, high income professionals are adopting an egalitarian, small family pattern, whereas poorer families must pool their resources in extended families.[55]

External migration, which covers to some extent the impact of industrialization, if extended for a long period of time, is quite an effective change inducing factor. A number of empirical research studies[56] (A. Kudat, 1975; Mübeccel Kiray, 1976) have shown that not only do women migrant workers assume the role of family head, but they also acquire a whole set of new prerogatives, completely absent in their home country. Among these new rights one can list the right to choose the type and place of work as well as the permanent domicile; the right to determine the amount of savings, investment and expenditure; the right to decide upon their children's education; and finally, the right to decide upon family size both in terms of children and adhering other members. Indeed, detailed empirical data indicates that it is the employed female migrant workers who decide which relatives of friends are to be invited for short or long stays abroad. To a great extent, the duration and type of employment abroad seems to determine the degree to which Turkish women adjust to a given society. Transitional employment situations seem to lead solely to the acquisition of new consumption patterns.[57]

As far as education is concerned, functional education programs geared at meeting the specific needs of a given environment introduce women to specialized jobs and professions, especially in large urban centers. These new situations also produce a number of important side effects, such as an awakening political interest, class consciousness, awareness of social and economic rights, and the need for self fulfillment. Instead of blindly adopting the bourgeois components of the passive wife and motherhood ideology, some modern young women in industry and the services sector are striving toward goals such as the acquisition of an independent personality and freedom of choice in terms of husband and number of children.

The difficulty in realizing these goals, when one considers the uninterrupted contradictions between cultural and traditional values, the limitations of legally bestowed rights, and the economic realities, is obvious. These obstacles are further enhanced by the deliberate efforts of a mass consumption oriented market; a sex segregation based bourgeois ideology; and, the intensive efforts of political organizations, anxious to mobilize large groups of women to devote themselves solely to religious practices. As Mernissi reminds us, enouragement of traditional saint's rituals by administrative authorities who oppose any trade unionist or political movements is a well-known tactic in Third World politics.[58]

8. Major approaches to the problems of social change and women's status

Having briefly sketched the major features of social change as they relate to Turkish women, it now seems necessary to present very briefly the major approaches to this problem as reflected in Turkey's mass media and press.

(a) The evolutionist, legalistic approach can be summarized as follows: Women's emancipation and the realization of an egalitarian, civilized, Western type of society can be basically achieved through radical, comprehensive legislative and administrative measures. This idea can be found in "A Vindication of the Rights of Women," published by Mary Wollstonecraft in 1872, in which she states, "The faults of women were the natural consequences of their education and station in society... Let women share the rights and they will emulate the virtues of men."[59] Equality before law, equal pay for equal work, together with equal opportunities for education as well as the right to vote, once transformed into legal provisions, will supposedly produce in the long run a new generation of women, eager to become active, participating citizens.

This approach places very little, if any, importance on deeply rooted structural changes. The major vehicle for change is considered to be an array of legislative measures, large-scale publicity for egalitarian value judgments and, more recently, insistence on women's participation in the labor market, and the reduction of family size with the help of family planning. This evolutionary model, reborn under the modern version of feminism, wants to transform woman's world into a unisex male one without questioning the real reasons for this capital delay.

(b) The radical, class-oriented, structural approach assumes that a woman's social, economic and cultural problems differ in nature according to the social class to which she is affiliated. These special affiliations determine the range of alternatives open to a person in economic space. In the specific framework of the Third World countries, unless basic changes are made in the economic and social spaces, proposals such as those which encourage women to work, heighten their level of education and the concomitant provision of social services, will not work. Legal reforms solely produce a social system in which women's political role always remains a "symbolic" one. This is mainly due to the fact that their political choices largely depend upon the influence of two major institutions, namely, the "family" and "religion" and the role both of these institutions perform. Adherents of the radical, class-oriented, structural approach blame the capitalist system for this situation and maintain that it is wrong to focus on women's problems. According to them, a new societal order will automatically bring about the desired solution.

Some protagonists of this approach have added an additional dimension to this problem which is connected with the prevailing world economic order and characterized by a hierarchy built around the current international division of labor and class structure. This hierarchy is dominated by the international flow of capital (multinational corporations) in the metropolitan centers. Multinational decisions fundamentally influence the political-economic life of peripheral countries in the Third World. Women remain almost entirely unrepresented at this level. Thus, the "international class system," the "national class structure" and "household politics" are interrelated.

(c) The cultural sex-role sterotype approach. Sigmund Freud's anatomy destiny paradigm has recently led a great number of social scientists (psychologists, anthropologists and sociologists), to deal with the cultural dimension of women's position in society. According to this approach, the core of the female problem today is a problem of identity. A great number of cultures, especially the Islamic one, do not permit women to accept or gratify their basic needs and to grow and fulfill their potential as human beings. This has led a number of social scientists to deal with cultural sex-role stereotyping, attempting to delineate the major problems in each phase, such as sex-role attribution in the primary and secondary socialization processes, as well as the assessment of occupational segregation as cause and consequence of such a socialization pattern. Experiences, such as government support for changes in traditional sex roles (Sweden); greatly increased participation by women in traditionally masculine occupations (Soviet Union) and, the development of strategies to eliminate sex-role stereotypes from the educational systems, have contributed to the growth of this approach.

Quite a few authors have combined the major ideas of these approaches. Without entering into a detailed discussion of these apparently juxtaposing views, while supporting the major theses of the structural approach, it seems imperative to agree on one important point. Regardless of the social model a society like Turkey adopts, it is of major importance that action be taken to modify and improve the status of its millions of "second class citizens." The realization of an egalitarian, free and democratic society, where men and women may develop their personalities, requires much more reliable, scientific knowledge, data and research. This intensified research will enable politicians, policy makers, legislators, opinion leaders, planners and scholars, to conceive more effective strategies and policies.

CONCLUSION

Options in the form of placing priorities on total sexual liberty, sex segregation in favor of women, insistence on the decisive importance of the women's rights movement or sentimental attachment to past legal reforms, are certainly not the proper vehicles for an efficacious and comprehensive emancipation of all Turkish women. It is also obvious that no social problem can be isolated and treated by one-sided recommendations, such as family planning, vocational training or rural development projects.

Every society needs for its advancement and for a harmonious balance between industrialization and rural development, intelligent, mature, knowledgeable men and women. The political solution to be adopted will no doubt remain a constant issue of debate and will not disappear from the agenda of public discussions. But during this process of selecting the most efficacious remedies, one point should not be overlooked. The veil cast upon the myriads of problems, consciously or unconsciously perturbing the great majority of Turkish women, has not been lifted. Turkish women deserve to be carefully studied, their problems to be exposed and discussed. More knowledge means more power. Turkish women and men are rich with innate abilities. It is the duty of Turkish researchers to help to detect the manifold obstructions which prevent the emergence of a free and equal young generation of women and men dedicated to the survival of Turkish democracy.

NOTES

1. Pervin Esenkova, "La Femme Turque Contemporaine, Education et Rôle Social". *IBLA*, Tunis 1951, p. 285.
2. Tezer Taskıran, *Cumhuriyetin 50. Yılında Türk Kadın Hakları,* Ankara, Basbakanlık Kültür Müstesarlığı Yayını, 1973, pp. 27—28. For the curriculum of Girl's Teacher Schools see Faik Resit UNAT, *"Türkiye Eğitim Sisteminin Gelismesine Tarihi bir Bakış",* Ankara, Milli Eğitim Basimevi, 1964, pp. 92—105.
3. Gotthard Jaeschke, "Die frauenfrage in der Türkei", *SAECULUM,* X, Heft 4, p. 361.
4. Jean Melia, *Mustapha Kemal ou le Renovateur de la Turquie,* Paris, 1929, p. 94.
5. Charlotte Lorenz, "Die Frauenfrage im Osmanischen Reiche mit besonderer Berücksichtigung der arbeitenden Klasse", *Die Welt des Islam* (6), 1918, p. 72.
6. Halide Edip Adıvar, *Mor Salkımlı Ev,* Istanbul, Atals Kitabevi, 1967, 2nd

ed., pp. 22—23.
Halide Edip, *Conflict of East and West in Turkey,* Labore Jamia Milia Extension Lectures, p. 193.

7. Tezer Taşkıran, op. cit., pp. 55. Also see Tezer Taşkıran, *Women in Turkey,* Transl. Nida Tektaş, Istanbul, Redhouse Publ. 1976, p. 45.

8. Muhaddere Taşçıoğlu, *Kadının Sosyal Durumu ve Kadın Kıyafetleri.* Ankara, 1958, p. 11. Charlotte Lorenz, *op. cit.,* p. 73.

9. Muhaddere Taşçioğlu, op. cit., p. 45 Füsun ve Tunç Tayanç, *Dünyada ve Türkiye'de Tarih Boyunca Kadın,* Ankata, Toplum Yayinevi, 1977, pp. 110—111.

10. Enise Yener, "Eski Ankara Kıyafetleri ve Giyiniş Tarzları", *Dil, Tarih ve Coğrafya F. Dergisi,* XIII, Vol. 3, 1955.

11. Niyazi Berkes, *Turkish Nationalism and Western Civilization,* London, 1959, p. 252, p. 303. Ziya Gökalp, *Türkçülüğün Esasları,* 1970.

12. Naciye Yücel, "Tıp Alanmda Türk Kadım" in *Cumhuriyetin 50. Yılında Çaltşma Alanlarında Türk Kadım,* Istanbul, Sermet Matbaasi, 1974, pp. 64—66.

13. The newspaper "Türkoğlu", published in Bolu, reports in its issues of October 30, 1921 about the military accomplishments of 12 women who fought battles with their own weapons. The same newspaper also reports the promotion of a woman called Fatma from corporal to the rank of sergeant. Tezer Taşkiran, *op. cit.,* p. 81.

14. Afet Inan, *Turih Boyunca Türk Kadımnın Hak ve Görevleri,* Istanbul, Milli Eğitim Basımevi, 1975, pp. 127—128, (Atatürk Serisi, No. 10).

15. Afet Inan, *op. cit.,* pp. 127—128. Also see Şirin Tekeli, *Kadının Siyasal Hayattaki Yeri Üzerine Karşilaştırmalı Bir Araştırma,* Doçent Thesis, unpublished, Istanbul, 1977, mimeographed, pp. 272—273.

16. Sirin Tekeli, *op. cit.,* footnote 39, pp. 418—419.

17. *Atatürk'ün Söylev ve Demeçleri II,* January 21, 1923, pp. 147—148.

18. Tezer Taşkıran, *op. cit.,* pp. 91—95.

19. Tezer Taşkıran, *op. cit.,* pp. 96—99. For a more detailed narrative see Afet Inan, *op. cit.,* pp. 134—138. For the full text see *Zabıt Ceridesi,* Devre, I Ietima Senesi, 4. cilt 28, pp. 222—350.

20. Tezer Taşkıran, *op. cit.,* p. 96.

21. Necmeddin Sadak, "Kadınlarımız ve Aile Hukukuna Ilişkin Kararlar", *Aksam, January 7, 1924.*

22. Şirin Tekeli, *op. cit.,* pp. 275—276.

23. According to a regulation issued in 1923, "Husband and wife may sit next to each other provided they are not acting against the law in public transportation vehicles. No police can prevent an honourable woman from sitting next to her husband."

24. Atatürk's Speeches, *op. cit.,* vol. 11., pp. 85—87.

25. T. B. M. M. Tutanakiart, (Parliamentary Records). February 17, 1926.

26. Türk Üniversiteli Kadınlar Derneği, Ankara, *Türkiye Kadın Yıh Kongresi, 1975,* Ankara, Ayyıldız Matbaast, 1978.

27. Nermin Abadan, *Social Change and Turkish Women,* Ankara, SBF, 1963, p. 23 (SBF. Yayin No. 171—153).

28. Tezer Taşkıran, *op. cit.,* pp. 72—73. Afet Inan, *Medeni Bilgiler ve Mustafa Kemal Atatürk'ün El Yazıları,* Ankara, 1969, pp. 3—4.

29. *Zabit Ceridesi,* Parliamentary Records, Vol. 17, devre III, Session 3, March 20, 1930.
30. Cited by Şirin Tekeli, *op. cit.,* pp. 282—284.
31. Mary R. Beard, *Woman as Force in History,* London, Collier-MacMillan, 1946, pp. 22—23.
32. Nermin Abadan, *op. cit.,* p. 9.
33. Sirin Tekeli, "Siyasal Iktidar Kaışısında Kadın", *Toplum ve Bilim,* No. 3, 1977, p. 69.
34. Deniz Kandiyoti, *Women's Place in Turkish Society, A Comparative Approach, Current Turkish Thought,* New Series, No. 30, Spring 1977. See also Deniz Kandiyoti, "Sex Roles and Social Changes: A Comparative Appraisal of Turkey's Women", *SIGNS,* Journal of Women in Culture and Society, Vol. 3, No. 1, Fall 1977.
35. Ismail Beşikçi, *Doğuda Deîşim ve Yaptsal Sorunlar,* Ankara 1969, p. 187.
36. Deniz Kandiyoti, *op. cit.,* p. 17.
37. TIB, *Türkiye'de Kadının Sosyo-Ekonomik Durumu,* Ankara, 1975, p. 65. Füsun ve Tunç Tayanç, *op. cit.,* p. 118.
38. Nermin Abadan-Unat, "Implications of Migration on Emancipation and Pseudo-Emancipation of Turkish Women", *International Migration Review,* Vol. II, No. 1, 1977, pp. 54—55.
39. P. Benedict, "The "Kabul Günü": Structured Visiting in an Anatolian Provincial Turkish Town", *Anthropological Quarterly,* Washington, D. C. 47 (1), 1974, pp. 28—47 Mübeccel Kıray, *Ereğli: Ağır Sanayiden Evvel Bir Sahil Kasabası,* Ankara, DPT 1964. Fatma Mansur, *Bodrum: A Town in the Aegean,* Leiden, E. J. Brill, 1972.
40. Indian Council of Social Science Research, *Status of Women, A Synopsis of the Report of the National Committee,* New Delhi, 1975, p. 10.
41. Kemal H. Karpat, *The Gecekondu, Rural Migration and Urbanization,* Cambridge, Cambridge University, 1976, Table 4, 3, p. 102.
42. Kemal H. Karpat, *op. cit.,* 116.
43. The proportion of female labor to the total of labor force declined from 40.76 in 1960 to 36.2 in 1975. Hamide Topçuoglu, "Türk Toplumunda Kadınım Sosyal Statüsü", *Türkiye Kadın Yılı Kongresi,* Ankara, 1978, p. 89, Table: 19.
44. Kemal H. Karpat, *op. cit.,* Table 6, 11, p. 154.
45. Emre Kongar, *Survey of Familial Changes in Two Turkish Gecekondu Areas,* Paper submitted to the Social Anthropological Conference, Nicosia, September 1970.
46. Gül Ergil, *Toplumsal Yapt Araştırmast,* (DPT No. 1607, SPD. 298) Ankara, p. 23.
47. Hamide Topçuoğlu, *op. cit.,* pp. 92—93.
48. Abadan-Unat, *op. cit.,* 33—34.
49. Mesut Gülmez, "Türk Kamu Görevlilerinin Sayısal Evrimi", *TODAIE Dergisi,* 1972, p. 44.
50. Hamide Topçuoğlu, *Kadınların Çalışma Saikleri ve Kadın Kazancının Ile Bütçesindeki Rolü",* Ankara 1957. Oya Çitçi, "Women at Work", *Turkish Public Administration Annual,* 1975.
51. Şirin Tekeli, *op. cit.,* p. 299.

52. Nermin Abadan, *Social Change and Turkish Women,* SBF, Ankara 1963, p. 17.
53. In 1973 there were 149 women judges in Turkey out of a total of 3,022 (4.8%: 95.2%). Again in 1970, out of 10, 670 lawyers, there were 1,952 women lawyers. (10.7%—89.3%). Tezer Taşkıran, *op. cit.,* p. 161. Compare with Ayse Öncü's paper "Women in the professions: why so many?" in the same volume.
54. Deniz Kandiyoti, *op. cit.,* p. 64.
55. Serim Timur, *Türkiye'de Aile Yapısı,* Ankara, 1972, p. 175, (Hacettepe Üniversitesi Yayinlari D-15).
56. Mübeccel Kıray, "The Family of the Immigrant Worker" in N. Abadan-Unat, Ed. *Turkish Workers in Europe, 1960—1975,* Leiden; E. J. Brill, 1976, pp. 214—216.
57. Nermin Abadan-Unat, see footnote 38, p. 54—55.
58. Fatima Mernissi, "Women, Saints and Sanctuaries", *SIGN,* Journal of Women in Culture and Society, Vol. 3, No. 1, Autumn 1977, p. 112.
59. Mary Wollstonecraft, *A Vindication of the Rights of Woman* New York, W. W. Norton, 1967.

7

SOCIOECONOMIC CHANGE, SEX ROLES AND THE FAMILY

INTRODUCTION

Turkey is the only Muslim country in the Middle East that has pursued a systematic policy to separate religion from state affairs. Each of its constitutions (1924, 1961, 1982) gives paramount importance to the principle of secularism. Moreover, by promulgating the Law for Unification of Instruction together with the abolition of the Caliphate, both on March 3, 1924, the right to an education for both sexes was assured. Finally, by adopting the Swiss Civil Code on October 4, 1926, Turkey became the first Muslim country to eliminate as a whole the rules of the Sharia and to introduce a Western-oriented complete legal code of behavior and interaction. For the last six decades this code has regulated almost all aspects of the private life of its citizens.

Such deep and entrenching reforms cleared the way for comprehensive and measurable changes in the status of women. Indeed, one of the main aspirations of Kemal Atatürk, founder of the Turkish Republic, was to transform Turkish women into responsible, self-confident citizens. Atatürk cherished the ideals of equality between the sexes and of a family life not based upon a lifelong tie of one-sided bondage. These ideals led Atatürk to focus on eliminating traditional Islamic norms and practices and introducing a secular, mixed educational system. In other words, Atatürk chose to use the revolutionary tools of legal reform and education to accomplish his goals of equality for Turkish women.

Yet, sixty years later a multitude of problems still beset Turkish women, especially those living in rural areas, that force us to reconsider certain issues. To what extent can "revolutions of legal systems" change the traditional lifestyle of the majority of women in a given country? Which major economic, social or political factors are directly or indirectly responsible for accelerating or retarding this process? Does religion, ideologically or morally, still maintain its decisive hold on the degree of women's social integration and political participation?

When we look at various sociological, anthropological or sociopsychological theories (Goode, 1964; Bott, 1957; Laslett, 1976; Shorter, 1976; Wallerstein, et al., 1979), all seem to show that shifts in sex roles or changes in the status of women depend directly on changes in the demographic structure, the economic system and the household composition. But social crises also affect the status of women (Boulding, 1977). According to this theory, rapid modernization or a crisis (such as war) seems to bring women into "male" positions under the guise of national mobilization of all resources. During these periods a breakdown of cultural norms pertaining to men's and women's tasks temporarily occurs. The crisis is useful in that it illustrates the importance of the time element necessary for change as well as the possibilities and limitations for change in a society with deeply rooted sex roles.

The Turkish case can be partly evaluated in light of the crisis theory (Abadan-Unat, 1980). Class formation is the most important factor here, but other major factors include the national liberation war, the decrease in women's seclusion and exclusion from public life, systematic educational efforts as a part of a comprehensive Western-oriented modernization program, the shift toward a capitalist economic system, the introduction of new technologies leading to a growth in the industrial and service sectors, the elaboration of national development plans and the persistence to abolish cultural dualism.

To assess the impact of these processes on sex roles, a short overview on the major socioeconomic structural changes seems imperative.

SOCIOECONOMIC CHANGES

The significant change of status for Turkish women, within the family or in larger context, is closely related to depeasantization and rapid urbanization. Social scientists such as Kiray and Kandiyoti have rightfully insisted that a new type of community life emerges only when major changes in economic life take place (Kiray, 1968; Kandiyoti, 1974).

Turkey, especially since 1950, has undergone rapid change in rural areas due to internal and external migration and mechanization of farming methods (Turkish SIS, No. 683, 1973:111). Indeed, since 1950, half a million agricultural laborers were replaced by 300,000 tractors.

Cities grew slowly before 1950; between 1927 and 1950 the urban population increased from 2.2 million to 3.9 million. After 1950 Turkey became one of the most rapidly urbanizing countries in the world; for the next thirty years the average annual increase in urban population was 5.7% (table 1). During the 1920s less than one-sixth of the population lived in cities and towns with more than 10,000 inhabitants. In 1950 only five cities had populations of more than 100,000; by 1980 this number rose to twenty-nine. This urbanization is not organic or healthy, but is artificial, resulting as it has from from a solely demographic change (Yazgan, 1967; Danielson and Keles, 1984).

Migration has been the driving force behind rapid growth in Turkey; in the 1980s over 700,000 rural dwellers were moving to urban areas each year (Tumertekin, 1970:157-69). In addition, external migration produced an explosive social movement in Turkey; in one decade, 1960-1970, approximately 1.5 million men and women moved to Western Europe (Abadan-Unat, 1975:79). This migration caused regional disparities as well; in 1980 western Turkey's urban centers accounted for 93%; 12.2 million people were living in cities with more than 100,000 inhabitants. Since most industry is located in large cities, western Turkey has far more industrial development than the less urbanized eastern provinces. In 1975 the province of Istanbul alone accounted for 49% of all major industries in the nation, while less than 3% were located in eastern Anatolia.

Employment in industry rose from 250,000 in 1927 to over two million in 1980. Industrialization, however, has not been able to keep pace with urbanization, resulting in a significant growth of the service sector (table 1).

The interplay of these forces produced a dual economic structure in Turkey's cities. Industrialization and urbanization gave part of urban Turkey a modern industrial economy, but the inability of the modern sector to keep pace with the flood of immigrants created a second economy—the "informal" or "traditional" sector. The demands of rural dwellers for low-cost housing could not be met by either the private market or government. As in other rapidly urbanizing societies, migrants responded by occupying illegally, and

Table 1
Types of Employment by Major Cities

City	Industry	Services	Other
Istanbul	38.9%	56.2%	4.9%
Ankara	20.1%	69.6%	10.3%
Izmir	34.7%	53.6%	11.7%

Source: *SIS*, 1970, No. 659.

becoming building squatter housing or gecekondus.

As villagers poured into the cities, the number of gecekondus expanded rapidly, from 100,000 units in 1950 to 1.25 million in 1983 (table 2). Nearly six million people lived in squatter housing in 1983; one survey indicated that 84% of these squatters originated in rural areas.

The high mobility of Turkey's people can be judged from the fact that in 1976 over 60% of city dwellers had been born in other provinces

Table 2
Squatter Housing: 1945-1980

Year	Number of units	Housing stock	Number of individuals	Percent of urban population
1945	10,000	4.0%	40,000	1.4%
1960	240,000	16.7%	1,200,000	16.4%
1970	600,000	21.4%	3,000,000	23.6%
1980	950,000	21.1%	4,750,000	23.4%

Source: Kent-Koop, *Konut '81*, Ankara 1982:23.

(1970 census).

These important changes are also reflected in the changing structure of the workforce. In 1950, 85.7% of the economically active population was employed in agriculture; this percentage went down in 1960 to 74.9%, while services went up from 6.9% to 10.3% and industry from 7.4% to 9.6% (table 3). This change also had repercussions in the distribution of economically active women.

Table 3
Occupational Distribution of Labor Force by Sex

Sector	1955		1975	
	Male	Female	Male	Female
Agriculture	46.6%	53.4%	50%	50%
Industry	87.1%	12.9%	88.5%	11.5%
Services	92.4%	7.6%	87.4%	12.6%

Source: *SIS,* Population Census Data 1970.

This distribution indicates the high share of women in agriculture; indeed 88% of active women are engaged in agriculture, but less than 4% and 8% are employed in industry and services, respectively. Of the active females in agriculture, only 1.5% are wage employees; the remainder toil under the status of "unpaid family member" (Ergil, 1977; Erder, 1981). That is, the overwhelming proportion of rural female labor carries on productive activities as a natural extension of household duties, as daughters and then mothers.

One should not overlook the fact that the 12-14 age group comprises 7.1% of the total economically active population. This finding demonstrates the utilization of child labor, especially girls (85% of the above mentioned age group). The share of "unpaid working women" in the category of "unpaid family workers" appears to increase with age (54.7% for age group 15-24, 74.3% for 25-44 and 90.9% for 45-64). The 86.6% of active females (1975) employed without renumeration do not reap the direct fruits of their labor in the form of personal monetary gains.

These figures explain why, in spite of significant increases in the labor force in urban industry and service sectors, Turkish women occupy a relatively unimportant place (on the order of 11%) here. Kazgan correctly points out that a social division of labor based on sex still appears to be an outstanding feature in Turkish urban society, since 85% of urban women of working age remain out of the labor force (Kazgan, 1981:136-37). This figure becomes even more significant when compared with the share of Turkish women working abroad—17.6% of the total Turkish labor force in West Germany, for example. It appears that a totally different environment, such as exists in Western Europe, creates a different set of incentives for women and alters their attitude toward household and market activity.

These figures force us to assess properly the educational level of Turkish women. In spite of systematic efforts to improve education for women, the problem of literacy remains a predominantly female problem (table 4).

Table 4
Literacy Rates by Sex in Turkey, 1927-1975

Census years	Male	Female	Difference
1927	17.4%	4.6%	12.8%
1935	29.3	9.8	19.5
1940	33.9	11.2	22.7
1945	41.9	18.1	23.8
1950	47.1	20.1	27.0
1955	55.6	25.6	30.0
1960	53.6	24.8	28.8
1965	64.0	32.8	31.2
1970	69.0	40.0	29.0
1975	75.1	48.1	26.8

Source: *SIS,* 1973; *SIS,* 1975:6-7

The problem of literacy is aggravated by regional disparities. Whereas the gap of literacy between men and women in metropolitan areas is quite close—Istanbul, 83.1% male, 68.7% female; Ankara, 84.4% male, 63.1% female—in eastern provinces this gap is much wider. Thus in Maras there are 64.8% literate males versus 17.2% literate women. In Mardin the proportions are 40.1% male to 9% female literate citizens.

The relatively lower socioeconomic status of women in general and of rural women in particular is on the one hand reflected by and on the other hand explained by the low degree of educational attainment among Turkish women. This fact is closely related to the female labor force participation rate. Two different patterns in the relationship between labor force participation and education in rural and urban areas of the country in regard to women can be observed. In urban areas, where women mainly participate in nonagricultural occupations, the proportion of females in the labor force is low, but there is a positive relationship between educational attainment and labor force participation (table 5). In rural areas; however, labor force participation does not increase by educational attainment, but on the contrary decreases (Özbay, 1982: 136).

Table 5
Distribution of Female Population by Education Level and Employment Status 1975 (Aged 12 and over)

School	Employed	Unemployed	Number of persons
Non-graduate	50.1%	49.9%	7,913,364
Primary	36.4	63.6	4,454,068
Junior high	15.4	84.6	521,594
Vocational at Jr. high level	34.0	66.0	13,530
High school	32.1	67.9	239,475
Vocational at H.S. level	57.2	42.8	192,331
College	71.4	28.6	67,093
Total	44.1	55.9	13,401,455

Source: *SIS,* 1976:6-7, 24-25.

When we examine the values toward education as displayed by Turkish women, a puzzling dualistic pattern emerges. Empirical data reveal three general observations: (1) relative to men, women display substantially lower levels of educational attainment; (2) relative to men, women who pursue education beyond the primary level show more persistence and achieve greater success; and (3) despite the low level of educational attainment for women, substantial numbers of them do obtain professional degrees and practice in what in the West are considered male-dominated occupations. Of Turkish physicians 14% are women; among lawyers this percentage goes up to 18.6%. In the United States the respective figures are 10% and 5% (Öncü, 1981:184). Apparently the high level of illiteracy among Turkish women does not prevent the coexistence of significant numbers of professional women.

The present and future implications of this dualistic structure, which no doubt influences the sex role distribution as well, will be discussed in the next section.

SOCIAL CHANGE AND SEX ROLES

Every culture has its stereotypes of masculinity and femininity, which pressure its own members toward conformity. Muslim societies have generated a culture based explicitly upon sexual segregation. Muslim sexuality is based on territorial rights that strictly allocate space to each sex: religion and power to the universe of men, and the domestic universe of sexuality and the family to women (Mernissi, 1975:81).

Although Turkey has repeatedly undertaken major efforts to break down the barriers between sexes, certain patterns of behavior continue, in different ways. For example, women of all ages do travel alone on trains and buses, but they try not to sit too close to a man; territorial segregation persists, even if in a very modified way.

In Turkey, as in all Islamic cultures, male honor is important; this concept demands the purity and chastity of all women closely related to a particular man. Nevertheless, as sexuality becomes more articulated in the press and in literature, sexual mores are weakening. As noted previously, the legal reforms of the mid-1920s have produced astonishing results that go in two directions—traditionalism and modernism—depending on the respective structural changes that have affected Turkey's social structure. This explains why a more detailed analysis seems imperative.

Sex Roles in Rural Turkish Society

Fast-developing societies like Turkey are characterized by distinct classes of women, usually of six or seven different types. Kandiyoti (1977) differentiates between (a) nomadic, (b) traditional-rural, (c) changing-rural, (d) small town, (e) squatter (gecekondu), (f) urban middle class professional or housewife. In this study we add a seventh: the migrant women abroad and their left-behind female relatives.

160

Nomadic women. A small percentage of Turkey's women belong to isolated nonintegrated nomadic tribes. At present the trend is toward a spatial settlement of almost all nomadic tribes in Anatolia, but this process will require some time to accomplish. Within such nomadic or half-sedentarized tribes, women play a decisive role in dairy production, weaving, etc., but outside their procreative role their power in decision-making is negligible. Males dominate all activities related to the public sphere, while women's authority remains confined to interfamily affairs. Nomadic women adhere totally to the rigid rules of the tribe; the degree of individuality depends on the innate capacity to resist an overall embracing type of control.

Traditional, rural women. As universally observed, the traditional lifestyle of peasant culture, closely linked to a subsistence economy, determines also the female status within that culture. This status remains constant, namely childbearing and growing authority with advancing age. Their labor goes largely unrecognized; males control specialized areas and public dealings. However, the impact of technological innovations and the widening of the communications network are also touching traditional villages. Furthermore, traditional peasant women feel integrated through various instruments and institutions—mainly the mass media and political elections. The high percentage of electoral vote-casting among village women indicates that even where political choices are heavily under the directives of the head of the family, women are conscious of their role as citizens.

Changing, rural women. In this group we find women whose setting is changing, often dramatically. Internal and external migration, farm mechanization or the entrance of the village into a cash crop economy substantially alters the function of fathers and mothers and redefines the status of women. The strong negative relationship between socioeconomic development and women's labor force participation is to be seen particularly in this group (Kazgan, 1981). Under certain conditions, development may negatively affect women's educational level; wherever seasonal migration and alternative job opportunities such as factory work for men are present, we see a greater concentration of women in small labor-intensive agricultural production. Such intensive work hinders women's schooling (Kâğitçibaşi, 1980).

Sex Roles in Urban Turkish Society

"Gecekondu" (squatter housing) women. Erder (1981) projects that in the year 2000 Turkey's female population will be 35.6 million; 26.7 million women—Turkey's total rural population today—will live in cities, mostly as a result of a fast depeasantization. Among these

new urbanites, the most dynamic part is represented by the Turkish gecekondu women (Senyapili, 1981). The women of the squatter housing districts are part of the peripheral labor force, which is based on kinship ties and networks. Like her spouse it is hard if not impossible to find employment in the formal, organized urban sectors. These women share the general characteristics of this labor force in that they are uneducated, untrained, unskilled and inexperienced. Yet the Turkish case represents some particularities which make their situation different from urban patterns of developing countries at comparable levels of development (such as Latin American countries) through the conspicuous absence of women in small trade, vending or peddling jobs that require spatial mobility and exposure in public places. Turkish gecekondu women also solicit to a very small percentage jobs as domestic help in private homes (Kandiyoti, 1982:104). In the early 1950s the only opportunity for illiterate, unskilled women was to work as maids; later, they entered unspecialized branches of the urban service sectors. In the gecekondu (squatter areas) of Istanbul and Ankara only 5.5% and 6%, respectively, of the active female population in the age group of 15-64 were working in 1976 and 1977 (Şenyapili, 1981:209). Thus the present employment pattern of the women in the gecekondu reflects a general withdrawal from the urban labor market and a tendency to enter unorganized, low paying, unspecialized jobs, while refraining from domestic jobs.

Urban female wage earners. Although 81% of the economically active urban women are not gainfully employed, the number of female wage earners is steadily increasing. Certain regions such as the Marmara and the Aegean as well as the three provinces with metropolitan cities show the most rapid growth (table 6).

Table 6
Female Wage Earners by Year and Region by Percentage

Year	Central Anatolia	Black Sea	Aegean and Marmara	Mediterranean	Eastern Anatolia	3 Metropolitan cities
1955	1.2	1.2	4.7	4.4	2.0	18.9 ·
1960	4.6	1.4	5.8	3.8	1.4	25.0
1970	6.0	5.3	11.0	10.7	4.0	40.8

Source: Gül Ergil, *Toplumsal Yapı Araştırması: Nüfus ile İlgili Gelişmeler* (Social Structure Study: Population Development Trends) State Planning Organis-ation, 1977, Table 13:47.

The indigenous female labor class has grown slowly, from 78,767 in 1943 to 143,000 in 1968. The heaviest concentration of these women are in light manufacturing industry, i.e., tobacco, textiles, apparel, food, beverages, packing, etc. Only about 9% of the workers were covered by social security in 1977; the majority were not unionized. Most were in the twenty-five and under age group.

Actually the most drastic swelling of Turkey's female labor class has taken place outside the national boundaries. The opening up of Western Europe's labor market created new job opportunities for men and women. While the number of female Turkish migrant workers in West Germany was as low as 173 in 1960, this number reached 143,611 in 1977 (Abadan-Unat, 1978). In 1978 there were about 215,000 Turkish migrant women employed in Europe, distributed as follows: Austria 31,800, West Germany 134,342, Switzerland 12,979, Belgium 5,175; the rest were scattered over France, Holland and the Scandinavian countries (SOPEMI, 1979).

In addition to these employed women, one should not overlook the large number of nonactive spouses. Their total number in Europe is about 451,550 of which 77% (349,232) reside in West Germany. Together with 816,876 children under eighteen, the total of Turkish migrants in Western Europe exceeds 2.2 million (SOPEMI, 1982). These large figures explain why the most significant changes in Turkey's social structure have primarily been affected by the massive toll of external migration parallel to the very fast rate of urbanization. Both factors are closely related to economic under-development and its corollaries, unemployment and under-employment.

Small-town women. This group embraces predominantly wives of small entrepreneurs or low-ranking civil servants. Small-town women are the least visible in the sense that they are the most homebound and secluded, the most restricted in movement and the least prominent in employment. Detailed case studies carried out in Turkish small towns permits us to have an insight into women of the provincial middle class, a group not assimilable to their metropolitan counterparts (Kiray, 1976, 1981; Fallers and Fallers, 1976; Benedict, 1974; Mansur, 1972; Magnarella, 1974).

Although the attitudes toward veiling, segregation and mixing with male visitors are more relaxed, women in small towns, because of the greater emphasis on public sphere and the absolute disappearance of female labor, are rather confined to their residential neighborhoods. The Boğazliyan study on left-behind family members of migrants (Abadan-Unat, et al., 1976) indicated that shopping, which traditionally has

163

been a man's job, represents a delicate problem to solve. While 51% of the migrants' wives were permitted to shop themselves, including going to the weekly marketplace, the remaining 40.6% delegated this task to male relatives or their own children. Under these conditions female leisure, which is almost nonexistent in rural areas, has resulted in larger social networks, which have facilitated the formation of the "kabul gün." This institution (one could call it an "acceptance day") consists of a visiting pattern by which women receive guests on a regular rotational basis. A wife's attendance at kabul güns reflects her husband's position in the community. Generally, only the wives of local and nonlocal salaried employees, ağas and wealthy merchants give and attend kabul güns (Benedict, 1974:131). For the remaining part of small-town women, gatherings of a religious nature such as recitations of the *mevlût* prayer offer an opportunity for social interaction (Kiray, 1981; Mansur, 1972). The mevlût is attended by women of all ages. Finally, one should not overlook the "drop-in" form of visits which constantly take place in immediate neighborhoods (Kiray, 1981).

Professional middle-and upper-middle-class women. In Turkey it seems that the public sector has attracted most of the educated professional women. Considering that the first female employees in the post offices were admitted only in 1914, after the entrance of the Ottoman Empire into World War I, the history of white-collar Turkish women is rather brief. Under the Ottoman rule, female civil servants were obliged to work in segregated rooms and could only discard their veils during working hours. Yet, the growth in the numbers of female bureaucrats has been spectacular. While in 1938 there were only 12,716 female civil servants (9.5%), this figure rose in 1970 to 123,812 and in 1978 to 277,622, representing 26.7% of the Turkish governmental bureaucracy. Differentiating between local and national government, the distribution reflects 82.8% in central governmental offices and state economic enterprises versus 17,210 in local administration (Citci, 1971:226). Thus one can state that a visible "bureaucratization" of qualified female manpower has taken place in Turkey (Gülmez, 1972; Citci, 1975). Indeed, during 1938-1976 the number of female civil servants increased nineteen times, while the number of male civil servants rose only sixfold. This increase carries with it also a rise in educational attainment. While 54% of all male civil servants are primary or secondary school graduates, 68.5% of women in government service are educated to high school (lycée) level or beyond (Abadan-Unat, 1981b). Nevertheless, these women have remained in "feminine occupations" such as secretarial work, switchboard operation, nursing and teaching.

Next to civil service, banking seems to be the preferred occupation, so much so that one can talk about a "feminization" of the banking sector. In 1982, of a total of 132,714 bank employees, more than one third (35%), namely 46,576, were women. Especially in metropolitan centers the proportion of female to male banking clerks rose from 43% in 1972 to 53% in 1981 (Nokta, 1983). Finally, the position of Turkish women in the professions must be scrutinized. A young Turkish woman sociologist, Ayşe Öncü, asks in one of her writings: "Why so many?" According to Öncü's findings (1981), one in every five practicing lawyers in Turkey is female and one in every six practicing doctors is female; 28.5% of the members listed in the Istanbul Bar Association for 1978 were female and the estimated proportion of female medical school diploma holders in the labor market in 1965-1970 was 2,570. Öncü explains these phenomena with a mode of recruitment under conditions of rapid expansion. Thus, women's entry into the professions is a direct outcome of elite recruitment as generally, over the years, all educational echelons were opened for the daughters of upper-class families. Women from elite backgrounds are much more acceptable and less threatening in highly prestigious professions than upwardly mobile men from humbler backgrounds who are likely to be more competitive and achievement oriented (Öncü, 1981:189).

Upper-class housewives seem to have largely benefited from Atatürk's reforms; a considerable number of them have completed a university education but have preferred to marry instead of taking up a career. For them the successful woman is still to be defined in exclusively domestic terms such as "good mother and wife." This strata attaches great importance to conspicuous consumption and displays a stylish Western dress, while still clinging to traditional values that center around a network of family members, neighbors and classmates.

Continuity and Change in Sex Roles

The first question to be discussed here is: have social reality, mores and tradition up to the present day resisted Westernizing legal norms? One answer to this is that sex roles are closely related to forms of production and social structure. Thus wherever noticeable structural changes such as rapid urbanization or a high rate of external migration occurred, important changes in the interpretation of sex roles took place and traditions faded out.

Empirical data of recent years reveal that four groups among Turkish women seem to have adopted significantly new attitudes and standards. Each group—the gecekondu women, the Turkish migrant women abroad, the female relatives of migrant workers left behind, and the middle-class professional women—is acquiring a different set of modernizing values. The salient issue in this regard seems to lie in a different outlook on life and women's function and place in society, rather than in the search for evidence of the emergence of a totally independent personality.

Contrary to the prevailing idea that employment outside the home is the only vehicle for emancipation, the Turkish case clearly shows that a change in mentality does not automatically stem from participation in economic activities, but is rather linked to a different position within the family and/or within the given social strata as well as the degree of financial controlling power.

Kuyas' survey on female labor and power relations (1982) has proven that as long as women are denied autonomy in their relation to production or in the appropriation of the exchange value of their labor power, the extension of their traditional roles to the labor market cannot be interpreted as a genuine resource. This hypothesis can be validated in regard to those Turkish migrant women who, after the recession of 1966-1967, were recruited for industrial work in West Germany without being obliged to register on a waiting list. Most of these women, who had a traditional social background and were mentally unprepared and to a considerable extent unwilling to go abroad, were strongly urged by their fathers, husbands or brothers to take up industrial or service openings abroad in order to secure jobs for their male relatives later. Once forced to live independently, a considerable number of these women acquired very different preferences. Thus a number of empirical research studies (Kudat, 1975; Kiray, 1976; Abadan-Unat, 1978, 1982) have shown that when migrant women abroad or those left behind become heads of the family, they also assume new responsibilities and act totally differently. Their readiness to use new rights is astonishing. Among them are the right to choose the type and place of work as well as the family's permanent domicile; the right to determine the amount of savings, investment and expenditure; the right to decide upon their children's education; and finally the right to decide upon family size both in terms of children and adhering other members. Indeed, detailed empirical data indicate that it is the employed female migrant worker who decides which relatives or friends are to be invited for a short or long stay. With these new rights, conflict also emerges. The most frequent sources for dispute are the allocation of the household income and the establishment of separate bank accounts (Kudat, 1975).

Parallel to those abroad, the left-behind family members also experience a sharp turn in their social status. Although occupying marginal positions abroad, at home the migrants are looked upon as successful social climbers. Their prestige exercises a spill-over effect on their families. Especially in case of establishing an independent, if fragmented, household, the left-behind women—whether mothers, spouses or sisters—are gaining in self-consciousness. The fact that they benefit from the remittances sent home and are not actively participating in any remunerated occupation is irrelevant; important is the fact that they enjoy a kind of financial independence they never possessed before. As heads of family they are obliged to enter into formal relations with banks, post offices and government agencies. All these obligations modify the self-weighted social values of these women and produce noticeable changes in the assessment of their functions in society. Abroad or at home, these women start to understand what "equality before law" and "to have legal rights" mean, even if this understanding sometimes cannot be verbalized in a rational form. A good example for such self-assertion is a remark made by a woman from Boğazliyan whose two sons were employed in Holland, "Previously the grocer of our village did not even let me enter his shop. Now, if I wish, I could buy out all his stapled merchandise!" (Abadan-Unat, 1977:46).

Next to a rise in self-confidence and evaluation of their social standing, these women are also demonstrating that they are determined to become "the architects of their own lives" by using birth control measures. A recent survey indicates that 78% of the working and 55% of the nonemployed migrant women are making use of contraception (Yasa, 1979:140).

Thus wherever wives are assuming new roles as heads of household and decision-makers in the absence of their husbands in the nuclear family, or wherever unmarried, single women have a gainful occupation without living with their immediate families, a sharp reversal of sex roles takes place, which, as Kiray correctly observes, "No law of the Republic could have produced on such a scale" (Kiray, 1976:224).

The third group of Turkish women to experience noticeable changes in sex roles is in the gecekondu area where former peasants are establishing themselves. Because very few of these women are gainfully employed, most are subject to the prescribed roles for women of any Muslim society—passivity, docility, acceptance of male control. Yet while most of these women lead secluded lives in ethnic-determined "islands of isolation," they do have access to the media, which serve as powerful instruments for introducing new values. The popular media messages constantly stimulate more comprehensive consumption of goods and the achievement of upward mobility through marriage. Television, as well as the "photo-fiction," which penetrate the gecekondu environment effectively impose a consumption-oriented value system (Senyapili, 1982: 295). Thus we might conclude that the culture that permeates the mass media by conveying understandable terminology, symbols and images is more effective than the educational institutions; the awakening to consumerism among gecekondu women equips them with a new urbanite understanding. Faithful to their particular community values, they perceive themselves in a more authoritative way. This evolution is reflected in Karpat's finding, where 69% of women versus 59% of men consider themselves to be the most trustworthy and reliable person (Karpat, 1976:154). In line with this high degree of self-reliance, gecekondu women insist on having a say in the choice of their future husband (47%) as well as to determine the education of their children. Thus while gecekondu women retain certain elements of village culture, they also emulate middle-class values. Because of their strong motivation to integrate into urban life, they represent one of the most dynamic elements in Turkey's modernization process.

The fourth group of women where a significant change in sex roles has taken place is represented by the middle-class professional women and the upper-class housewives. In regard to the unemployed housewife, Kandiyoti's research (1981) has shown that from the intergenerational point of view, the major breakthrough has taken place in the mother's generation. Yet, these women felt the necessity to reconcile traditional and newer demands. Thus although predominantly oriented toward Western standards, the first generation of the Republican era seems to have added some roles instead of undergoing a radical mental change. This also explains why we find a higher degree of psychosocial change among the second and third generations. The area where mothers and daughters seem to differ most is in premarital sexual standards. While 84% of mothers believe that virginity until marriage is a must, this percentage drops to 38% for daughters. Again, while 45% of mothers believe that women should avoid responsible positions and jobs, this proportion is 11% for their daughters (Kandiyoti, 1981:251-52).

In a similar vein, Horner's concept about "fear of success" seems to have only a limited application among middle-class women with high education belonging to the second generation. Actually, the detailed study of sexual segregation has compelled some social scientists such as Fallers and Fallers for Turkey (1976) and Papanek for Pakistan (1971, 1973) to forward the proposition that women who are self-sufficient and psychologically more independent in their segregated worlds have less difficulty separating their professional and sexual identities in a work situation. This observation gains particular importance in regard to women professionals versus women government employees. The first group, which includes judges, lawyers, notaries, physicians, university professors, architects and engineers, encounters practically no noticeable obstacles in public life. Their clientele looks upon them as asexual officeholders; respect for the office such professional women occupy overshadows their personal characteristics.

This projection is less clearcut with low- and middle-management government officials. They look upon their occupation less like a career and more like a job. That is why the second group considers itself primarily homemakers and mothers; they justify their entrance into the labor market on a purely economic basis.

Only the elite group consisting of highly skilled professional women consider self-sufficiency and full deployment of their innate capacities as the most sought-after goal. Particularly striking is that Turks of both sexes assume that a highly skilled educated woman will pursue a lifetime career just as a man would and that she will be fully as professional as a man in that position (Fallers and Fallers, 1976:254). Here the calculation that education is a form of investment that should not be wasted enters into consideration.

After having attempted to explain the modalities that induced some Turkish women to evaluate their role in society according to dynamic standards, a general statement about the trend of continuity in sex roles seems necessary. The basic values of the traditional outlook lie in the sex-anchored division of labor and its concomitant spatial segregation. Thus food preparation for the family, cleaning and childcare are almost exclusively women's work in conservative environments such as rural life in general, small-town life and in the lower-middle-class housewives' milieu. In villages dependent on the cultivation of some kind of subsistence crop, the traditional lifestyle of peasant culture does not admit women into the male world. However, depending on the geographic and economic conditions, these peasant women are (a) totally involved in home production, (b) additionally engaged in traditional crafts such as carpet-weaving, (c) may eventually also work full time in the fields. Because traditional socialization stresses the temporary presence of girls at home, parents prepare their daughters for marriage and home by equiping them with qualities such as submissiveness, obedience, shyness and passivity. Few girls in such traditional settings are motivated to pursue education beyond the compulsory primary school. In 1974 the State Planning Organisation estimated the proportion of girls with village origin as 2.6% among all students applying for university entrance exams (DPT, 1977:17). This explains why the Hacettepe study of 1975 found 40% among a sample of 2,322 village women agreeing with the statement, "Girls don't need to go to school or have a job" (Özbay, 1979:176). Familism as a dominant ideological value remains at the base of Turkish society. It applies as much to rural as to small-town and low-middle-class, urban women. These values are so strong that they seldom if ever enter into conflict with national goals. Thus all the Five Year Development Plans have so far not been able to change the main purpose of "girl's technical education," which has not gone beyond preparing girls to become good housewives and training them for vocations "suitable" for girls (Kazgan, 1979a).

The main goal in changing the social status of women in Turkey was to offer equal educational opportunities for girls. But prevailing attitudes in traditional settings toward education as well as an assessment of the kind of landownership and agricultural production, which necessitates a heavy involvement of women, creates serious obstacles for the promotion of women. The projection presented by Özbay suggests that, with the decline of independent producers on the land, "feminized" agricultural production will increase. This will mean that the educational gap between the sexes in rural Turkey will probably increase. Furthermore, this situation will become a major obstacle to improving women's status (Özbay, 1981:147). Thus drastic changes in sex role distribution aside from far-reaching socioeconomic changes such as those caused by migration, urbanization and industrialization are not to be expected.

THE FAMILY IN TURKEY

Much of sociological inquiry on social change in recent years has asserted that, as a direct consequence of industrialization and urbanization, the extended family will be superseded by the independent nuclear family. This generalization has been sustained by observations that extended families are more prevalent in rural areas and even more so in underdeveloped, agricultural societies. Yet, comparative and historical research indicate that there is no causal relationship between the nuclear family, urbanization and industrialization.The most convincing example seems to be Japan, where a signficant number of extended families continue to exist in spite of its fast rate of modernization. Survey and census data of India, China and Egypt have revealed that the majority of families live in nuclear households; only the wealthy were able to maintain an extended family in one household.

Thus in recent years myths attached to these hypotheses have been increasingly criticized and exposed (Duben, 1982:73-74).

Family Structure

Based on the extended empirical survey of Serim Timur, a relatively sound profile of the structure of Turkish families can be presented. According to this survey, 60% of all families in Turkey are nuclear, 19% are of the "patriarchal extended" type, 13% are "transient extended," 8% are "dissolved families or nonfamily households" (Timur, 1972:33). Although in both patriarchal and transient extended families three generations live together, in the first the patriarch father is the household head, and in the second the son is the chief bread winner.

There is a close relationship between urbanism and the size of families; nuclear families increase and patriarchally extended families decrease with the degree of urbanism. The transient extended family does not vary by community size.

Timur's data indicate that in rural areas landowning farmers live mostly in extended families, whereas the landless farm workers have the largest proportion of nuclear families. Accordingly, the proportion of nuclear families is 44% among farmers, 64% among sharecroppers and 77% among farm workers. In urban areas the highest proportion, 77%, is among professionals. Among businessmen and industrial entrepreneurs only 64% live in nuclear households. Other findings are confirming that the nuclear family household is most prevalent among the smallest landholders, those with less than five hectares, whereas the extended family household is associated with the largest landholders (Tekeli, 1978:322, Kandiyoti, 1976:65). Family size is closely related to large land holding, but not with education or income. Timur's findings have also supplied evidence that the prevailing family type is not static but dynamic. Accordingly, there seems to be a cyclical development of the extended family, where a married man passes through three stages: following his marriage he first lives for a while in his father's household, then establishes his own independent nuclear family and as patriarch again offers temporary residence to his own son, when he establishes his family.

There is also a close relationship between the size of the family and the form of its establishment, including the selection of spouses and the age at marriage. Large and extended families are maintained where wedding festivities requiring large spending as well as the payment of the traditional bride price obliges members of the new family to stay at least provisionally for some time with the elder family members.

In regard to the selection of the spouses and the decision to establish a new household, the greatest authority to be held by father or mother appears within the patriarchal extended family (50%) and the least in the original nuclear one (12%). The great importance economic interests play at the formation of new households becomes evident in the widely practiced custom of marriage between relatives. Such marriages account for 17% in metropolitan areas, up to 36% in villages and 37% in eastern Anatolia. The most often selected spouses are cousins.

Bride price. As pointed out previously, there is a functional relationship between family type and formation of marriage. In extended families the choice of a bride is made by the head of the family, and economic transactions accompany the marriage. In other words, marriage here is conceived as an alliance between families. Bride price payment permits heads of families to control the marriage of their offspring and also represents a kind of reciprocity in terms of indemnity for the loss in production of an element of the economic unit—in case the daughter is to be given away. In Timur's survey only 13% of the women said they made their own choice and 9% said they had to elope. Half of the men said they had decided for themselves.

As one would expect, prearranged marriages are more prevalent in rural areas due to the tendency of breaking up the transient extended family only after having met to a certain degree the expenditures undertaken for the wedding and the setting up of a new home. Thus the highest percentage for prearranged marriages is to be encountered in villages (63%) and the lowest level in metropolitan areas (19%) (Timur, 1972:83). From the regional point of view, parallel to the dominance of extended families, the two regions with the highest percentage of bride price practice are eastern Anatolia (77%) and the Black Sea (72%) areas. These regions are characterized by the high degree of female labor participation in production.

Form of marriage. Under the Swiss Civil Code, nonregistered marriages have no legal validity. Yet many Turkish citizens still prefer the informal or consensual marriage, or *imam nikahi* in Turkey's popular language. This concept is based solely on the pronouncement of a prayer with the intention to communicate the desire of the partners to establish marital union; no procedure takes place. Failure to comply with the civil marriage laws is partly due to complications in completing the required formalities. Another important factor is the persistence of eventually taking a second wife, even if the first marriage has been legal. (It cannot be overlooked that the concept of Christian monogamous marriage inherent in the Turkish Civil

Code is as alien to the traditional legal culture of Muslim Turks as polygamy is to Westerners.) While such marriages have in no sense been eradicated, their percentage of all marriages has declined significantly. This trend is in large measure the product of certain economic and legal incentives such as government pensions and legal inheritance entitlements for the spouses and children. Proof of an official marriage must be presented in order to participate in these entitlements. Timur's survey indicates that the percentage of polygamous marriages—usually bigamy in the form of one legal wedding and one informally chosen wife—is very small: 1% in cities and towns, 3% in villages (Timur, 1972:73).

At this point, a second question must be confronted: which factors support the practice of two ceremonies—a religious and a civil one? Timur's data indicate that in Turkey 35% of marriages have been solely civil, whereas 49% opted for a double ceremony and 15% were realized solely through religious prayers. Here again metropolitan areas rate highest in exclusively civil marriages (54%), while in one-fifth of the villages religious ceremony has been considered most desirable (Timur, 1972:91-92). The answer lies in psychocultural reasoning. As Williams states, the betrothed are culturally disposed to wanting a solemn blessing. Especially in the countryside, where the civil ceremony is not attended by the compensating resplendence of town weddings, the couple is apt to prefer prayers. Those who hold such beliefs find that two separate ceremonies are required to satisfy the competing demands of secular law and religious belief (Williams, 1982:163).

Age of marriage and fertility. Following the adoption of the Swiss Civil Code, the legal age of marriage was at first eighteen for males and seventeen for females. This requirement was culturally inappropriate and was amended in 1938, under popular pressure, to seventeen and fifteen for males and females, respectively, requirements that seem to coincide with the practice of the majority. Both Timur's and Kǎgitçibasi's surveys confirm that over 50% of Turkish women marry between the ages of fifteen and seventeen, and men marry at about age 22.

The early age of marriage obviously leads to a high level of fertility, which varies according to economic and social development. While the average number of children in rural areas of Turkey is 6.12%, it is around 3.88% in urban areas. Further broken down, we see that it totals 3.30% in Ankara, 2.91% in Izmir and 2.65% in Istanbul. A close relationship between fertility and education can be observed. While the average level of fertility among illiterate women is 4.2%, this average falls to 3.2% among literate, to 2.8% among primary school graduates, to 2% among secondary graduates and to 1.4% among university graduates (Timur, 1972:176).

Fertility also has been a topic of investigation as related to social change and development. The findings of Kăgitçibasi's research, which was part of a large-scale nine-country survey, have shown that socioeconomic factors affect people's perception, values and family dynamics. In turn, these factors, as social-psychological mechanisms, affect fertility behavior. Specifically, it has been found that with socioeconomic development and especially education, the economic value of children decreases, whereas the psychological value of children increases.

Of the three dimensions, the most important value appeared to be the economic contribution at young ages, and support in the future. Psychological value was perceived in the form of providing companionship, love and joy, and strengthening marital bonds. Finally, the social/normative value is reflected in children continuing the family name and contributing to society. Wherever social security is lacking and social welfare institutions are inadequate, and the needs of agriculture production are great, the value of sons is perceived very high; producing sons becomes a major goal. Here, the economic value of children is closely associated with the number of children. In rural areas 38% of women with two children in least developed areas want more children, whereas only 10% of those in most developed areas want more (Kağitçibasi, 1982:168). The degree of sex differentiation in this context was most vividly expressed in a forced-choice question, where son preference was found to be 84% as contrasted with a daughter preference of 16%. Sons were preferred by 92.5% of the men and 75% of women (Kağitçitasi, 1982:168).

Until the early 1960s, the Turkish government's official stand was to encourage population increase. After 1963, as part of the First Five Year Development Plan, the Ministry of Health set up an administrative unit for family planning and in 1965 a new law legalized the sale of contraceptives and the dissemination of information concerning them. However, the implementation of a family planning policy did not yield important results, as predominantly women who had behind them an average of four to five live births and eight to ten stillbirths volunteered for the use of intrauterine devices (IUD) and other contraceptives. Furthermore, the percentage of IUD use remained remarkably low; it did not exceed 8% in rural areas or 10% in urban areas (U.N. Fertility and Family Planning in Europe, 1976:155). The Turkish parliament passed in September 1983 a strongly worded amendment to the Turkish Penal Code that permits the termination of unwanted pregnancies up to

174

three months through abortion and the performance of abortion upon demand in public hospitals. Married women are obliged to submit a written permission from their husbands.

Power structure in the family. Family modernity and the power structure in the family are closely related to the prevailing family type. In both urban and rural areas, patriarchally extended families represent the most traditional, and nuclear families the least traditional. Timur's survey has attempted to measure modernity within the family by using the following indexes: visiting friends with the husband, permission to go out without a covered head, wearing short-sleeved dresses, permission to shop by herself, permission to visit female friends alone. The various modalities of behavior which were asked all relate to the degree of autonomy a woman is granted by her family in terms of dress code, going out of the house unchaperoned and socializing with persons other than relatives. The results indicate that where a patriarchal family relationship prevails, traditional behavior of women is expected, even in metropolitan centers such as Istanbul, Izmir and Ankara. Thus, the degree of modernity in the three big cities was 62% versus 3% in the villages, 28% versus 24% for transitional and 10% versus 72% for traditional families.

One of the most blatant examples of the impact of family type on the status of women reveals itself in eating patterns. In nuclear families living in villages, 91% eat together; in extended families of rural background this percentage is only 71%. In 23% of these families there is segregation at mealtime and in 5% of these the daughters-in-law eat separated even from other female members of the family (Timur, 1972:112-13). Regionally, this custom prevails in eastern Anatolia and the Black Sea while it does not play any importance in western Anatolia.

Given the overall segregated way of life in Turkish society, it seems rather logical that predominantly in rural areas and to some extent in urban areas as well, decisions concerning the selection of friends to visit, leisure time activities, type of dresses to be worn, spending of income and expenditure on food, are predominantly determined by the male head of the family. Independence of action is normally only encountered in metropolitan areas and in cases of fragmented, incomplete families with a female head of family.

Nevertheless, it would be erroneous to evaluate husband-wife relationships solely according to a dichotomy of traditional-modern family structure typology. Thus Olson's attempt to introduce a new dimension in this field by elaborating a so-called "duo-focal family structure" appears to be a fruitful approach. According to Olson a

Turkish marriage tends to be "more nearly a juxtaposition of two networks than the uniting of two individuals" (Olson, 1982:52). By and large, the husband is not the wife's primary confidante and parner. In other words, the partnership marriage built on strong emotional ties is a recent phenomenon in Turkish society, even where economic conditions have created a nuclear household.

Whether a married woman remains in her hometown/village or moves elsewhere, she will build a new network of female relatives, neighbors and peers, and her husband will do the same thing among the males. Even among the urban elite this bipolarity takes place, where husbands as a rule attend clubs, coffeehouses and restaurants with their friends. For the majority, marriage in Turkey is not likely to involve a unitary, highly "joint" relationship in which spouses look to each other as a primary source of advice, companionship, emotional support and entertainment. Rather, they continue to rely on the members of their own, primarily unisexual, social networks to satisfy these needs, as they did before marriage. These networks seem to disappear with increased geographical and social mobility, social isolation and residence in metropolitan area and professional activity.

Thus we may conclude that in Turkey the nuclear family system is not yet a complete unit with clear boundaries, but is more or less enmeshed in a visible, functionally extended family network.

In this light, it seems extremely important to inquire to what extent social change affected intrafamilial relationships. Kiray's analysis of Eregli's work shows that as social changes increase, the wife's subservience diminishes. Women, particularly mothers, function as buffers to provide a smooth change within family relationships, while also serving to adjust and integrate the changing family into their changing society.

Kiray's survey also proved that in major conflicts between father and son regarding the son's use of leisure time, marriage and choice of residence, an alliance between mother and son in rejecting the father's authority provided the channel to force the father to accept new modes of behavior. Another new change is coexistence after marriage with the children. While in the past custom required that sons take care of their parents, nowadays the trend is for separate homes for sons, and parents eventually living with the daughter and son-in-law. This change in attitude, of course, greatly enhances the prestige of daughters. Hence, in the absence of institutions that could provide security to the aged, the daughter acquires new function as a buffer mechanism and provides the balance required in a changing environment.

All in all, women in changing Turkey are able to assume new roles with the help of two behavioral characteristics learned from traditional relationships. The first is the skill in asserting her influence in an effective, though roundabout way; the second is her ability to adjust to a hostile environment with modesty but also with definite determination (Kiray, 1982:455).

Divorce

In all societies, marriage and divorce represent important legal institutions; they regulate the legitimacy of children and the unification or splitting up of property. But, aside from its legal implications, marriage and divorce are at the same time a kind of barometer with which social change and its repercussions on sex roles can be measured. In Turkey divorce seems to be encouraged by the interaction of four social conditions: (1) equality of both sexes before law, which secures women the right to initiate separation or divorce, (2) changes in fertility and mortality, (3) economic vulnerability, and (4) opportunities for separating households.

The spread of public health education, family planning and other services has significantly reduced infant mortality and fertility in Turkey. Women's traditional role of childbearing has substantially changed and alternative sex role expectations have emerged. Industrialization has produced marital stress and conflicting role expectations for women. Finally, soaring inflation and heavy costs of living have also raised the cost of divorce.

The Turkish Civil Code, in line with its source of inspiration, the Swiss Civil Code, has adopted some specific grounds for divorce: adultery, attempt on life, cruel treatment, infamous crime, dishonorable life, abandonment and insanity as well as one of a general nature—incompatibility (Arts. 129-34). These same grounds can be claimed in case of a demand for separation, which temporarily absolves the partners of the marital obligation of cohabitation (Art. 135).

In order to assess the frequency with which divorce is pronounced in Turkey, statistical records must be used; but they do not include the number of dissolved informal marriages. Divorce rates are commonly given in two indices. The first is known as the Crude Divorce Rate, showing the number of divorces per 10,000 population (table 7). The second, the Refined Divorce Rate, reflects the number of divorces per 10,000 married females. In Turkey both rates show a steady increase from 1936 to 1956, followed by a gradual decline. When compared to the experience of most developed countries since the 1950s, Turkey's reversal of the general tendency toward divorce since 1956 seems unusual.

Table 7
Crude Divorce Rate in Selected Countries, 1976
Per 10,000 Population

United States	50.2
USSR	33.5
West Germany	26.7
England	25.6
Canada	23.4
Finland	21.4
Romania	16.8
Switzerland	15.1
France	12.7
Japan	11.1
Israel	9.5
Iran	5.4
Syria	4.9
Turkey	3.5

Source: 1977 U.N. Demographic Yearbook.

From this table and other statistics it is clear that the official crude divorce rate for Turkey is the lowest rate in the world.

Some general patterns have emerged in the 1970s in Turkish cases. More than 50% of all divorce cases occur in childless marriages. Almost half of the divorced male population falls between the ages of 25 and 34. Of the divorced female population, almost half are in the 20-29 age group. Almost half of the divorces occur in the first four years of marriage. Finally, there is a clear trend for divorce among the urban population as compared to rural (table 8).

From the regional point of view, there is a clear east-west gradient in divorce rates, with rates rising consistently from east to west. Provinces with higher divorce rates are indicating lower fertility, smaller household size, higher literacy and education level—all indicators pointing toward a change in the traditional female role. There seems to be a close relationship between pressure on urban job markets, housing and urban services and the ability to maintain separate households. In addition to limited growth of personal income, there are also restrictions in housing. Few single persons can afford to set up a separate household; and the pressure on a married couple to maintain a house in spite of marital stress becomes very strong. Thus one may say that economic necessity has reinforced family structure.

Table 8
Number of Divorces by Permanent Residence of Couples

Year	Urban	Percent of total	Rural	Percent of total
1974	6,613	57	4,934	43
1977	8,884	66	4,542	34
1979	9,733	67	4,807	33

Source: *Bosanma Istatistikleri* (Divorce Statistics), Ankara 1973; 1978; 1980.

A detailed study on divorce in Turkey by Levine has indicated that divorce is more associated with developed agriculture than with industrialization. In relation to education, men and women who have the lowest divorce rates are those who are completely illiterate, while those who have the highest divorce rates are those who are just literate (Levine, 1982:332). Levine defines this group as the "urban poor."

Is there a relationship between divorce and sex roles? In rural, agricultural communities in Turkey there are still solidly anchored conservative roles for men and women. When these people migrate to the urban areas, roles change only slowly. However, in an urban, industrial society, men and women are expected to play interchangeable roles. In such transition periods people are confused in their behavior; such confusion may frequently become the reason for divorce and may partly explain the Turkish experience.

Nevertheless it has to be stated that avoidance of making use of divorce reinforces the authoritarian, patriarchal family. Therefore one may argue that divorce represents a struggle against conservatism, an act of female emancipation. Whether in each case divorce secures women a better position in the socioeconomic and social realm is debatable. For Levine, at least, increase in divorce represents an intensification of the social struggles for economic development and increasing social equality (Levine, 1982:344). by 1970, incompatibility was listed as grounds in 80% of divorces. Although men and women have sought divorce in roughly equal numbers, an increasing tendency for divorce to be awarded to women is noticeable. In 1960, divorces awarded to the plaintiff wife accounted for 44.9%; in 1979 this percentage rose to 58.4% (Williams, 1982:539). The following factors may explain this tendency: first, in a mutual consent case the normal strategy calls for the wife to file the suit. Second, a gradual but real increase in the economic independence of educated women can be noticed. Finally, time, education and improved communication have raised women's (and men's) general awareness of their legal rights.

Honor Crimes and Blood Feud
The difficulties rural women face in regard to social change and a new code of behavior are closely related to the values of their communities. In traditional Turkish culture a central value is placed on the concept of honor. Honor may refer to a man's reputation as a participant in the community (*seref*) or may refer to his reputation as determined by the chastity of the women in his family *(namus)*. Threats to *namus* may originate in the behavior of a man's wife or unmarried daughter or sister, or in gossip concerning the man's ability to control his women. Any threat to *namus* calls for punishment and lost *namus* can be completely restored only by killing the male offender and perhaps the guilty woman as well. Normally, the defense of honor is a man's duty, but might exceptionally be also expected from the woman. Interestingly enough, the practice to legitimize endogamic marriage in almost all Mediterranean countries has logically lead to the dictum that "Killing in defense of family honor...is a socially expected and approved behavior" (Safilios-Rotschild, 1969). French anthropologist Tillion explains that as soon as marriage between cousins is admissible, the network of the blood related kinship constitutes a source of permanent social control, which again leaves little if no independency for its members, mostly, of course, the female ones (Tillion, 1966). Furthermore, "honor crimes" are far from purely personal events; on the contrary they are and must be publicly known and communally validated. In other words, honor crimes are community expected and approved actions. Excellent examples can be found in Turkish and Greek fiction, such as Halide Edip's "Kill the Whore" (Vurun Kahpeyi) and Kazancaki's "Zorba, the Greek"; in each case a widow has to pay for her nonapproved infatuation to a man by being stoned by the community.

Blood feud may be considered a special case of the honor crime. The reasons are manifold: loss of someone's *seref* or *namus* (honor), land dispute, etc. Whatever the origin, once the initial killing has occurred, members of the victim's clan feel honor bound to avenge

180

his death. The duty for women is to raise their children with feelings of unextinguishable hatred and revenge. This leads to a self-perpetuating cycle of vengeance. The tradition survives most strongly in the more traditional segment of Turkish society—isolated villages and small towns as well as certain shantytown districts. According to the most recent statistics, strongholds of "vendetta" are mostly (a) the less developed regions of Anatolia, namely the southeast (26.1%); (b) the Black Sea coast (25.6%); and (c) central Anatolia (16.6%) (*SIS*, Criminal Statistics, 1981: 237-47).

A recent study on this subject by two women social psychologists (S. Ozgur and D. Sunar) tried to explain the high incidence of honor crimes and related homicides, as well as common murders. According to these authors, individuals who are tightly knit into the relational system of family, clan and village, and those groups who occupy low status positions might tend to solve their stress situations by simply eliminating the major adversary.

The clash of urban global culture versus parochial, traditional culture is best expressed in Kemal's fiction, "The Murder of Demirci," where the leader of the clan gives his nephew the following advice: "Never leave your clan. You may stay hungry or thirsty, you may even have to beg, still don't give up your tribe!" (Kemal, 1974:301).

These strong ties explain an important feature of the high juvenile delinquency rate among blood feud convicts. Unsal's recent survey reveals that in a sample of 100 criminals involving vendetta action, 50% of the offenders were between 12-16 years of age, another 19% were between 17 and 21, and 23% were between 22 and 31 years old. Thirty-nine percent came from families of five to seven members, 30% from families of 8-10 persons, 71% were bachelors, 59% were the second, third or fourth child in the family. Finally, the most important characteristic: 80% were living in absolute economic dependency on their family, and 53% of their origins were mountain and forest villages.

For these youngsters the fear of social ostracism has been extraordinarily high; 44% claimed that if they did not save the family's "honor," nobody would "look in their face." This situation explains also why two-thirds (65%) of those interviewed in Unsal's survey refuse to go back to their family and home town, once released from imprisonment. The major reason given was to avoid a new provocation, a new induced crime, a second condemnation.

Two important factors, then, are visible in cases of honor crimes: the oppressing force of communal approval or rejection and the compulsion for women to raise and educate their sons for revenge—a socialization pattern that prohibits any kind of softening of mores and the establishment for more tolerant and permissive rules. It is obvious that with the fast-changing social and economic fabric of Turkish society and the strengthening of administrative security measures, blood feud and honor crime practices will decline. But this process will take time; the free development of boys and girls to achieve independent personalities will continue to be hindered for some time.

THE FAMILY AND TURKISH LEGAL CULTURE

This chapter has concentrated mostly on empirical data obtained with the help of applied social sciences such as sociology, psychology, and anthropology. Since, however, Turkey's social reforms came about from an attempt to replace an Islamic legal system with a Western legal system, it seems imperative to assess the evolution of the Turkish legal culture. This concept has been defined by Friedman as the "network of values and attitudes relating to law which determines when, why and where people turn to the law or away" (Friedman, 1969:1004). By using this yardstick we can evaluate the way legal reforms have functioned in Turkey. First, a historical perspective will be discussed.

The Pre-Islamic Period

Little is known about the legal life of the early Turkic people. The information that is available is based upon early Chinese writings and modern archeological and ethnographic research.

Turks placed strong emphasis on the importance of the family. The patriarchal family with the father as the ultimate authority was the norm. Although women were under the guardianship of father or husband—with the exception of taking military and official positions—they assumed important roles. In the ruling class a woman occupied an almost identical position with her spouse. Because society was so often at war, women enjoyed a certain freedom in managing the affairs of the family. Women were neither closeted in harems nor obliged to cover themselves before men. The only condition required for marriage was consent of the guardians and the couple. The state was not involved in the marriage contract.

Islamic Law in Ottoman Turkey

During the tenth and eleventh centuries, Turks all over Central Asia and the Middle and Near East were gradually, but not forceably, converted to Islam (Kinross, 1977:16). By this time Islamic Law had undergone more than four hundred years of development, and the Ottoman

Turks inherited a Holy Law that admitted no further creative development. Thus, while Islamic Law experienced further refinements in some areas, the Sunni norms governing marriage and divorce (and inheritance) remained set and static. Ottomans adopted this law so thoroughly that the old Turkish legal culture lost its distinct identity, resulting in a lessened status of Turkish women in both society and family. In the nineteenth century, with the advent of the Tanzimat edict in 1839, imitative self-defense reforms, strongly influenced by the Westernizers, were adopted. In 1871 a commission was established to rewrite the Holy Law of obligations and contracts using relevant western codes as a guide, but its product, the ''Mecelle,'' did not touch the core of the Sacred Law, the Law of the Family. Nevertheless the Ottomans developed institutions by which they could monitor, if not regulate, the institution of marriage. The iman was required to notify state authorities of all marriages, and thus the iman's role became that of an official marriage registrar (Cin, 1974:287).

At the beginning of the twentieth century, in 1917, a special code for marriage and divorce was drafted. Although this code, adopted by the last Ottoman parliament and later repealed in 1919 under pressure from Islamic reactionaries, fell far short of bringing progressive rights. It approved of marriages at the age of nine for girls and ten for boys, and of polygamy. The only progressive aspect of this code was the prohibition of ''cradle marriages'' and the acceptance of certain conditions for the oath of repudiation—the right of divorce, recognized one-sided only the husband. This explains why Atatürk refused to discuss this project in the National Assembly after the creation of the Turkish Republic (Abadan-Unat, 1981:12).

Adoption of the Swiss Civil Code

Atatürk, determined to fight against the conservative forces gathered around the Ministry of the Sharia, succeeded in passing legislation that changed the ideological scope of public life. On March 3, 1924 he secured the right to an education for both sexes by abolishing the Caliphate and passing a Law for the Unification of Instruction.

Determined not to wait for long-term evolutionary processes, Atatürk proceeded to use codification to accelerate social change. On February 17, 1926, the Turkish parliament adopted a slightly modified version of the Swiss Civil Code (found by the commission to be the most suitable to the principle of secularism). For Atatürk and his supporters, the granting of equality before law for men and women was the realization of a promise given long before, a symbol to the world that the new Turkey was adamant about ''reaching a level of contemporary civilization" (Atatürk, 1926).

The Turkish Civil Code, which became effective on October 4, 1926, made polygamy illegal and gave equal rights in divorce; thus formally ensuring the freedom and equality of women. In divorce, custody of the children was now given to both parents (Art. 262); a judge decided which parent should have custody (Art. 264). In practice, custody for children under ten years of age is usually given to the mother. In case of death, custody is entrusted to the remaining spouse. Marriage by proxy was abolished and marriage, in order to be valid, had to take place in the presence of the bride. Equality in heritance was granted (Art. 439) and equality in regard to testimony was accepted.

Finally, the new code prescribed a minimum age for marriage. At first the limit was eighteen for men and seventeen for women, but later, in 1938, these limits were reduced to seventeen and fifteen, respectively; the absolute minimum age in special circumstances was kept for men, but lowered to fourteen for women (Art. 85).

How egalitarian is the Turkish Civil Code? Its model, the Swiss Civil Code, imbued with certain democratic values, nevertheless reflected a traditional point of view. Meanwhile, Swiss cantons realized gradual amendments that substantially improved the code. In Turkey a special commission has been working on certain amendments for the past twenty years without presenting a new draft to the public.

At present there is no absolute equality between husband and wife; the husband is head of the family. The wife cannot represent the marital union (Art 154). The husband alone is entitled to choose a domicile and the wife must follow him (Art. 152, II). The wife is required to participate in the expenses of the household by contributing financially or by assuming tasks in the household (Art. 190). If the wife wants to assume a profession or work outside the household, she must obtain the tacit approval or consent of the husband (Art. 195). However, the wife is free to dispose of her material goods; in marriage the rule is separation of property and goods.

How did this legal transplantation function? Although Turkey's choice to adopt a Western legal code provided a favorable climate for change in the status of women, it assumed real importance only where socioeconomic structural changes totally changed the outlook of both sexes. Here the Code plays an important role in serving as an instrument for the recognition of rights. In areas with a predominant feudal character, however, the Code has had little impact. Thus legal dualism still exists to some degree. Proof of this is most evident in the situation of those children—fruits of de facto marital unions—who are deprived of their civic identity unless a legal correction takes place. This vital problem was solved in two ways: from 1933 to 1956, so-called "amnesty" laws legally recognized the paternity of such children and issued birth certificates to a total of 7,724,419 children in 1950 (Abadan-Unat, 1963:23). After 1960 the lawmakers, realizing that the need and right of each individual to secure a judiciary remedy in case of personal identity is under constitutional guarantee, adopted Law No. 2526, which introduced a simplified procedure for recognizing paternity. At the same time the constitutions of 1961 and 1982, recognizing the paramount importance of the family and of mother and child in particular, entrusted the state to take special measures of protection.

With the changing social structure of Turkish society, demands for radical changes in the Turkish Civil Code in the way of more equal rights have been advanced in the press and through the mediation of women's associations. During the Women's Year in 1975 the following demands were proclaimed by twenty-seven women's associations:

1. The status of family should not be confined solely to the husband.
2. The wife should not be obliged to adopt the husband's family name.
3. The prerogative of a husband to forbid his wife the practice of a profession or employment should be abolished.
4. Legal, educational and administrative measures should be implemented aiming at the abolishment of the "bride price."
5. The prohibition of a religious ceremony before a civil marriage has been registered should be reinforced.
6. In order to equalize tax obligations, individual income tax declarations for husband and wife should be required.
7. The right to join the armed forces should be reinstituted.
8. Women civil servants and workers should be able to take one paid year leave of absence after childbirth.
9. The agricultural Social Insurance bill should be passed in priority in order to assure peasant women social security rights.
10. The living conditions of prostitutes should be improved.
11. Female children, who have been apparently "adopted" but are in fact employed in domestic service (besleme) should not be left without legal protection, their exploitation should be strictly forbidden (Abadan-Unat, 1981; 15).

As one can detect, some of these demands reflect serious social problems while others represent imperfections in a functioning legal system.

At present the Turkish parliament has incorporated on the agenda of the legislative year 1985-1986 a very comprehensive bill to modify various sections of the Turkish Civil Code. The bill contains a number of progressive amendments all in favor of equalizing the status of women and men. However, a systematic mobilization of public opinion in favor of the bill has not been realized so far.

CONCLUSION

The Turkish society is a highly complex, heterogeneous one with a diversity of ethnic, cultural and religious conglomerations differentiated along social class, rural-urban and development dimensions. Various lines of historical-cultural influence have molded this society, the main ones being nomadic-Turkish, Anatolian, Islamic Middle Eastern and the Mediterranean.

Furthermore, such rapid social change involves, on the one hand, modifications of social structure and on the other hand modifications in attitudes, beliefs and values. More specifically, shifts in the demographic composition of the rural and urban areas, increased differentiation and specialization of production, industrial growth and other related changes in economy and social structure precipitate modifications in family structure, functioning and dynamics. It is obviously impossible to describe such a complex phenomenon within the scope of one chapter. The major topics to which special attention has been devoted are (a) major socioeconomic changes as related to demographic growth, urbanization, labor force participation and education, (b) change within sex role distribution in accordance to a rural-urban typology, (c) structural aspects of Turkish family life involving bride price practice, form and age of marriage, fertility patterns, power structure in the family, divorce, blood feud and honor crimes, and finally (d) the impact of Turkish legal culture on women and the family as influenced by the adoption of the Swiss Civil Code.

All available empirical data indicate that the change of the traditional agrarian society through the waves of rural to urban migration and international migration has produced the most noticeable changes. Thus one may observe that concomitant to geographic mobility, there is also a factor we may call "psychological mobility."

The dynamic nature of the family in Turkey as it undergoes modification reveals itself in the prevalence of nuclear families, the life cycle of the rural family as well as in the establishment of matrilocal households due to economic necessity. However, even when conjugal families live in separate households, there is still the material support of what can be called the "functionally extended family."

Today, civil marriage is practiced with or without an additional religious ceremony. Rural marriages appear to assume more of a social than individual or conjugal character, and seem rather to serve as an establisher of economic and social ties.

The second class status of women in the Middle East is also seen in Turkey. In recent years the position of the "woman" has improved more than that of the "young woman" who is still subject to strict social control. Clearly defined sex roles, division of labor and separate social networks may both help the woman endure the status difference and yet at the same time serve to reinforce and perpetuate this difference. Education and professionalization of women appear to be the key to psychological mobilizers rather than mere participation in the labor force. Women's work is hardly the modernizer it is assumed to be. The most striking changes in regard to sex role distribution are closely linked to fast urbanization and international migration.

Finally, in evaluating the revolutionary experiment of using the law as an instrument of social change, one must start by accepting that the Turkish Civil Code is not perceived as being ideal. For conservatives it has remained alien to tradition and custom; for progressives it is not egalitarian enough. The first group would eventually wish to return to the Sharia. The adherents of this view, although strong in certain areas, have thinned out greatly in recent years. At the other end of the spectrum, the second group argues that the more progressive and modern aspects of the intent of the law have been intentionally neglected by a conservative judiciary. Between the two poles lies the majority view that the Code is essentially well-suited to the needs of the people. The merit of the majority view lies in the effort of the judiciary, who succeeded in introducing a foreign system of family law into the Turkish legal culture. That a civil court of law, however costly, inconvenient and time-consuming, rather than a council of elders or an iman should decide matters of family law is largely accepted as a fact of modern life in Turkey. Thus, one can conclude that the Turkish Family Law has been able to shed its Swiss identity and acquire its own Turkish identity as a constituent element of Turkish legal culture. Finally, one can agree that the idealistic vision of the modernized society of Atatürk has provided Turkey's increasingly aware womanhood with an excellent framework for further emancipation, freedom and social participation.

BIBLIOGRAPHY

Abadan—Unat, N. 1963. *Social Change and Turkish Women*. Ankara: Ankara University.

_____. 1964. *Batı Almanya'daki Türk Iscileri ve Sorunları* (Turkish Workers and Their Problems in West Germany). Ankara: DPT.

_____. 1964. Turkish Migration to Europe (1960-1975), A Balance Sheet of Achievements and Failures, *Batı Almanya'daki Türk Iscileri ve Sorunları,* 61, table 37; 125, table 113; 131, table 121; 140, table 135; 200. table 208. In *The Turkish Workers in Federal Germany and Their Problems.* Ankara: DPT.

_____. 1967. Turkey. In *Women in the Modern World,* R. Patai, ed. pp. 94-95. New York: Free Press.

_____. 1971. La Recession de 1966/67 en Allemagne Federale et ses repercussions sur les ouvriers turcs. *The Turkish Yearbook of International Relations* 46.

_____. 1975. Educational Problems of Turkish Migrants' Children. *International Review of Education.* Special issue 31:312.

_____, ed. 1976. *Turkish Workers in Europe, 1960-1975.* Leiden: E. J. Brill.

_____. 1977. Impact of Migration on Emancipation and Pseudo-Emancipation of Turkish Women. *International Migration Review* 2, 1:32-33.

_____. 1978a. The Modernization of Turkish Women. *The Middle East Journal.* pp. 291-306.

_____. 1978b. Women's Movements and National Liberation: The Turkish Case. Paper presented at the 9th World Congress of Sociology, ISA, Uppsala, August 14-19.

_____. 1979. Die Politischen Auswirkungen der turkischen Migration in Inund Ausland. *Orient* 123.

_____. 1980-81. Movements of Women and National Liberation: The Turkish Case. *Journal of the American Institute for the Study of Middle Eastern Civilization* 1, 3-4:4-16.

_____. 1981. Social Change and Turkish Women, 1926-1976. In *Women in Turkish Society.* Leiden: E. J. Brill.

_____, ed. 1981. *Women in Turkish Society.* Leiden: E. J. Brill.

_____. 1981. Women in Government as Policymakers and Bureaucrats: The Turkish Case. In *Women, Power and Political Systems,* M. Rendel, ed. pp. 94-115. London: Croom Helm.

_____. 1981. The Effects of International Labor Migration on Women's Role: The Turkish Case. In *Sex Roles, Family and Community in Turkey,* 0. Kağıtçıbaşı, ed. Bloomington, Indiana: Indiana University

Turkish Studies 3.

Abadan-Unat, N., et al. 1976. *Migration and Development*. Ankara: Ajansturk.

Adelman, I. and C. T. Morris. 1973. *Economic Growth and Social Equity in Developing Countries*. Stanford, California: Stanford University Press.

Adıvar, Halide Edip. 1967. *Mor Salkimli Ev*. Istanbul: Atlas Kitabevi. 2nd ed. pp. 22-23.

Adler, S. 1975. People in the Pipeline. Unpublished dissertation, Massachusetts Institute of Technology.

Akpınar, U. 1977. Angleichungsprobleme turkischer Arbeiterfamilien. In *Turkische Migrantenfamilien*. G. Mertens and U. Akpinar, eds. pp. 135-300. Bonn: Sonderheft 2.

Arıburun, K. 1951. *The Istanbul Open Air Meetings During the War of Independence (Millı Mücadelede Istanbul Mitingleri*, Turkish). Ankara.

   Atatürk'ün Söylev ve Demecleri II, (Atatürk Speeches and Declarations) 21 January 1923:147-48.

Basgöz, I. 1976. Toronto'ya Göcümüz. *Özgür İnsan* 29:80-85.

Baumgartner-Karabak, A., and G. Landesberger. 1978. *Die Verkauften Braeute: Turkische Frauen zwischen Kreuzberg und Anatolien*. Hamburg: Reinbeck.

Beard, Mary R. 1946. *Women as Force in History*. London: Collier-MacMillan.

Beck, L. and N. Keddie, eds. 1978. *Women in the Muslim World*. Cambridge: Harvard University Press.

Benata, F. 1970. *Le Travail Feminin en Algerie*. Alger: SNED.

Benedict, P. 1974. The Kabul Günü Structured Visit in an Anatolian Provincial Town. *Anthropological Review* 47:28-47.

_____. 1974. *Ula, An Anatolian Town*. Leiden: E. J. Brill.

Benedict, P., et al. 1974. *Turkey—Geographic and Social Perspectives*. Leiden: E. J. Brill.

Beneria, L. 1978. Production, Reproduction and the Sexual Division of Labor. *ILO Working Paper,* series WEP 10 (WP .2) July.

Benhert, H., L. Florn and H. Fraistein. 1974. Psychische Storungen bei auslaendischen Arbeitnehmer. *Nervenarzt* 45:76-87.

Berger, J., and J. Mohr. 1975. *A Seventh Man. The Story of a Migrant Worker in Europe*. New York: Penquin.

Berkes, Niyazi. 1959. *Turkish Nationalism and Western Civilization*. London.

Beşikçi, Ismail. 1969. *Doğuda Degişim ve Yapıtsal Sorunlar*. Ankara. p. 187.

Blumer, H. 1957. Collective Behavior. In *Review of Sociology Analysis of a Decade,* J. Gittler, ed. p. 127. New York: Wiley & Sons.

Bott, E. 1957. *Family and Social Network*. London: Tavistock.

Boulding, E. 1977. *Women in the Twentieth Century World.* New York: Wiley & Sons.

Bundesanstalt fur Arbeit. 1973. *Repreasentativuntersuchung '72.* Beschaeftigung auslaendischer Arbeitnehmer.

Bundesministerium fur Jugend, Familie und Gesundheit. 1977. *Situationsanalyse nichterwerbstaetiger Ehefrauen auslaendischer Arbeiternehmer in der BDR.* pp. 180-81.

Castles, S., and G. Kossack. 1973. *Immigrant Workers and Class Structure in Western Europe.* London.

Çaka, C. 1948. *War and Women in History* (in Turkish, *Tarih Boyunca Harp ve Kadın*). Ankara.

Choucri, N. 1977. Migration Processes Among Developing Countries: The Middle East. Paper for APSA Meeting, September 1-4.

CIME. 1979. *Fourth Seminar on Adaptation and Integration of Permanent Immigrants.* May 8-11. Geneva.

Cin, H. 1974. *İslam ve Osmanlı Hukukunda Evlenme.* (Marriage in Islamic and Ottoman Law). 1974. Ankara: Ankara Universitesi.

Çitçi, 0. 1975. *Turkish Public Administration Annual.* Ankara.

——————. 1979. Türkiye'de kadın sorunu ve çalışan kadınlar' (The Problem of Women in Turkey and Working Women). Unpublished Ph.D. thesis. Ankara.

Coşar, O. S. 1973. Çakırcalı Mehmet Efe. *Milliyet,* June 9.

Danielson, M. N. and R. Keles. 1985. *Urban Development and Politics in Turkey, Government and Growth in Ankara and Istanbul.* New York: Holmes and Meyer.

DIE, 1976. *1975 Nüfus Sayımı.* DIE. Ankara.

Dirks, Sabine. 1969. *La Famille Musulmane Turque.* Paris and The Hague: Mouton.

Duben, A. 1982. The Significance of Family and Kinship in Urban Turkey. In *Sex Roles, Family and Community in Turkey,* C. Kağıtçıbaşı, ed. Bloomington, İndiana: Indiana University Turkish Studies 3.

Edib, Halide. 1963. *Conflict of East and West in Turkey.* 3rd edition. Lahore: Sh. Muhammad Ashraf.

Epstein, Cynthia Fuchs. 1970. *Woman's Place.* Berkeley: University of California Press.

Engelbrektsson, U. 1978. *The Force of Tradition, Turkish Migrants at Home and Abroad.* Acta Universitatis Gothoburgen sis.

Erdentuğ, N. 1964. Bazı Devrek Köy Toplumlarında Kadının Mevkii. (The Status of Women in Some Devrek Type Village Communities). *Antropoloji Dergisi* 1:2.

Ergil, D. 1978. Sociological Analysis of Honor Crimes in Turkey. *METU Studies in Development* 12:26-65.

Ergil, G. 1977. *Toplumsal Yapi Arastirmasi. Nüfus ile İlgili Gelismeler* (Social Structure Study: Population Development Trends). State Planning Organization.

Erder, L. 1981. The Women of Turkey: A Demographic Overview. In *Women in Turkish Society,* Abadan-Unat, ed. pp. 41-58. Leiden: E. J. Brill.

Erder, T. 1981. *Situation and Problems of Unpaid Working Women in Turkey.* Council of Europe, CDSO (81) 49.

Esenkova, Pervin. 1951. La Femme Turque Contemporaine, Education et Role Social. *BLA* Tunis, p. 285.

Fairchild, H. P. 1925. *Immigration.* New York: Macmillan.

Fallers, L. and M. Fallers. 1976. Sex Role in Edremit. In *Mediterranean Family Structures,* J. Peristiany, ed., pp. 243-60.

Freedman, M. ed. 1967. Levels of Change in Yugoslav Kinship. *Social Organization.* Chicago: Aldine.

Friedman, L. M. and S. Macauley, eds. 1969. *Law and the Behavior Sciences.* New York: Bobbs-Merril.

Galtung, J. 1971. A Structural Theory of Imperialism. *Journal of Peace Research* 8:81-117.

Gonzalez, N. L. S. 1961. Family Organization in Five Types of Migratory Wage Labour. *American Anthropologist* 63:1264-1280.

Goode, W. J. 1963. *World Revolution and Family Patterns.* New York: Free Press.

_____. 1964. *The Family.* Englewood Cliffs, NJ: Prentice-Hall.

Gülmez, M. 1972. Türk Kamu Görevlilerinin Sayisal Evrimi. (The Numerical Evolution of Turkish Public Servants. *Amme Idaresi Dergisi* 6, 3, September.

Gürel, S. and A. Kudat. 1978. Türk Kadınının Avrupa'ya Göcünün Kişilik Aile ve Topluma Yansıyan Sonuçları. *SBF Journal* 33:3-4, 115-18.

Gokalp, Ziya. 1970. *Türkçülügün Esasları.*

Hauser, P.M., and L. F. Schnore. 1965. *The Study of Urbanization.* New York.

Helling, G. 1966. *The Turkish Village as a Social System.* Omaha.

Holtbrugge, H. 1975. *Turkische Familien in der BDR, Erziehungsvorstellungen und familiale Rollen und Autoritaetsstruktur.* Verlag der Sozialwissenschaftlichen Kooperative, p. 116.

Indian Council of Social Science Research. 1975. *Status of Women, A Synopsis of the Report of the National Committee.* New Delhi.

International Organization for Labour—ILO. 1974. *Some Growing Employment Problems in Europe, Report I.* Geneva: ILO. 97.

ILO. 1977. *The Effects of Technological Changes on Conditions of Work and Employment in Postal and Telecommunications Services.*

Inan, A. I. 1965. *Fiili Birleşmelerle bunlardan doğan çoçukların tesciline dair kanun, yönetmelik ve sözleşmeler* (Les Lois, l'administration et les conventions concernant l'enregistrement des enfants des unions illegitimes). Ankara.

_____. 1969. *Medeni Bilgiler ve Mustafa Kemal Atatürk'ün El Yazilari.* Ankara.

_____. 1975. *The Rights and Duties of Turkish Women in History.* (Tarih Boyunca Türk Kadınının hak ve görevleri) Ankara: Başbakanlik Besımevı, p. 81.

Jelin. E. 1977. Migration and Labor Force Participation of Latin American Women: The Domestic Servants in the Cities. In *Women and National Development: The Complexity of Change.* Wellesley Editorial Committee, p. 133. Chicago: Illinois University Press.

Johansen, U. Die guten Sitten des Essens und Trinken. *Sociologus* 23, 1:41-70.

Kağıtçıbaşı C. 1975. *Value of Children.* Paper presented at the Second Turkish Demography Conference, Cesme, Izmir, Sept 29-Oct 1.

_____. 1980. Women and Development in Turkey. Paper presented at the International Seminar on Rural Women and Development, Cairo, December.

_____. Value of Children, Women's Role and Fertility in Turkey. In *Women in Turkish Society,* N. Abadan-Unat, ed. pp. 74-95. Leiden: E. J. Brill.

_____, ed. 1982. *Sex Roles, Family and Community in Turkey.* Indiana University Turkish Studies 3:151-80.

Kandiyoti, D. 1974a. Some Social, Psychological Dimensions of Social Change in a Turkish Village. *The British Journal of Sociology* 25,1:47-62.

_____. 1974b. Social Change and Social Stratification. *Journal of Peasant Studies* 12:206-19.

_____. 1976. Characteristics of Turkey's Industrial Workers in the Istanbul-Izmit Complex. Paper presented at the OPSSME Workshop, Khartoum, 20.

_____. 1977. Sex Roles and Social Change: A Comparative Appraisal of Turkey's Women. *Signs* 3:57-73.

_____. 1981. Dimensions of Psycho-Social Change in Women: An Inter-Generational Comparison. In *Women in Turkish Society,* N. Abadan-Unat, ed. pp. 233-58. Leiden: E. J. Brill.

Karal, Enver Ziya. 1975. Kadın Hakları Sorunu ve Atatürk. *Türk Dili* 32, 290:608.

Karpat, K. 1976. *The Gecekondu: Rural Migration and Urbanization.* London: Cambridge University.

Kazgan, G. 1978. Türkiye 'de Kadın Eğitimi ve Kadın Çalısması (Women's Education and Work in Turkey). *Toplum ve Bilim* 5:37.

_____. 1981. Labour Force Participation, Occupational Distribution,

Educational Attainment and the Socioeconomic Status of Women in the Turkish Economy. In *Women in Turkish Society,* N. Abadan-Unat, ed. pp. 131-59. Leiden: E. J. Brill.

Keles, R. 1972. *Türkiye 'de Kentleşme, Konut ve Gecekondu* (Urbanization, Housing and Gecekondu in Turkiye). Istanbul: Gercek Yayinevi.

_____. 1974. *Urbanization in Turkey.* New York: Ford Foundation.

Kent-Koop. 1982. *Konut '81.* (Housing '81). Ankara.

Kinross, J. 1977. *The Ottoman Centuries: The Rise and Fall of the Turkish Empire.* New York: Morrow.

Kıray, M. 1964. *Ereğli: Ağır Sanayıden Evvel Bir Sahil Kasabasi* Ankara: DPT.

_____. 1968. Values, Social Stratification and Development. *Journal of Social Issues* 24, 2:87-102.

_____. 1976. Changing Roles of Mothers: Changing Intra-Family Relations in a Turkish Town. In *Mediterreanean Family Structures,* J. Peristiany, ed. pp. 261-71. London: Cambridge.

_____. 1976. The Family of the Migrant Worker. In *Turkish Workers in Europe 1960-1975,* N. Abadan-Unat, ed. p. 234. Leiden: E. J. Brill.

Koçer, Hasan Ali. 1978. Türkiye'de Kadın Eğıtimi. *A. Ü. Egitim Fakultesi Dergisi,* p. 116.

Kongar, Emre. 1970. Survey of Familial Changes in Two Turkish Gecekondu Areas. Paper submitted to the Social Anthropological Conference, Nicosia, September.

Koutopoulos, K. M. 1972. Women's Liberation as a Social Movement. In *Toward a Sociology of Women,* Constantina Safilios-Rotschild, ed. p. 355. Xerox Corp.

Kudat A. 1975. Structural Changes in the Migrant Turkish Family. In *Manpower Mobility Across Cultural Boundaries: Social, Economic and Legal Aspects,* R. E. Krane, ed. p. 88. Leiden: E. J. Brill.

_____. 1975. *Stability and Change in the Turkish Family at Home and Abroad:* Comparative Perspectives. Pre-print Series No. P/75-6. Berlin: Science Center of Berlin. 18.

_____, et al. 1975. *Yurt Dısına İşgücü Göçünün Yöresel Boyutlari* (The Regional *Dimensions of Turkey's External Migration*) Mimeo. Table 27.

Kuyaş, N. F. The Effects of Female Labor on Power Relations in the Urban Turkish Family. In *Sex Roles, Family and Community in Turkey,* C. Kağıtçıbaşı, ed. pp. 181-205. Bloomington, Indiana: Indiana University Turkish Studies 3.

Laslett, P. and R. Wall, eds. 1976. *Household and Family in Past Time.* London: Cambridge University Press.

Lerner, D. 1958. *The Passing of Traditional Society.* Glencoe, IL: The Free Press 49.

Levine, N. 1982. Social Change and Family Crisis: The Nature of Turkish Divorce. In *Sex Roles, Family and Community in Turkey,* C. Kağıtçıbaşı, ed. pp. 323-348. Bloomington, Indiana: Indiana University Turkish Studies 3.

Litvak, E. 1965. Extended Kin Relations in an Industrial Democratic Society. In *Social Structure and the Family: Generational Relations,* E. Shanas and G. F. Streib, eds. Englewood Cliffs, NJ: Prentice Hall.

Lorenz, Charlotte. 1918. Die Frauenfrage im Osmanischen Reiche mit besonder Berucksichtigung der arbeitenden Klasse. *Die Welt des Islams* 6:82.

Maehrlaender, U. 1974. *Soziale Aspekte der Auslaenderbeschaeftigung.* Bonn: Verlag Neue Gesellschaft. Tables 12 and 13.

Magnarella, P. J. 1974. *Tradition and Change in a Turkish Town,* New York: Schenkman.

_____. 1979. *The Peasant Venture, Tradition, Migration and Change among Georgian Peasants in Turkey.* New York: Schenkman.

Mansur, F. 1967. The Position of Women in Turkish Society. Unpublished manuscript.

_____. 1972. *Bodrum: A Town in the Agean.* Leiden: E. J. Brill.

Mehrlaender, U. 1974. *Soziale Aspekte der Auslaenderbeschaeftigung.* Freidrick Ebert Siftung, Bd. 103, 207.

Meister, M. 1975. Wie in einem Gefaengnis. Gastarbeitertochter berichten von ihrem Leben in der BDR. *Korrespondenz: die Frau.*

Melia, Jean. 1929. *Mustapha Kemal ou le Renovateur de la Turquie,* p. 94.

Melon, J. and M. Timsit. 1971. Etudes statistique sur la psychopathologie des immigres. *Acta Psychiat. Belg.* 71.

Mernissi, F. 1975. *Beyond the Veil: Male-Female Dynamics in a Modern Muslim Society.* Cambridge, MA: Schenkman.

_____. 1977. Women, Saints and Sanctuaries. *SIGN,* Journal of Women in Culture and Society 3, 1:112.

Neumann, U. 1977. Turkei. In *Auslaendische Kinder, Schule und Gesellschaft im Herkunftsland,* U. Boos-Nunning and M. Hehmann, eds. pp. 258-59. Dusseldorf: Publikation Alfa.

Nikolinakos, M. 1973. *Politische Okonomie der Gastarbeiter.* Rowohlt Verlag. p. 142-43.

Nolkensmeier, I. 1976. Spezifische Probleme der auslaendischen Frauen in der BDR. Paper presented in Geneva.

Nokta. 1983. No. 26:50. Istanbul (weekly).

OECD. 1979. Continuous reporting system on migration.

Olson, E. A. 1982. Duofocal Family—Structure and an Alternative Model of Husband-Wife Relationships. In *Sex Roles, Family and Community in Turkey,* C. Kagitçıbaşı, ed., p. 33-72. Bloomington, Indiana: Indiana University Turkish Studies 3.

195

Öncü, A. Turkish Women in the Professions. Why So Many? In *Women in Turkish Society,* N. Abadan-Unat, ed., p. 181-93. Leiden: E. J. Brill.

Özbay, F. 1981. The Impact of Education on Women in Rural and Urban Turkey. In *Women in Turkish Society,* N. Abadan-Unat, ed., p. 160-80. Leiden: E. J. Brill.

——————. 1982. Women's Education in Rural Turkey. In *Sex Roles, Family and Community in Turkey,* C Kağıtçıbaşı, ed. pp. 133-49. Bloomington, Indiana: Indiana University Turkish Studies 3.

Özek, M. 1971. Soziale Umstrukturierung als Provokationsfaktor depressiver Psychosen. In *Probleme der Provokation depressiver Psychosen.* Graz: Internationales Symposium.

Özgür, S. 1980. Social Psychological Patterns in Homicide: A Comparison of Male and Female Inmates. Unpublished MA thesis, Boğaziçi University.

Paine, S. 1974. *Exporting Workers: The Turkish Case.* London: Cambridge University Press, pp. 26-27, table 1.

Ronneberger, F. 1976. *Turkische Kinder in Deutschland* (Turkish Children in Germany) Seminar der Sudosteu‌ opa-Gesellschaft, November 15-17.

Rosen, B. C. 1973. Social Change, Migration and Family Interaction in Brazil. *American Sociological Review* 38:198-212.

Rustow, Dankwart A. 1969. Atatürk as Founder of State. *Abadan Armağanı.* Ankara: SBF Yayini., p. 545.

Safilios-Rotschild, C. 1974. *Women and Social Policy.* Englewood Cliffs, NJ: Prentice Hall.

Schaniberg, A. 1971. The Modernizing Impact of Urbanization: A Causal Analysis. *Economic Development and Cultural Change,* p. 101.

Secretariat d'etat aux travailleurs immigres. 1975. *La nouvelle politique de l'immigration,* p. 109.

Sedak, Necmeddin. 1924. *Kadınlarmız ve Aile Hukukuna İlişkin Kararlar. Akşam,* January 7.

Seidel, H. 1979. Auslaendische Arbeitnehmer in der BDR. Ein statischer Uberblick. *Deutsch Lernen.*

Senyapili, T. 1981. A New Component in Metropolitan Areas. The Gecekondu Women. In *Women in Turkish Society,* N. Abadan-Unat, ed. pp. 194-214. Leiden: E. J. Brill.

Shorter, E. 1976. *The Making of the Modern Family.*

Statistical Figures Related to Higher Education Enrollment in 1974/75. 1975. Ankara: State Statistical Institute, 119.

Statistical Yearbook of Turkey, 1973. 1974. Ankara: DIE State Statistical Institute.

Stirling, P. 1965. *Turkish Village.* New York: Science Editions.

Suzuki, P.T. A Themal Analysis of Turkish Films Viewed by Turkish Researchers in West Germany. *Document.*

Taşçıoğlu, Muhaddere. 1958. *Kadının Sosyal Durumu ve Kadın Kıyafetleri.* Ankara.

Tadesse, Z. 1979. *Women and Technology in Agriculture: An Overview of the Problems in Developing Countries.* UN Institute for Training and Research.

Taşkıran, T. 1973. *Turkish Women Rights* (Turk Kadin Haklari). Ankara: Başbakanlık Besimevi.

Teber, S. 1980. *İşçi Göçü ve Davranış Bozuklukları.* İstanbul.

Tekeli, Sirin. 1977. Siyasal Iktidar Karşışinda Kadın. *Toplum ve Bilim* 3:69.

——————. 1977. *A Comparative Study on the Status of Women in Politics.* Unpublished manuscript, Istanbul., pp. 272-73.

Tekeli, S. and E. Erder. 1978. *İç Göçler* (Internal Migration). Ankara: Hacettepe University Publication D-26.

Tessler, M. A. 1978. Women's Emancipation in Tunisia. In *Women in the Muslim World,* L. Beck and N. Keddie, eds. Cambridge: Harvard University Press.

Tezgider, G. 1978. Çalışan kadınların sorunları üzerine bir inceleme (Problems of Working Women). *Calisma dergisi* October.

Thomlinson, R. 1976. *Population Dynamics, Causes and Consequences of World Demographic Change.* New York.

TIB. 1975. *Turkiye'de Kadının Sosyo-Ekonomik Durumu.* Ankara.

Timur, S. 1972. *Turkiye'de Aile Yapısı* (Family Structure in Turkey). Ankara: Hacettepe Universitesi Yayınları, D-15.

——————. 1978. Determinants of Family Structure in Turkey. 1978. In *Women's Status and Fertility in the Muslim World,* J. Allman, ed., p. 227-42. New York: Praeger.

Tillion, G. 1966. *Le Harem et les Cousins.* Paris: Seuil.

Toffler, A. 1970. *Future Shock.* New York: Random House.

Topçuoğlu, Hamide. 1957. *Kadınların Çalışma Saikleri ve Kadın Kazancının İlçe Bütçesindeki Rolü.* Ankara.

Tümertekin, Erol. 1975. Gradual Internal Migration in Turkey. *Review of the Geographical Institute of the University of Istanbul. 1970-1971,* No. 13:157-69.

Tunalıgıl, Baha. 1975. Kırsal kesimde kadın. *Politika,* 11 April.

Türk Üniversiteli Kadınlar Derneği. 1978. *Turkiye Kadın Yılı Kongresi, 1975.* Ankara: Ayyıldız Matbassı.

Turkish State Institute of Statistics (SIS), *1970 Census of Population.*

——————. *1975 Census of Population.*

——————. *Divorce Statistics, 1968-1973, 1976.*

_____. *Criminal Statistics, 1970.*

Turkiye'de Toplumsal ve Ekonomik Gelismenin 50 Yılı. 1973. Ankara: Devlet İstatistik Enstitüsü, p. 111.

United Nations. 1976. *Fertility and Family Planning in Europe Around 1970. A Comparative Study of Twelve National Surveys.* New York.

UN Seminar on the Effects of Scientific and Technological Developments on the Status of Women. 1969. Isai, Rumania, August (St/TAO/HR/37).

Veblen, T. 1934. *The Theory of the Leisure Class.* New York: An Economic Study of Institutions 89.

Wallerstein, I., et al. 1979. *Household Structure and Production Processes.* Binghamton: Fernand Braudel Center.

Weber, R. 1970. Rotationsprinzip bei der Beschaeftigung von Auslaendern. *Auslandskurier* 5, 10.

White, E. H. 1978. Legal Reform as an Indicator of Women's Status in Muslim Nations. In *Women in the Muslim World,* L. Beck and N. Keddie, eds. Cambridge: Harvard University Press.

Williams, H. P. 1982. The Role of Adjudicatory Law in Divorce Proceedings in Turkey. Unpublished Ph.D. Dissertation, Tufts University.

Wilpert, C. 1977. Zukunftserwartungen der Kinder Turkischer Arbeitnehmer. In *Auslaendische Kinder,* U. Boos-Nunning and M. Hehmann, eds., pp. 258-59. Dusseldorf: Publikation Alfa.

Wollstonecraft, Mary. 1967. *A Vindication of the Rights of Woman.* New York: W. W. Norton.

World Conference of the UN Decade for Women. *Technological Changes and Women Workers: The Development of Microelectronics.* 1980. Copenhagen, July 14-30. A/Conf. 94/26:19.

_____. *The Effects of Science and Technology on Employment of Women.* A/Conf. 94/29:8-9.

Yasa, I. 1955. *Hasanoğlu Köyü* (Village of Hasanoğlu). Ankara: Todaie.

_____. 1979. *Yurda Dönen Işçiler ve Toplumsal Degisme* (Returning Migrant Workers and Social Change). Ankara: Todaie.

Yaşar, K. 1974. *Demirciler Çarşışı Cinayeti* (The Murder on the Market of Demirci). Istanbul.

Yazgan, T. 1967. Turkiye'de sehirlesmenin nüfus ve işgücü bünyesine tesirleri (The impact of urbanization on population and manpower). Unpublished Ph.D. Dissertation, Istanbul University.

Yener, Enise. 1955. Eski Ankara Kıyafetleri ve Giyiniş Tarzları. *Dil, Tarih ve Cografya F. Dergisi* 13, 3.

Yenisey, L., et al. 1976. The Social Effects of Migrant Labour in Boğazlıyan Villages. *Migration and Development.* Ankara.

Youssef, Nadia H. 1976. Women in the Moslem World. In *Women in the*

World, B. Ilglitzin and R. Ross, eds. p. 204. Oxford: Clio.

Youssef, N., M. Buvinic, and A. Kudat. 1979. *Women in Migration: A Third World Focus.* Washington, D.C.: International Center for Research on Women, pp. 43-46.

Yücel, Naciye. 1974. "Tip Alanınde Türk Kadını." In *Cumhuriyetin 50. inci Yılında Çalışma Alanlarında Türk Kadını,* Sermet Matbassı, pp. 64-66. Istanbul.

Zabit Ceridesi. 1930. Parliamentary Records, Vol. 17, Devre III, Session 3, March 20.

INTERNATIONAL STUDIES NOTES
of the International Studies Association

— an international forum of international importance —

INTERNATIONAL STUDIES NOTES is published to provide a challenging *multi-disciplinary* forum for exchange of research, curricular and program reports on international affairs. It is designed to serve instructors, scholars, practitioners, and others concerned with the international arena.

Recent and future topics include: Terrorism; Science, Technology and Development; Soviet Power; Nuclear Conflict; Internationalizing the College Campus; Visits with Past Secretaries of State; Teaching Strategies in International Relations; Polar Politics.

Recent contributors have included Louis René Beres, James Seroka, Phillip A. Taylor, George Modeski, George Mannello, Steve Smith, Sylvia Lee Weed, Tom Bateman, Earl L. Backman.

— RECOMMEND A SUBSCRIPTION TO YOUR LIBRARIAN —

INTERNATIONAL STUDIES NOTES of the International Studies Association is published quarterly by the University of Wyoming and Bemidji State University and is edited by Joan Wadlow and Leslie Duly.

Subscription Rates: One year $20.00; two years $36.00.

Send Manuscripts to: Joan K. Wadlow, Academic Affairs, University of Wyoming, University Station Box 3254, Laramie, Wyoming 82071 (307-766-4106).

Send subscriptions to: Leslie Duly, Academic Affairs, Bemidji State University, Bemidji, Minnesota 56601 (218-755-2015).

Journal of Peace Research

A quarterly journal edited at the International Peace Research Institute, Oslo (PRIO)

Vol. 22, No. 3, 1985

Focus On: *Raimo Väyrynen:* Is There a Role for the United Nations in Conflict Resolution?

Bent Sørensen: Security Implications of Alternative Defense Options for Western Europe

M. Rafiqul Islam: Secessionist Self-Determination: Some Lessons from Katanga, Biafra and Bangladesh

Erich Weede: Some (Western) Dilemmas in Managing Extended Deterrence

Ron Smith, Anthony Humm & Jacques Fontanel: The Economics of Exporting Arms

Paul F. Diehl: Armaments without War: An Analysis of Some Underlying Effects

Gerald M. Steinberg: The Role of Process in Arms Control Negotiations

Review Essay: *Ingmar Oldberg:* The USSR – Evil, Strong, and Dangerous?

To: Norwegian University Press
PO Box 2959, Tøyen, 0608 Oslo 6, Norway

Journal of Peace Research
ISSN 0007-5035

☐ Enter my/our subscription for 4 issues of **Journal of Peace Research.**

Rates 1985 (postage included).

Nordic countries only: ☐ Institutions NOK 230,-. ☐ Individuals NOK 195,-.

All other countries: ☐ Institutions USD 38.00. ☐ Individuals USD 33.00.

Airmailed to subscribers in the Americas.

Name: _____

Address: _____

Individuals must order direct from publisher.
☐ Cheque enclosed.   ☐ Please send invoice.

JOURNAL OF INTERNATIONAL AFFAIRS

Summer 1985　　　　　　　　　　　　　　　　　　　　　Volume 39/1

Will defense replace deterrence or will space become a battleground?
Will factories of the future orbit the earth?
Is space the common heritage of mankind?
The military, political and economic implications of space technology are examined in:

TECHNOLOGY IN SPACE

Published since 1947, the Journal has a readership in over 70 countries.

Subscription Rates:	One Year	Two Years	Three Years
Individual	$11.00	$21.00	$31.00
Institutions	$22.00	$43.00	$64.00

Foreign subscribers, except Canada, add $3.50 per year postage.
single issue price: $5.50
All checks must be in U.S. dollars and drawn on U.S. banks.
Issues sent only upon receipt of payment.
Mail all orders to: **Journal of International Affairs**
Box 4, International Affairs Building　•　Columbia University　•　New York, New York 10027

— At the forefront of facts and issues —

WORLD POLITICS

A Quarterly Journal of International Relations

revista mexicana de
POLITICA
EXTERIOR

PUBLICACION TRIMESTRAL

Suscríbase a:

revista mexicana de
POLITICA
EXTERIOR

Publicación trimestral del Instituto Matías Romero de Estudios Diplomáticos, Organo Académico de la Secretaría de Relaciones Exteriores, que da a conocer, a través de ensayos, notas e informes, reseñas, cronología de noticias, discursos y documentos, los hechos que dejan constancia del quehacer de México en el Mundo, así como los lineamientos más relevantes de su política exterior.

Precio del ejemplar

$ 450.00

Adjunto cheque o giro bancario núm. _____ *del Banco* _____ *por la cantidad de* _____ *a nombre de la* REVISTA MEXICANA DE POLITICA EXTERIOR, por concepto del importe de mi suscripción por un año.

Nombre _____
Dirección _____
_____
Ciudad _____
Código Postal _____ Estado _____
País _____

Suscripción anual

México: $ 1,500.00

E.U.A., Canadá, Centroamérica y Sudamérica: 25 U.S. dólares
Otros países: 34 U.S. dólares

Para suscripciones favor de enviar este cupón a:

Dirección General de Archivo, Biblioteca y Publicaciones
Secretaría de Relaciones Exteriores
Ricardo Flores Magon N° 1
Ex-Convento de Tlatelolco
C.P. 06995
México, D.F.

Conflict

All Warfare Short of War

Edited by George K. Tanham

This quarterly journal focuses on conflicts short of formal war, including guerrilla warfare, insurgency, revolution, and terrorism. Articles also cover non-physical conflicts, such as those of an economic, social, political, and psychological nature. Issues will attempt to address some of the less visible and less publicized conflicts occurring in the world today.

Selected Articles from the Volume 5:

Issued Quarterly, Volume 6 $60.00

CR Crane, Russak & Company, Inc.

3 East 44th Street, New York, N.Y. 10017, (212) 867-1490

CAIRO PAPERS IN SOCIAL SCIENCE
بحوث القاهرة فى العلوم الاجتماعية

The CAIRO PAPERS IN SOCIAL SCIENCE provides a medium for the dissemination of research in social, economic and political development conducted by visiting and local scholars working in Egypt and the Middle East. Produced at the American University in Cairo since 1977, CAIRO PAPERS has published more than 20 issues of collected articles and monographs on a variety of topics. Beginning January 1983, issues will appear on a quarterly basis. Future topics include:

> THE POLITICAL ECONOMY OF REVOLUTIONARY IRAN
> URBAN RESEARCH STRATEGIES FOR EGYPT
> THE HISTORY AND ROLE OF THE EGYPTIAN PRESS
> SOCIAL SECURITY AND THE FAMILY IN EGYPT
> THE NATIONALIZATION OF ARABIC AND ISLAMIC
>   EDUCATION IN EGYPT: DAR AL-ULUM AND AL-AZHAR
> NON-ALIGNMENT IN A CHANGING WORLD

In addition, we plan to publish a special index of survey research conducted by Egyptian research centers and agencies which will be offered at a discount rate to our subscribers.

```
************************************************************************
```
NAME: INSTITUTION:

ADDRESS:

CITY: STATE OR COUNTRY:

VOLUME SIX ORDERS
    INDIVIDUAL (US $15 or L.E.8)   INSTITUTIONAL (US $25 or L.E.10)
                                         Please indicate if standing order:

BACK ORDERS
    SINGLE ISSUES (US $4 or L.E.3)   _____VOLUME 4 (US $15 or L.E.8)
Please indicate title and author:

Enclosed is a check or money order for_____payable to THE AMERICAN UNIVERSITY IN CAIRO (CAIRO PAPERS).

Signature or authorization:

```
************************************************************************
```
Inquiries or orders originating in the   Those originating elsewhere should
USA should be sent to: be sent to:

CAIRO PAPERS IN SOCIAL SCIENCE   **CAIRO PAPERS IN SOCIAL SCIENCE**
American University in Cairo   **American University in Cairo**
866 U.N. Plaza   **P.O. Box 2511**
New York, N.Y. 10017   **Cairo, Egypt**

THE ANNALS
of The American Academy *of*
Political *and* Social Science

RICHARD D. LAMBERT, *Editor*
ALAN W. HESTON, *Associate Editor*

CHINA IN TRANSITION

Special Editor: Marvin E. Wolfgang

As China and the United States move together through the 1980s and 1990s, the legal, economic, and ethical issues facing China are also significant to the United States. Population and migration control . . . criminal justice and civil rights . . . investment of capital in hotels, in high technology, and in nuclear power . . . all are topics of major concern.

This issue, prepared for the 87th annual meeting of the American Academy of Political and Social Science, furthers our understanding of the problems and potentials of China. Academic and political science experts examine legal education, internal politics, population control, urbanization, rural agriculture, and modernization. They also explore the relationships among China, the USSR, and the United States. Original and intriguing, these papers constitute a timely portrait of a country in the midst of dramatic change.

Volume 476   November 1984

Enter your Academy membership today!

A subscription to **The Annals** is available to individuals only through membership in The American Academy of Political and Social Science, one of the world's oldest and most distinguished professional associations. Each bimonthly volume of **The Annals** presents current, insightful articles on a single emerging social issue, all invited by an expert guest editor. Each volume also contains **The Annals'** timely Book Department—a knowledgeable review of new literature in the social sciences.

Your one-year Academy membership includes six bimonthly volumes of **The Annals.**

One-year Academy membership:
$26 — **The Annals** paper edition
$39 — **The Annals** cloth edition

One-year institutional subscription:
$45 — **The Annals** paper edition
$60 — **The Annals** cloth edition

Please send orders to **The Annals,** in care of

SAGE PUBLICATIONS
The Publishers of Professional Social Science
275 South Beverly Drive, Beverly Hills, California 90212

Established 1928

Isn't it time to subscribe?

Pacific Affairs

An International Review of Asia and the Pacific

Pacific Affairs
University of British Columbia
Vancouver, BC, Canada V6T 1W5

Published Quarterly

Subscription rates: for individuals, $25 per year; for institutions, $30 per year.
Add $5 for postage outside Canada.

COOPERATION AND CONFLICT

NORDIC JOURNAL OF INTERNATIONAL POLITICS

Published quarterly for the Nordic Cooperation Committee for International Politics, including Conflict and Peace Research, by Norwegian University Press, Oslo, Norway. It is the only journal in the English language devoted to studies of the foreign policies of the Nordic countries and to studies of international politics by Nordic scholars. Editor: Arild Underdal, Norwegian School of Management, (BI), P.O. Box 69, 1341 Bekkestua, Norway.

Contents Vol. XXI, No. 1, March 1986

Subscription rates: (Nordic area NOK, rest of the world USD).
Institutions USD 32.00/NOK 195,–. Individuals USD 26.00/NOK 156,–.

Orders can be placed with Norwegian University Press, Subscription Division, P.O. Box 2959 Tøyen, 0608 Oslo 6, Norway, and US Office: P.O. Box 258, Irvington-on-Hudson, NY 10533, USA.

COOPERATION AND CONFLICT

I wish to become a subscriber from No. 1, 1986

☐ Institutions USD 32.00, NOK 195,– (Nordic area)   ☐ cheque enclosed
☐ Individuals USD 26.00, NOK 156,– (Nordic area)   ☐ please send invoice

Name: . . . .

Address: . . . .

. . . .

Issues will be sent to you as soon as payment is received.
Norwegian University Press, P.O. Box 2959 Tøyen, 0608 Oslo 6, Norway

Proofing, typesetting, layout and printing

by

CROSSBRIDGE LIMITED, TAIWAN BRANCH
9F, 118 Tun Hwa N. Road
Taipei, Taiwan, R. O. C.